Preface

THIS STUDY IS the third in a series that began in the fall of 1961 with an assessment of the freshman classes entering a national sample of 246 institutions in the fall of 1961. Data provided by these 127,000 freshmen at the time of matriculation were analyzed and reported in *Who Goes Where to College?* (Chicago: Science Research Associates, 1965). A one-year followup study of some 30,000 of these students was carried out in the summer of 1962 and reported in a second book, *The College Environment* (Washington: American Council on Education, 1968).

The current report, based on a followup carried out in the summer of 1965—four years after matriculation—involved some 36,000 of the original students. It is our belief that longitudinal data such as these provide a unique opportunity to determine how the student's persistence in college, career plans, achievements, and educational aspirations are affected by the type of college he attends.

In many respects, this series of studies has served as a model or prototype for a major program of research on higher education which is now underway at the American Council on Education. Longitudinal data being obtained through this Cooperative Institutional Research Program, which currently involves more than 400 institutions and nearly a million students and faculty, will make it possible ultimately to examine the comparative effects of different educational practices on a wide variety of student outcomes.

This project was made possible in part by a two-year grant to the American Council on Education from the National Science Foundation.[1] A portion of this grant was provided by the U. S. Office of Education and the National Institute of Mental Health through a transfer-of-funds to the National Science Foundation. R. E. Iffert (U. S. Office of Education), Herbert Rosenberg (National Institute of Mental Health), and William Jaracz (National Science Foundation) represented their respective agencies in the early conceptualization of the project and assisted in the design of the followup questionnaire. We are especially indebted to Justin Lewis and William Jaracz of the National Science Foundation for the expert manner in which they handled the difficult task of coordinating the varying interests of three sponsoring agencies.

Additional financial support for this project was provided from the general operating funds of the American Council on Education and from the

---

[1] An earlier version of this manuscript was submitted to the National Science Foundation in February 1968, as the final report under Grant GR-22.

Center for Advanced Study in the Behavioral Sciences, which provided fellowship support for the senior author during the major writing phase of the project in 1967–68.

A project of this magnitude requires the coordinated efforts of many key persons. In the Office of Research of the American Council on Education, we received valuable assistance in data processing from Gerald Richardson, William Mong, Janet Griffith, and Richard Bain. We are also indebted to Barbara Blandford and Janet Liechty of ACE, who helped both in managing many logistical problems and in typing portions of the manuscript, and to Irene Bickenbach of the Center for Advanced Study in the Behavioral Sciences, who carried the main burden of typing the manuscript.

We should also like to express our appreciation to Laura Kent for her expert editing of the entire manuscript, and to Gerald F. Koch of National Computer Systems for maintaining, under conditions of considerable time pressure, high standards of quality control in the design, printing, mailing, and processing of questionnaires.

Finally, we are indebted to the several hundred college administrators and the many thousands of college students who willingly contributed their time and energies to make this project possible.

Center for Advanced Study in the
Behavioral Sciences and American
Council on Education

April, 1968

ALEXANDER W. ASTIN
ROBERT PANOS

THE EDUCATIONAL
AND VOCATIONAL DEVELOPMENT
OF COLLEGE STUDENTS

The Educational
and Vocational Development
of College Students

ALEXANDER W. ASTIN
ROBERT J. PANOS

American Council on Education

Contents

List of Tables

1
Background and Design of the Study

ADVANCED FORMAL EDUCATION is the principal social mechanism for developing skilled manpower in most countries of the world. In the United States, this critical task of selecting and training high-level talent is not accomplished, as in many other countries, by means of a highly centralized and homogeneous system of institutions, but rather by means of the largely uncoordinated efforts of a great many diverse and independent institutions. While the American system, in all its diversity, may not be the most efficient from the point of view of manpower planning and control, it offers a unique opportunity to investigate the relative effectiveness of different approaches to undergraduate education.

The major purpose of the study reported in this book was to assess the significance of institutional diversity in the production of skilled manpower by comparing the effects of different college environments on the undergraduate student's educational aspirations and career plans. The specific objective was to identify institutional characteristics and educational practices that affect the student's chances of completing college, going to graduate school, and pursuing a career in a particular field. It was assumed that, in addition to their immediate value as an aid in educational planning and manpower development, the results of this study would contribute to a better understanding of the processes of career choice and career development and of the interaction between the undergraduate student and his college environment.

This study was in some respects the natural outgrowth of a long series of studies of undergraduate institutions begun during the early 1950s. We shall first review briefly this history of previous research and then describe the design of the present study.

RESEARCH ON COLLEGE IMPACT

Among the earliest systematic attempts to compare the effects of different undergraduate institutions were the studies of "Ph.D. productivity" conducted by Knapp and Goodrich (1952) and Knapp and Greenbaum (1953). These investigators found that baccalaureate recipients from certain undergraduate institutions were much more likely to win graduate fellowships or to go on to get the Ph.D. degree than were graduates of other institutions. At many institutions, for example, fewer than one graduate in a hundred went on to get the Ph.D.; at a few others, the proportion was as high as one

1

in four graduates. These investigators also demonstrated that Ph.D. productivity varied considerably by geographic region and type of institution. Moreover, the highly productive institutions, in comparison with the less productive ones, tended to have higher faculty-student ratios, larger libraries, and richer endowment funds. As one might infer from these institutional characteristics, Knapp and Greenbaum's list of 50 "top-ranking" institutions in Ph.D. productivity consisted almost entirely of prestigious private institutions. The authors were generally inclined to interpret the high Ph.D. productivity of these institutions as attributable to specific environmental influences on the students.

Similar findings concerning the Ph.D. outputs of chemistry departments in different undergraduate institutions were reported at a conference held several years later at College of Wooster (Wooster Conference Report, 1959). The authors of this report produced data showing a relatively high correlation between a department's output of Ph.D.'s in chemistry and its expenditures for research.

The interpretation of these results was called into question when it was shown that the highly productive institutions were much more likely to enroll highly able and highly motivated students than were the less productive institutions (Holland, 1959; Astin and Holland, 1962). Thus, the observed differences among institutions in their student "outputs" (proportion of graduates who go on to get the Ph.D.) may result, in part at least, from differences in their student "inputs" (the characteristics of the students that they enroll) rather than solely from differences in institutional impact on the students. These later studies also showed that, unless such initial differences in student inputs are taken into account, it is difficult to determine whether observed differences in student outputs are due to environmental influences, to differential inputs, or to some combination of the two.

These earlier studies were subsequently reevaluated under conditions in which it was possible to make some adjustments for differential student inputs to the various institutions (Astin, 1961, 1962c). Briefly, this procedure involved calculating each institution's "expected" Ph.D. output from the sex, intelligence, and field of study of the entering freshmen.[1] The expected Ph.D. output was then compared with the actual Ph.D. output in order to determine whether the institution was in reality producing Ph.D.'s at a rate commensurate with the potential of its entering freshmen.

The results of these studies showed clearly that an institution's output of Ph.D.'s is highly dependent on its input of students. Furthermore, several of the earlier "top-ranking" institutions turned out to be highly *underproductive* relative to their student inputs. These studies also suggested that certain educational practices which were previously thought (Thistlethwaite, 1959, 1960) to increase the student's desire to get the Ph.D. were artifacts resulting from uncontrolled differences in student inputs.

In the years since these initial studies, an increasing number of investigators have devoted their efforts to intensive examination of differential college impact on the student's educational aspirations (Astin, 1962c, 1963a; Davis, 1966; Thistlethwaite, 1966), on his intellectual achievement (Nichols, 1964), on his persistence in college (Astin, 1964), on his personality and values (Nichols, 1967; Plant, 1958), and on his career choice (Astin, 1963c, 1965b; Holland, 1962, 1966b). Although they employed a variety of designs and statistical methods, virtually all these studies have demonstrated that in order to compare the effects of different institutions, it is essential to control for differential student inputs. They have also shown that, while different types of institutions do appear to have differential effects on their students, the magnitude of these effects is small compared with the effects of the student input.

Even though this increased research activity has produced several suggestive findings concerning the nature of differential institutional influence on student development, their validity and generalizability have been questioned either because the methodology employed was inadequate or because the samples of institutions and students were biased. Specifically, most of these studies have dealt solely with highly able students attending relatively prestigious institutions.

A recognition of the need for a longitudinal study involving a representative national sample of colleges and of students was largely responsible for the initiation of the study reported in this book. Actually, this study is the third in a sequence that began with a survey of entering freshmen at 248 institutions conducted in the fall of 1961 (Astin, 1965d). The second in the series, conducted in 1962, was designed to obtain information about the environments of these institutions (Astin, 1968a). In addition to the data from these first two studies, the current study utilizes data collected from the same students in 1965, four years after they had entered college.

COLLECTION OF DATA

The analysis of differential college impact can be viewed as requiring three types of data: *input* or pretest information showing the status of the student when he first enters college, *output* or criterion information showing the status of the student after he has been exposed to the environment of the institution, and *environmental* information describing the institutional characteristics to which he is exposed.

Student Input Data

The initial data for this project were collected in the fall of 1961, when a brief questionnaire (see Appendix A) was administered to each member of the entering freshman class at a stratified national sample of 246 accredited four-year colleges and universities.[2] Originally undertaken to explore some of the problems suggested by the earlier reexaminations of the Ph.D. productivity studies, the project was designed primarily to obtain comparable input information on the entering freshmen classes at each institution, prior to their experience at colleges. It was assumed that such information would be useful both in understanding how student talent is distributed among different types of institutions within the American system and in carrying out future longitudinal studies of differential institutional impact.

Each of the 127,212 entering freshmen in 1961 reported information concerning his socioeconomic background, his academic and extracurricular achievements in high school, and his future vocational and educational plans. We expected that such input information would be relevant to the study of differential institutional impact on the student's educational aspirations and vocational goals. While it might have been desirable to collect a wider range of information—for studies of institutional impact on the student's personality, attitudes, values, and behavior, for example—we decided to limit ourselves to questions directly related to educational achievement and career plans. Part of our reasoning here was that institutions would be more inclined to cooperate if the questionnaire was kept short. As it turned out, a relatively high rate of participation (80.8 percent of all institutions invited) was obtained. An analysis of participants and nonparticipants among all invited institutions did not reveal any significant biases relating to identifiable institutional characteristics.

A total of 52 input measures was computed for each of the 246 entering student bodies on the basis of the information provided by the students on the questionnaire. Examples of such measures are the percentage of men in the student body, the percentage of students who were elected presidents of their high school class, the percentage who planned to become scientists, and the percentage who planned to obtain the Ph.D. degree. The diversity among the 246 institutions with respect to most of these 52 student input measures was considerable (see Astin, 1965d, Table 3). For example, although an average of 42 percent of all the entering students planned eventually to do graduate work, the range among institutions was from a low of 6 percent of the freshmen in one entering class to a high of 98 percent of those in another. Similarly, the percentage of students whose fathers were either professionals or executives ranged from a low of zero percent at one college to a high of 75 percent at another.

A factor analysis of the 52 student input measures revealed that most of the information they contained could be accounted for in terms of six general characteristics:

1. Intellectualism (academic ability, high educational aspirations, interest in science).
2. Estheticism (interest and ability in art, music, and writing).
3. Status (socioeconomic level, interest in enterprising careers).
4. Leadership (past achievement in leadership, drama, and speech).

5. Pragmatism (high interest in engineering and technical fields; low interest in education and social science).

6. Masculinity (high percentage of men, high percentage of students planning professional careers, low percentage of students planning careers in education and social science).

Types of institutions also differed greatly with respect to their entering freshman classes. In general, technological institutions, teachers colleges, and private nonsectarian institutions had the most unique student inputs.

Student Output Data

Output or criterion information was obtained from these same students in the summer of 1965, approximately four years after the initial survey. This particular time was selected for the followup primarily because it is frequently a major turning point in the development of those students who have completed their undergraduate training in four years; often, they must at this time make major decisions about future career, further education, or possible marriage. For students who have not completed their undergraduate training in the four-year period, this time—when normally they would be graduating—may represent a point for reflection and stock-taking.

In order to reduce project costs, a subsample of 60,505 students was randomly selected for the followup survey. All students from those institutions enrolling fewer than 300 freshmen in 1961 were included in the followup; samples of approximately 250 students were selected at random from the larger institutions. The arbitrary figure of 250 was chosen with the expectation that the rate of return would be about 50 percent and that the 100–125 student returns for a given college would thus yield a reasonably stable estimate of how the class had changed during the four years. Larger samples of approximately 500 students were selected from several of the large complex universities.

Followup information was collected by means of a mailed questionnaire (see Appendix B), which was sent out in late August of 1965. Its major purpose was to secure output information pertaining to the student's educational achievement, educational aspirations and plans, and career goals. Thus, several items from the original 1961 survey were repeated verbatim:

1. Probable future occupation (free response).

2. Final (or most recent) undergraduate major field of study (free response).

3. Highest degree planned (none, associate, bachelor's, master's, Ph.D. or Ed.D., M.D. or D.D.S., LL.B., other).

Additional criterion information included (1) how many years of undergraduate education the student had completed during the four years since matriculation, (2) whether or not he had obtained the bachelor's degree, (3) whether or not he intended to go to graduate school, and (4) whether or not he had authored any published scientific papers or literary works. The questionnaire also contained a variety of other items about the student's experiences during his undergraduate years. Some of the results derived from this information are presented in Chapter 2.

Many of the questionnaires were mailed to addresses provided when the student first entered college in the fall of 1961. Approximately half of the 60,505 addresses had been updated in the fall of 1962, and further updating was done in the spring of 1965. Names and addresses of the 60,505 students were visually checked against institutional rosters, and any changes in the student's home address were made. Approximately half of the original sample were identified in these rosters, and approximately half of their addresses required updating.

The followup questionnaire was designed to be processed by an optical scanning device[3] in order to reduce the errors and expenses associated with keypunching. These questionnaires were mailed out from Minneapolis during the last week of August, 1965, with a postage-paid return envelope addressed to the American Council on Education in Washington. Approximately five days later, a reminder postcard was sent to each student, in accordance with a procedure found successful in the initial followup study conducted by Project Talent (Flanagan and Cooley, 1966). About one month after the initial mailing of questionnaires, a double-flap postcard was sent to each nonrespondent (see Appendix B). Its purpose was to exhort the nonrespondent to complete either the original questionnaire or the attached short-form questionnaire, which contained the four critical criterion items (career choice, years of study completed, final field of study, highest degree sought). Several special studies were conducted to determine the characteristics of nonrespondents and the comparative effectiveness of various nonrespondent followup techniques. The results of these special studies are given in Chapter 2 and Appendix D.

Since first-class postage was used in the initial mailing, all undelivered questionnaires were presumably returned to the Council. Although some 5,850 questionnaires, representing nearly 10 percent of the sample, were initially returned undelivered, another 1,200 of the short-form questionnaires sent to nonrespondents four weeks later were also returned as undeliverable. Thus, it appears that approximately 11 to 12 percent of the students never received either questionnaire. An attempt to update undeliverable addresses by sending lists of names to each institution proved to be largely unrewarding: New addresses were obtained for less than 10 percent of this group.

A total of 30,506 students completed and returned the initial long form of the followup questionnaire. An additional 5,899 students completed the short form, bringing the total percentage of respondents to 60 percent. Thus, approximately 68 percent of the students who actually received questionnaires completed and returned them.

Environmental Data

Environmental data were obtained from several sources, including publications such as the U. S. Office of Education's *Education Directory, Part 3: Higher Education* and the American Council on Education's *American Universities and Colleges* (Cartter, 1964). Additional data about the student's environmental experiences during college were obtained at the time of the followup conducted in 1965. The principal environmental measures, however, were obtained from the earlier followup conducted in the summer of 1962. Details concerning environmental measures are reported in a later section of this chapter.

STUDENT VARIABLES

The various sources of student data described above were used to construct input and output measures for assessing the student's educational and vocational development during the college years.

Output Measures

A total of 28 output or dependent variables, based on the information provided by the students in the 1965 followup, were defined in the study. (Because some categories were later collapsed, the total turned out to be 26.) Each variable was coded as a dichotomy: for example, the criterion of completing the baccalaureate degree was scored "1" (the student had completed his degree at the time of the followup) or "0" (the student had not completed his degree at the time of the followup). Similarly, the student's intention to enter graduate school was coded either "1" (he intended to obtain a graduate degree) or "0" (he did not intend to obtain a graduate degree). The specific output variables are described in detail in Chapters 3 and 4.

In addition to these 28 dependent variables based on the questionnaire information, scores on the Area tests of the Graduate Record Examinations (GRE) administered in the spring of 1965 were obtained for a smaller sample of students. These three Area tests, which are administered through the Institutional Testing Program of the Educational Testing Service, cover three broad areas of general educational development: social science, humanities, and natural science. Their principal objective is "to assess the student's grasp of basic concepts plus his ability to apply them to a variety of types of material which are presented for his interpretation" (Centra and Parry, 1967). Each test requires 75 minutes to administer. By searching the files of the Educational Testing Service, we found that 39 of the 246 institutions had administered the Area Tests as part of the Institutional Testing Program during 1965.[4] The presidents of all but one of these institutions gave us permission to obtain their students' scores.[5]

In matching the GRE data with other student data in our files, we limited our search to a subsample of 2,553 students (1) who entered one of the 38 institutions in the fall of 1961 and (2) for whom scores on the National

Merit Scholarship Qualifying Test were available from an earlier study (Astin, 1968a). This second restriction allowed us to exert some control over the differential aptitude levels of the students at the time that they entered college. A careful visual check of our list of names against the rosters provided by the Educational Testing Service yielded 669 students for whom scores on all three Area tests were available.[6]

The analyses involving these GRE data, which differed somewhat from the analyses of the other 28 output variables are described in detail in Chapter 3.

Input Measures

The student input variables, based on data provided by the student when he first entered college in the fall of 1961, are shown below.

    1. Sex (scored as a dichotomy)

    (2–19). Eighteen high-level extracurricular achievements from high school, each scored as a dichotomy:

    2. Placed (first, second, or third place) in a school science contest

    3. Placed in a regional or state science contest

    4. Placed in a national science contest

    5. Won prizes or awards in art competition

    6. Exhibited or performed a work of art at their high schools

    7. Exhibited or performed a work of art at a place other than their high schools

    8. Participated in a national music contest

    9. Received a rating of good or excellent in a state music contest

    10. Received a rating of good or excellent in a national music contest

    11. Had leads in high school or church-sponsored play

    12. Placed in a regional or state speech or debate contest

    13. Placed in a national speech or debate contest

    14. Edited their school papers or literary magazines

    15. Had poems, short stories, or articles published in a public newspaper or magazine (not a school paper) or in a state or national high school anthology

    16. Won literary awards or prizes for creative writing

    17. Was elected to one or more student offices

    18. Was elected president of high school class

    19. Received an award or other special recognition for leadership

    20–34. Probable major field of study (scored as 15 mutually exclusive dichotomies)

    35–64. Probable future occupation (scored as 30 mutually exclusive dichotomies)

    65–80. Father's occupation (coded as 16 mutually exclusive dichotomies)

81. Highest degree planned (4 levels: less than bachelor's, bachelor's, master's, or doctoral-level degree)

82. High school average (9 levels: D through A+)

83. Size of high school graduating class (8 levels: less than 50 through 600 or more)

84. Father's education (6 levels: grammar school, some high school, high school graduate, some college, college graduate, or postgraduate degree)

Because the length of the 1965 followup questionnaire was not limited by the same administrative considerations that forced us to keep the original input questionnaire brief, we decided to collect information on five additional input variables.

85. Mother's education (same categories as father's education)

86. Student's marital status at the time of entrance to college (scored as a dichotomy: married vs. not married)

87. Income of parents (9 levels: less than $4,000 per year through $25,000 or more)

88–92. Race (scored as 5 mutually exclusive dichotomies: White, Negro, American Indian, Oriental, other)

93–95. Religion in which the student was reared (scored as 3 mutually exclusive dichotomies: Protestant, Roman Catholic, Jewish)

In order to utilize as much information as possible, each category of variables 81 through 87 was scored as a separate, mutually exclusive dichotomy in certain of the analyses (see the later section in this chapter on Data Analysis, pp. 13–17).

ENVIRONMENTAL VARIABLES

Environmental measures were of two broad types: (1) the characteristics of the institution itself (its size, selectivity, permissiveness, etc.) which, presumably, affect all the students at a given institution and (2) special educational experiences *within* the college (living in a dormitory, participating in an honors program, etc.) to which all students at a given institution may not be exposed. This second category comprises *within*-college environmental variables, whereas the former category comprises *between*-college environmental variables.

Between-College Measures

The principal measures of institutional environments were developed from an earlier followup of the students conducted in the summer of 1962, following completion of the freshman year in college. Since this earlier environmental study has been described in detail elsewhere (Astin, 1968a), the results will be summarized very briefly here.

The general intention of the 1962 followup study was to use the students as observers of the college environment by asking them to make detailed reports on the characteristics of their institution. Questionnaires on the college environment were sent to the same 60,505 students as were surveyed in 1965; approximately 50 percent usable returns were received. The principal purpose of this 1962 questionnaire, called the Inventory of College Activities (ICA), was to identify and measure some of the important differences among college environments. In contrast to previous research on the subject (Astin, 1962a; Astin and Holland, 1961; Pace and Stern, 1958; Pace, 1963), this study attempted to view the college environment as an array of potential "stimuli." A stimulus was defined as any behavior, event, or other observable characteristic of the institution which is potentially capable of changing the student's sensory input and whose existence or occurrence can be confirmed by independent observation. The questionnaire included a list of 250 such stimuli covering four different areas: the peer environment, the classroom environment, the administrative environment, and the physical environment.

Variations among the environments of the 246 institutions were measured in terms of the relative frequency of occurrence of each of the 250 stimuli as reported by the students. For many of the stimuli, the diversity within the sample was indeed remarkable, ranging from very frequent occurrence at some institutions to virtual nonoccurrence at others. For example, the percentage of students who reported voting in a student election during their freshman year ranged from only 9 percent at one institution to 92 percent at another. Similarly, the percentage of students who reported that their instructors called them by their first names varied from a low of 2 percent to a high of 97 percent.

Factor analyses of the correlations among the 250 stimulus items, in which the institution was used as the sampling unit, revealed 27 distinct patterns of environmental stimuli that differentiated among the 246 institutions. These 27 environmental measures, which account for the bulk of the information contained in the original pool of 250 items, are listed below:

A. The Peer Environment
    1. Competitiveness *vs.* Cooperativeness
    2. Organized Dating
    3. Independence
    4. Cohesiveness
    5. Informal Dating
    6. Femininity
    7. Drinking *vs.* Religiousness
    8. Musical and Artistic Activity
    9. Leisure Time
    10. Career Indecision
    11. Regularity of Sleeping Habits
    12. Use of the Library

13. Conflict with Regulations
14. Student Employment
15. Use of Automobiles

B. The Classroom Environment
    16. Involvement in the Class
    17. Verbal Aggressiveness
    18. Extraversion of the Instructor
    19. Familiarity with the Instructor
    20. Organization in the Classroom
    21. Severity of Grading

C. The Administrative Environment
    22. Severity of Administrative Policy against Drinking
    23. Severity of Administrative Policy against Aggression
    24. Severity of Administrative Policy against Heterosexual Activity
    25. Severity of Administrative Policy against Cheating

D. The Physical Environment
    26. Spread of the Campus
    27. Friendliness of the Dorm Counselor or Housemother

An additional factor, which proved difficult to label but which might tentatively be called "Rate of Cheating," was also identified in the classroom environment (see Astin, 1968*a*, p. 61). This factor was employed in some of the analyses described later, bringing the total number of ICA stimulus factors to 28.

The questionnaire also contained 75 items concerning the student's subjective impressions of his college environment (e.g., "There is a lot of school spirit here"). A factor analysis of these items revealed an additional eight measures of the college "image," which were only moderately related to the 27 stimulus factors. These "image" factors are:

1. Academic Competitiveness
2. Concern for the Individual Student
3. School Spirit
4. Permissiveness
5. Snobbishness
6. Emphasis on Athletics
7. Flexibility of the Curriculum
8. Emphasis on Social Life

In the current study, the institution's scores on each of the 35 environmental variables were converted to normalized standard scores (Astin, Richardson, and Salmon, 1967).

Several additional measures of college characteristics were employed in certain of the analyses which permitted the use of a larger number of variables. These included a measure of the size (total enrollment) of the institution, its operating budget (per student expenditures for educational and general purposes), the percentage of men in the student body, the college's selectivity (an estimate of the average academic ability of the entering freshman class) (Astin, 1965a), and six measures of the curricular emphasis of the institution based on Holland's (1959) classification of occupations:[7]

1. Realistic Orientation (engineering, agriculture)
2. Scientific Orientation (natural science & mathematics)
3. Social Orientation (education, nursing, social science)
4. Conventional Orientation (accounting, secretarial science, business)
5. Enterprising Orientation (prelaw, political science, history, business administration)
6. Artistic Orientation (fine arts, music, writing, languages, speech)

The final group of measures of institutional characteristics included the standard typological classifications ordinarily used for administrative purposes. These classifications, which were scored as separate 1–0 dichotomies, are:

1. Curricular emphasis (4 dichotomies: teachers colleges, technological institutions, liberal arts colleges, universities)
2. Type of control (4 dichotomies: private-nonsectarian, Protestant, Catholic, public)
3. Sex (men's college, women's college, coeducational college)
4. Race (Negro vs. non-Negro)
5. Geographic region (4 dichotomies: Northeast, Southeast, Midwest, West-and-Southwest)
6. Size of town (4 dichotomies: large city, medium-sized city, suburb, small town)

In all, 21 "type" characteristics were identified. One of the more theoretical objectives of the current study was to determine if the differential effects of institutions can be accounted for by the more sophisticated "stimulus" measures or whether these simple institutional "types" have effects on students that cannot be explained by the more elegant measures. Conversely, the administrative type characteristics may tend to obscure many important institutional differences that can be measured by the more sophisticated variables. The results of these special analyses are discussed in Chapters 3 and 4.

Within-College Measures

The 1965 followup questionnaire obtained information on five classes of within-college environmental experiences: the manner in which the student financed his undergraduate education, his living arrangements during the undergraduate years, his participation in vocational counseling as an undergraduate, his getting married after entering college, and his participation in the Undergraduate Research Program of the National Science Foundation. The following 13 dichotomous measures resulted:[8]

1. Received a major portion (at least 50 percent) of financial support from parents
2. Was financed in part by a scholarship
3. Was financed in part by a loan from the college
4. Was financed in part by work during the school year
5. Lived with parents during the freshman year
6. Lived in a dormitory during the freshman year
7. Lived in a private room or apartment during the freshman year
8. Lived in a fraternity or sorority house during the freshman year
9. Received one or more hours of vocational conseling as an undergraduate
10. Received 4 or more hours of vocational counseling
11. Received 10 or more hours of vocational counseling
12. Got married after entering college
13. Participated in the Undergraduate Research Program of the National Science Foundation

Although it might have been preferable to examine the effects of living arrangements beyond the freshman year, such studies would have necessitated excluding students who had dropped out of college after the first year. Thus, in the interest of conserving effort and project costs, we limited this investigation to the freshman year.

DATA ANALYSIS

The major purposes of the analysis of data were, first, to measure changes in the students during their undergraduate years as revealed by a comparison of their responses in 1961 and in 1965 and, second, to identify characteristics of the institution and of the students' educational experiences that may have contributed to these changes. Since earlier studies on differential college impact suggest that the conclusions to be drawn from such studies depend on the method of analysis used, several different methods were employed.

The principal consideration in selecting methods for analyzing the data was to produce maximally valid results concerning probable environmental influences on the student. Because of the large number of variables and the quantities of data, however, considerations of technical feasibility and computer costs were also important. Although some of the decisions made at various stages required a compromise among these various considerations, it should be stressed that our primary goal was to enhance the validity and meaningfulness of the findings.

Our approach was in many ways similar to the approach described earlier in the studies of Ph.D. productivity. The first step of this two-stage process involves statistically adjusting differential institutional outputs on the basis of their differential student inputs; the second step involves searching for environmental effects by relating the "adjusted" student output (i.e., adjusted for input) to the institution's environmental characteristics. The basic purpose of this type of analysis is to isolate environmental effects that cannot be attributed to some artifact of differential student inputs. Thus, in the studies of Ph.D. productivity described earlier, many of the institutions that at first appeared to be quite successful in stimulating their graduates to go on and get the Ph.D. degree turned out to be producing considerably fewer graduates who get the Ph.D. than they should, judging from the characteristics of their entering students.

Once appropriate controls for differential inputs have been applied, the relationship between the adjusted output and the environmental characteristics of the institution can be evaluated with greater confidence. Of course, statistical controls of this type do not yield data that necessarily prove causation, but they do serve to rule out many alternative interpretations of the findings that would otherwise suggest themselves. The adequacy of the controls depends both upon the methodology employed and upon the exhaustiveness of the list of student input variables. If certain potentially important student input variables are not included in the analyses, the confidence that can be placed in the results is reduced accordingly. It was for this reason that the dependent or outcome variables chosen for this study (e.g., career choice) were limited largely to those for which a prior response—a "pretest" at the time of entrance to college—was available from the 1961 survey.

The statistical procedure used for controlling the effects of student input characteristics on each of the 28 outcome variables was linear multiple regression analysis. For these analyses, a sample of 3,821, representing every eighth subject from the initial sample of students who returned the long form of the questionnaire, was selected. This relatively large sample was considered necessary in order to minimize errors that might be caused by the relatively large number of variables and the relatively low base rates (frequency of response) on many of them. Separate regression analyses were carried out on each of the 28 dependent variables in the following manner: Student input variables were added to the regression equation in a stepwise manner until none of the remaining input variables was capable of producing a reduction in the residual sum of squares in the criterion which exceeded $p = .05$.

Although it would have been desirable to perform all 28 regression analyses at the same time, we were initially prevented from doing so because our regression program was limited to a matrix of only 100 variables. Including all 28 output variables in this matrix would thus have limited us to a total of 72 input variables. In order to avoid the necessity of eliminating additional input variables and thereby increasing the risk that our controls of differential inputs would be inadequate, three separate analyses were performed. The first 100×100 analysis involved the 15 career choice criteria (see Chapter 4) and 85 student input variables. The second 100×100 analysis involved eight criteria pertaining to educational attainment (see Chapter 3).[9] The last analysis with the sample of 3,821 students was performed with a somewhat larger matrix (126×126) which was made possible by improvements in the program. This last analysis included seven criteria concerning the student's final major field of study in college (see Chapter 4), the criterion of completing four years of college (see Chapter 3), and some 114 student input variables. It was impossible, however, to score each category on each student input variable as a separate dichotomous variable.

Each of the 28 analyses was first performed with all input variables in the original correlation matrix and then repeated excluding the five additional input variables (race, mother's education, etc.) obtained from the long-form followup questionnaire. The reason for performing the analyses in two ways was to determine if the five additional input variables contributed significantly to the prediction of the various output criteria. As it turned out, several of them entered some, but not all, of the 28 analyses. On this basis, it was decided to use the final regression equations that were based on all 89 input variables.

Each of the 28 regression analyses yielded a set of weights that could be applied to certain of the input variables to maximize prediction of the dependent (output) variable. This set of weights, when applied to the appropriate student input variables, yields an "expected" output variable which, when subtracted from the actual output variable, yields a residual output variable that is statistically independent of the input variables.[10] An array of 28 such residual output scores was obtained for each of the 36,405 subjects by applying these sets of weights to his input variables and subtracting the resulting expected output variable from his actual output variable.

An additional regression analysis was performed using these residual output scores. For this purpose, a subsample was drawn from the one-eighth sample of 3,821 students used in the multiple regression analyses just described. This subsample of 1,590 were students for whom scores on the National Merit Scholarship Qualifying Test were available (Astin, 1965d). The purpose of this analysis was to determine if the effects of the student's academic ability on the various output criteria had been adequately controlled in the earlier analysis. An additional objective was to assess the impact of several of the within-college environmental experiences mentioned earlier. These two purposes were carried out in one analysis, primarily to reduce computing costs.

The students' residual criterion scores were averaged within each college, separately for each of the 28 criterion variables. It is important to note that, in cases where the college has no differential effect on a particular outcome variable, its mean residual score will be near zero. For intance, the mean residual score for a particular criterion (e.g., dropping out of college) will be near zero when the actual percentage of students who drop out during the four years is equal or nearly equal to the percentage of dropouts that would be expected on the basis of the students' input characteristics. On the other hand, if the mean of the residuals is a relatively high positive value, the institution presumably has the effect of influencing students to drop out, since the actual percentage of dropouts exceeds the percentage that would be expected on the basis of the students' input characteristics. Conversely, a negative mean residual indicates that the institution tends to retain students.

The final step in the sequence of analyses was to identify possible environmental influences by correlating the institutions' mean scores on these residual criteria with various environmental characteristics. This series of analyses was similar in method to the initial analysis of student input variables: Environmental characteristics of the institutions were permitted to enter the regression equation until no additional environmental characteristic was capable of producing a significant reduction in the residual sum of the squares in the criterion variable.

A somewhat different methodology was used in the second series of college effects analyses: The institution was the unit of analysis, both in the control of differential student inputs and in the analysis of differential environmental effects. Thus, each student input and output variable was first aggregated separately for each institution. Input variables (e.g., percentage of entering students seeking the Ph.D.) were entered into the regression equation in a stepwise fashion until no additional input variable was capable of significantly reducing the residual sum of squares. At this stage in the analysis, when differential student inputs were presumably controlled, the environmental variables were permited to enter the analysis.[11]

The principal objection to this last form of analysis is that controlling differential student inputs tends to throw out the baby with the bath water. As a large body of evidence (Astin and Holland, 1961; Astin, 1963b, 1968a) shows, the college environment is highly dependent on the characteristics of the entering student body. Thus, when student input characteristics are controlled using the institution as the sampling unit, most of the distinctive environmental characteristics of the insitution may be removed before their effect can be assessed. This method of analysis is particularly prone to this error if the magnitude of the environmental effect is proportional to the institution's score on the input variable.

The effect can be demonstrated using once again the example of Ph.D. productivity. For purposes of illustration, let us assume that the student's desire to obtain the Ph.D. is increased if he attends an institution where a relatively high proportion of his fellow students plan to obtain a Ph.D. This institutional influence would have the effect of increasing the between-institution correlation of the percentage of entering students seeking the Ph.D. with the percentage of graduating students seeking the Ph.D. Although the control of student input using the student as the sampling unit might reduce the apparent magnitude of this environmental effect, it would not obliterate it. But when the institution is used as the sampling unit, the risk arises that the institutional effect will be removed along with the effect of differential student inputs.

An advantage to this method is that it tends to isolate the effects of those environmental characteristics that are independent of the student input to the institution. In other words, while those environmental characteristics that are highly dependent on the student input are not likely to show up as affecting the student output measures, the effects of those environmental characteristics that are independent of or only partially dependent on student input will not be obscured under this method of analysis. Since many institutions, particularly those that are not selective in their admissions, do not have direct control over the characteristics of their student inputs, this method tends to isolate institutional characteristics which are subject to more direct administrative control. Thus, results from analyses in which institutions are used as the unit of sampling may have more practical application than results based on the former type of analysis.

The results of our analyses are presented in the ensuing chapters as follows: Chapter 2 gives a descriptive summary of the class of 1965, including information on their college activities and on how they viewed their college environments. Chapters 3 and 4 present the results of the regression analyses, identifying the student input and college environmental variables that affected the various output measures. Chapter 3 deals with the student's educational attainment and achievement, whereas Chapter 4 deals with his career plans. The final chapter provides a summary of the findings by type of institution, discusses some of the implications of the findings for educational policy and practice, and suggests possibilities for future research.

REFERENCES

1. Studies of the educational backgrounds of Ph.D. recipients (Astin, 1962c; Harmon, 1961) have shown that these three characteristics substantially affected the student's chances of eventually obtaining a Ph.D. degree. An undergraduate man majoring in business, for example, has about one chance in 250 of eventually obtaining the Ph.D., whereas an undergraduate man majoring in chemistry has better than one chance in six. Obviously, an institution enrolling a high proportion of men planning to major in chemistry is likely to produce a considerably higher proportion of Ph.D.'s than is an institution enrolling a high proportion of men interested in becoming businessmen, no matter what the differential impact of these institutions may be once the students have matriculated.

2. The entire population was stratified according to Ph.D. outputs and the sample randomly selected within strata. Since the distribution of Ph.D. outputs of institutions was positively skewed, relatively higher proportions of institutions were selected from the higher strata in order to create a more heterogeneous sample.

3. National Computer Systems, Minneapolis, Minnesota.

4. We are indebted to Gerald V. Lannholm of the Educational Testing Service for assisting us in obtaining the data.

5. Letters requesting clearance to obtain the GRE data from ETS were sent from ACE President Logan Wilson to each of the 39 college presidents. After two followup letters, we secured responses from all 39 institutions.

6. Our failure to find GRE scores for all subjects in our lists resulted from several factors, including dropouts, transfers, clerical errors (including misspelled names), and absenteeism on the day of the testing.

7. These six measures of curricular emphasis, together with the size of the institution and the selectivity, comprise the Environmental Assessment Technique (EAT) developed previously by Astin and Holland (1961).

8. Two other within-college variables were lost because of irretrievable errors in data processing: participation in "honors" programs and the use of a commercial loan to support college costs.

9. Different combinations of input variables were used, depending upon the output variables being predicted. Thus, in predicting the career choice outcomes, we used all of the dichotomous 1961 choices of careers and majors and scored the other input variables continuously. In predicting the criteria of educational attainment, on the other hand, we used a more limited number of initial careers and majors and substituted certain relevant continuous variables (e.g., high school grades) scored dichotomously.

10. In terms of classical test theory, these residual scores would not be independent of the students' "true" input scores, if their obtained (actual) input scores contained random errors. Under these circumstances, the correct procedure would be to compute all intercorrelations using the standard deviations of the "true" rather than the obtained input scores. We were not able to perform such analyses, however, because of the difficulty in estimating the proportion of "true" variance in our dichotomously scored input variables.

11. Since the environmental variables were included in the original correlation matrix (179×179), these were actually residual environmental scores (i.e., partial rather than part correlations) that entered the analysis during this final stage.

2

A Descriptive Summary
of the Class of 1965

IN THIS CHAPTER, we present descriptive information about the Class of 1965. Thus, the chapter focuses on normative rather than inferential aspects of the college experience. Although such descriptive data do not explore causal relationships among the variables represented, they are useful in learning more about the student and in suggesting ideas and hypotheses that can later be tested.

Because of the possibility that tabulations of some of the data from the followup questionnaire may have been affected by biases in the sample of respondents, the first section of the chapter is devoted to a discussion of the weighting procedure used to compensate for such bias. The second section deals with the validity of the data. The third presents weighted descriptive data concerning the personal and background characteristics of the Class of 1965. The next four sections present weighted descriptive data concerning the students' undergraduate experiences and activities and their impressions of their colleges. The final section summarizes the material.

WEIGHTING THE DATA

A series of analyses were performed to determine the extent and possible effects of bias in the sample of respondents. Although response biases did not appear to have any appreciable effect on relationships among the various items, the fact that on many items (e.g., plans for graduate study) the mean scores of early respondents differed considerably from those of later respondents indicated the need to adjust the data in order to obtain tabulations more representative of the entire population of entering freshmen of 1961. We computed three sets of weights: one to adjust for differences between respondents and nonrespondents in the sample of 60,505 students to whom the followup questionnaires were sent, a second to adjust for the percentage of students among all 1961 entering freshman at each institution in the sample to whom questionnaires were mailed in 1965,[1] and a third to adjust for the disproportionate sampling of institutions from the various stratification cells of the original sampling design (see Astin, 1965d, pp. 102–5).

A stepwise multiple regression analysis was used to identify the biasing variables among respondents. This analysis was carried out on a sample of

4,003 students randomly selected from the original mailing list of 60,505. For each student, a dichotomously scored dependent variable was defined to indicate whether the student was a respondent or a nonrespondent. A pool of 97 precollege input variables served as the independent variables. They included sex, extracurricular achievements in high school (16 dichotomies), probable major field of study (14 dichotomies), probable future occupation (27 dichotomies), father's occupation (18 dichotomies), highest degree planned (5 dichotomies), high school grade average (9 dichotomies), father's education (6 dichotomies), and size of high school graduating class (3 dichotomies). The final regression equation included only those input variables whose independent contribution at each step to the reduction of the residual sums of squares was statistically significant at the .05 level of confidence, which was used as the cutoff point in the stepwise procedure.

The biasing variables in the sample of respondents were: high school grade average, father's education, highest degree planned, and publication of original work while attending high school. More specifically, students whose high school grades ranged from D through B, whose fathers had only some high school education, who planned to get less than a bachelor's degree, and who had not published original writing were less likely to complete and return the followup questionnaire. On the basis of this analysis, three of the biasing variables were recoded: The nine levels of high school grade average were collapsed into seven levels (D; C; C+; B−; B; B+ and A−, A, or A+), the six levels of father's education were collapsed into four levels (grammar school; some high school; high school graduate or some college; and college graduate or postgraduate degree), and the five levels of highest degree planned were redefined as a dichotomy (less than a bachelor's degree vs. bachelor's degree or higher).

The biasing variables defined a $7 \times 4 \times 2 \times 2$ four-way table into which the 36,405 respondents were sorted. Individual weights for each of the 112 cells consisted of the ratio between the number of students to whom questionnaires were mailed and the number who completed and returned them. In order to obtain more stable weights within some of the cells, it was necessary to collapse two of the variables: highest degree planned and publication or nonpublication of original work during high school. The individual weights for the final 28 cells, adjusted so that the total weighted N equals the actual number of respondents, are shown in Table 1. Weights of less than 1.00 indicate that the rate of response among students in the cell was higher than the overall rate of response; weights of more than 1.00 indicate that the rate of response in that cell was lower than the overall rate.

The weights in Table 1 clearly show that high school grade average was monotonically related to response bias: The higher the student's average, the greater the likelihood that he completed and returned the questionnaire. Although father's education was also related to the probability of obtaining a response, the relationship was not monotonic. The slight reversals in the

TABLE 1

Weights Used to Adjust for Response Bias

FATHER'S EDUCATIONAL LEVEL	STUDENT'S HIGH SCHOOL GRADE AVERAGE						
	(D)	(C)	(C+)	(B−)	(B)	(B+)	(A−, A, A+)
Grammar school or less	(9)[a]	(207)	(277)	(319)	(598)	(530)	(704)
	1.73	1.51	1.34	1.14	1.09	0.94	0.87
Some high school	(11)	(281)	(458)	(498)	(889)	(749)	(986)
	2.47	1.52	1.30	1.15	1.08	0.97	0.86
High school graduate or some college	(37)	(819)	(1401)	(1706)	(3006)	(2581)	(3492)
	1.86	1.42	1.22	1.10	1.03	0.93	0.84
College graduate or higher	(39)	(576)	(986)	(1298)	(2262)	(2313)	(3474)
	1.31	1.24	1.07	1.01	0.93	0.88	0.81

[a] Numbers in parentheses indicate sample size. Total $N = 30,506$; Men = 17,150; Women = 13,356. The sample size of 30,506 includes those students who returned usable completed long-form questionnaires to the ACE Office of Research; an additional 5,899 students provided only criterion information but did not return the longer questionnaire.

first two rows of Table 1 (at the lower levels of father's education) indicate that students whose fathers dropped out of high school were less likely than were other students, including those whose fathers had only a grammar school education, to return a questionnaire. The pattern of weights shown in Table 1 otherwise conforms to common-sense expectations that the less academically able students from relatively less educated families are least likely to return a mailed questionnaire. These results clearly indicate that it is essential to obtain some estimate of response bias in mail surveys and to adjust the data among the returns. For example, although 70 percent of the students who returned a questionnaire indicated that they planned to pursue graduate training, we estimated that only 59 percent of the students in the population were so inclined at the time of the followup survey. Similarly, 72 percent of the respondents indicated that they had completed four or more years of college, yet we estimated that only 65 percent of the students in the population had completed four or more academic years.

The marginal tabulations presented in this chapter were obtained by applying the product of the individual's weight and his two institutional weights to his data vector in an attempt to estimate the population parameters of these descriptive summary statistics. Thus, insofar as is possible, given our sample and pool of items, the data reflect the results that would have been obtained if (1) the response rate had been 100 percent, (2) followup questionnaires had been sent to the entire 1961 entering freshman class at each institution in the sample, and (3) our sample of institutions had included all regionally accredited four-year colleges and universities in the fall of 1961. The weighted summary data presented in this chapter are based on the responses of 30,506 students who returned the initial long form of our questionnaire; an additional 5,899 students filled out a short form giving criterion

information but did not return the longer questionnaire. The weighting procedure was applied only to the data obtained from those students who
returned the longer form.

VALIDITY OF THE DATA

Because the data presented in this chapter are based on student self-
reports, the question naturally arises: To what extent do the results reflect
inaccurate or deliberately distorted self-descriptions?

Our starting point is the assumption that the student is willing to cooperate: that is, to be sincere and honest. Furthermore, the information
presented here is based chiefly on responses to questions of fact rather than
to questions calling for opinion. Most of the information requested is
presumably known to the student and could, in theory, be verified by an
independent observer. Therefore, it is reasonable to suppose that a person
would deliberately given inaccurate information only if the task aroused conflict and defensiveness. The nature of the items, however, does not appear to
be such as to invite falsifying; the items are not "content threatening."
Under these circumstances, we have assumed that our results represent a
reasonably accurate descriptive summary of the Class of 1965.

BACKGROUND AND PERSONAL CHARACTERISTICS OF THE STUDENTS

Fifty-six percent of the students in the population were men; 44 percent
were women. Slightly more than one-third of the Class of 1965 were married
at the time of the followup survey. Of these, 5 percent had been married before starting college, over 58 percent while in college, and 36 percent after
leaving college. In addition, 38 percent of the married group had one or more
children. A summary of marital status by sex is shown in Table 2. The data
in the table support the notion that marriage is a more likely outcome of
college attendance for women than for men and that women are more likely
than are men to leave college as a consequence of marriage.

The students were asked to estimate their parents' current annual income
and to indicate both parents' educational levels (see Table 3). Only 7 percent
of the Class of 1965 reported that their parents' incomes were less than
$4,000; more than twice as many said that their parents' incomes were over
$19,000. The modal (21 percent) interval reported was $7,000–$9,999.
Almost half the students' fathers had received at least some college training,
and 42 percent of the mothers had continued their formal education beyond
the high school level. These data are shown in Table 3.

Data on race and religious background are summarized in Table 4.
Slightly more than 96 percent of the students reported their racial background as Caucasian. Almost 3 percent indicated that they were Negro, 0.1
percent American Indian, 0.4 percent Oriental, and 0.3 percent "other."
Since the proportion of Negroes in the population is about 11 percent, it is
clear that the American Negro is under-represented among the college-

TABLE 2

Marital Status

(percentages)

ITEM	MEN	WOMEN
Have you ever been married?		
No	70.5	58.9
Yes: now living with spouse	29.0	40.0
separated	0.2	0.4
divorced	0.3	0.6
widowed	0.0	0.1
When were you married?		
Before entering college	6.2	4.1
While in college: in 1961	2.2	2.1
in 1962	5.5	7.4
in 1963	14.4	15.8
in 1964	24.4	19.4
in 1965	18.0	8.0
After leaving college	29.4	43.1
How many children do you have?		
None	60.7	62.2
One	30.4	27.7
Two	6.7	8.5
Three or more	2.2	1.6

TABLE 3

Parental Income and Parents' Educational Level

(percentages)

ITEM	MEN	WOMEN
Estimated Current Annual Parental Income:		
Less than $4,000	7.6	6.8
$4,000–$6,999	20.1	18.2
$7,000–$9,999	22.7	19.5
$10,000–$12,999	18.8	19.2
$13,000–$15,999	11.1	11.9
$16,000–$18,999	5.7	6.1
$19,000–$21,999	3.5	3.9
$22,000–$24,999	2.2	3.0
$25,000 or more	8.3	11.3
Father's Education:		
Grammar school	14.8	12.1
Some high school	15.4	13.2
High school graduate	25.8	23.0
Some college	18.2	20.5
College degree	14.5	16.4
Postgraduate degree	11.3	14.8
Mother's Education:		
Grammar school	9.1	6.1
Some high school	12.9	11.2
High school graduate	38.9	36.8
Some college	19.5	22.6
College degree	15.8	18.3
Postgraduate degree	3.8	5.0

trained, particularly the Negro male; nearly twice as many Negro women as men were members of the Class of 1965, even though men outnumber women in the total college population.

TABLE 4
Racial and Religious Background
(percentages)

ITEM	MEN	WOMEN
Racial Background:		
Caucasian	97.4	95.4
Negro	1.8	3.8
American Indian	0.1	0.1
Oriental	0.5	0.3
Other	0.2	0.3
Religious Background:		
Protestant	66.2	68.2
Roman Catholic	21.9	21.6
Jewish	6.7	5.3
Other	3.2	2.9
None	2.0	2.0
Present Religious Preference:		
Protestant	53.4	59.3
Roman Catholic	19.8	21.6
Jewish	6.0	4.7
Other	5.1	4.7
None	15.7	9.7

Over two-thirds of the students indicated that they came from Protestant family backgrounds, and 22 percent reported Roman Catholic backgrounds. Although only 2 percent checked "none" for their family religious background, 13 percent said that they themselves have no religious preference at present. These data suggest a tendency, more pronounced among men than among women, for young adults to reject their parents' religious beliefs. Most of the defection appears to occur among students from Protestant families; only minor discrepancies between parents' and students' choices appeared for the Catholic and Jewish faiths. Although these data suggest that one outcome of college for many Protestant students may be a rejection of orthodoxy, it should be noted that similar trends have recently been observed among students from Protestant families even at the time of matriculation (Astin, Panos, and Creager, 1967a, 1967b).

FINANCES, EMPLOYMENT, AND HOUSING

Who pays for college expenses? How much money do college students earn? Where do the students live during college? Answers to these and related questions are presented in this section.

Finances

Data concerned with the financing of undergraduate college and living expenses are shown in Table 5. Eight of the twelve items listed in Table 5

TABLE 5
The Financing of Undergraduate Expenses
(percentages)

SOURCE OF FINANCIAL SUPPORT	MEN						WOMEN					
	None	1–20%	21–40%	41–60%	61–80%	81–100%	None	1–20%	21–40%	41–60%	61–80%	81–100%
Support from parents	8.3	20.5	12.4	16.6	18.4	23.8	4.1	12.4	8.3	11.7	16.6	46.9
Support from spouse	87.3	7.0	2.6	1.8	0.9	0.5	81.8	8.8	3.1	2.3	1.4	2.6
Scholarship or fellowship:												
From college	70.0	18.3	5.5	3.2	1.4	1.7	67.2	21.2	6.3	3.5	1.2	0.6
State or local government	87.5	8.1	2.1	1.3	0.7	0.3	86.1	8.1	2.5	1.7	1.1	0.7
Federal government	94.5	2.1	1.2	1.1	0.6	0.5	93.9	2.5	1.2	0.8	0.5	1.0
Own earnings	6.5	39.9	21.2	15.1	8.3	9.1	21.8	52.0	12.7	7.0	3.0	3.4
Loans:												
Federal government	78.8	12.8	5.0	2.5	0.8	0.2	76.0	12.2	5.4	4.0	1.8	0.6
State or local government	94.8	3.0	1.0	0.7	0.3	0.2	96.1	2.0	0.8	0.6	0.3	0.2
From college	93.7	5.3	0.7	0.2	0.0	0.0	94.3	4.6	0.6	0.3	0.1	0.2
Commercial	92.5	5.0	1.3	0.4	0.4	0.3	96.1	2.0	0.8	0.6	0.3	0.2
Other	93.4	4.0	1.2	0.8	0.3	0.2	94.0	3.6	1.1	0.5	0.4	0.4
Other sources	61.8	29.1	3.8	2.2	1.3	1.8	67.0	23.7	3.6	1.9	1.7	2.1

turned out *not* to be a source of financial aid during the undergraduate years for more than 75 percent of the Class of 1965. Predictably, parents were by far the largest single source of financial aid to the college student: Over 93 percent of the Class of 1965 reported that "support from parents" helped pay for some part of their college and living expenses. The only other source of undergraduate financial support reported by a majority of students was their own earnings: Over 87 percent helped pay their own way. It would appear that the expense of going to college was a financial burden borne largely by the parents and the students themselves.

The summer earnings of the Class of 1965 are given in Table 6. Slightly more than 11 percent earned $1,000 or more during the summer of 1962 (at the end of their freshman year); more than twice as many reported earnings of $1,000 or more during the summer of 1965. As would be expected, men earn substantially more money than women; over half the men, as compared with only 17 percent of the women, earned $700 or more in 1965. However, any notion that this differential in earning power is attributable to employer discrimination against women should be tempered by the recognition that women have a much easier financial go of it while in college than do men (see Table 5). Furthermore, parents with limited resources may be less likely to send their daughters to college. The notion that women who go to college come from relatively affluent families is supported by the data in Table 3 which show that more men than women came from the lower end of the socioeconomic scale. Thus, women may have less need for remunerative employment than do men.

The modal interval (34 percent) reported by the Class of 1965 as their

TABLE 6
Earnings Through Summer Employment
(percentages)

ITEM	None	$1–$99	$100–$199	$200–$299	EARNINGS $300–$499	$500–$599	$600–$699	$700–$999	$1,000– or More
Summer 1962									
Men	9.4	2.8	4.4	7.0	14.8	12.7	12.9	18.0	18.0
Women	28.8	7.8	8.8	11.8	16.8	10.8	7.8	5.4	2.0
Summer 1963									
Men	11.2	2.9	3.5	5.7	11.8	11.4	11.3	18.8	23.3
Women	29.8	6.9	8.0	10.4	16.1	10.3	8.4	7.3	2.9
Summer 1964									
Men	11.5	2.8	4.3	5.7	11.0	9.3	9.8	16.0	29.7
Women	35.0	7.1	6.8	7.7	13.7	8.4	7.9	8.7	4.7
Summer 1965									
Men	13.4	2.7	3.7	5.2	9.2	7.7	8.0	15.6	34.5
Women	41.8	6.4	5.0	6.1	10.2	6.7	6.3	9.3	8.0

TABLE 7

Estimated Average Monthly Income (before Deductions) for 1966

(percentages)

INCOME	INCOME FROM OWN WORK		TOTAL FAMILY INCOME[a]	
	Men	Women	Men	Women
None	14.6	18.0	11.9	8.8
Under $100	18.3	8.9	10.2	3.8
$100–$249	18.5	10.3	15.8	6.7
$250–$499	24.4	48.4	25.9	31.7
$500–$749	16.2	9.1	19.5	23.6
$750–$999	1.9	0.6	7.6	12.0
$1000–$1249	1.2	0.4	3.1	5.1
$1250–$1499	0.9	0.5	0.8	1.3
$1500 or more	4.0	3.8	5.1	6.9

[a] Not parental family.

anticipated 1966 average monthly incomes (before deductions) was $250–$499. As many as 5 percent expected to earn a monthly salary of $1,000 or more from their own work during 1966, and more than twice as many expected to be earning at least $1,000 a month from their total family income (not parental family) during 1966. These data are shown in Table 7. Although the typical male student expected to earn considerably more than the typical female student, the women expected a much larger total family income during 1966 than did the men. This finding suggests that college women tend to marry men whose earning potential for the immediate future is considerably greater than is that of their male classmates.

Undergraduate Employment Status

Students were asked also about the nature of the jobs they held both during the academic year and during the summer. During the 1961–62 academic year, 10 percent of the Class of 1965 were employed; of these, one-fifth reported that their jobs were career related. During the 1965–66 academic year (the time of the followup), three-fourths of the employed members of the Class of 1965 were doing career-related work. During the summer of 1962, over 60 percent of the students were employed, and almost one-third of these reported that their jobs were career related. During the summer of 1965, almost one-half of those who were employed were working in career-related jobs. These data, shown in Table 8, indicate that over the college years, the working members of the Class of 1965 tended more and more to take jobs that were related to their career choices.

Student Housing

Although 64 percent of the students lived in a college dormitory during their freshman year at college, only 25 percent were living in dormitories during the academic year 1964–65. This decrease is monotonic and apparently linear. The only other category of housing which showed a similar monotonic (but positive) trend over the years was the percentage of students

TABLE 8

Career-Related Employment Status during the College Years

(percentages)

| | MEN | | WOMEN | |
ITEM	Career-Related Job	Noncareer Job	Career-Related Job	Noncareer Job
Academic year 1961–1962	21.0	79.0	19.3	80.7
Summer 1962	18.2	81.8	19.6	80.4
Academic year 1962–1963	27.3	72.7	31.3	68.7
Summer 1963	24.8	75.2	26.8	73.2
Academic year 1963–1964	35.3	64.7	38.2	61.8
Summer 1964	33.1	66.9	36.8	63.2
Academic year 1964–1965	45.7	54.3	53.7	46.3
Summer 1965	46.4	53.6	50.6	49.4
Academic year 1965–1966	68.3	31.7	81.2	18.8

living off campus in their own apartments. As Table 9 indicates, women were more likely to live in a college dormitory throughout the college years than were men, a finding which lends support to the popular belief that *in loco parentis*—as applied by college officials—perpetuates our society's double standard with regard to treatment of the sexes. Because the rules and regulations regarding student housing are one part of the college environment that can be manipulated fairly easily by college and university officials, it would seem advisable that institutional researchers attempt to discover how these various housing arrangements affect the student's development.

EDUCATIONAL ACHIEVEMENT AND PLANS

In this section, we shall describe the student's educational achievements during the undergraduate years and his educational plans. (The personal and environmental factors affecting these achievements and plans are explored in detail in the next chapter.) Among the specific questions that concern us here are the following: How many students get a terminal degree within four

TABLE 9

Living Accommodations during the College Years

(percentages)

| | MEN | | | | WOMEN | | | |
RESIDENCE	1961–1962	1962–1963	1963–1964	1964–1965	1961–1962	1962–1963	1963–1964	1964–1965
With parents	24.4	26.5	24.7	20.9	20.3	23.1	21.4	18.6
Private apartment	7.6	16.0	23.8	33.5	2.8	7.8	14.3	23.0
College dormitory	57.3	36.2	26.0	19.4	72.9	54.1	41.8	31.4
Fraternity (sorority) house	7.1	14.5	14.2	10.9	0.8	7.9	9.7	8.4
Other student housing	2.1	2.4	3.1	4.1	2.1	2.9	3.3	3.3
Other	1.5	4.5	8.1	11.1	1.2	4.2	9.5	15.3

years after their matriculation? How many students drop out of or transfer from college during the undergraduate years? What reasons do the dropouts give for leaving college? How many students plan to go into graduate study? When do the students expect to complete their formal education?

Persistence in College

As Table 10 indicates, we estimated that 65 percent of the students in the population had completed four or more years of college at the time of the survey. Thus, over one-third of the Class of 1965 did not complete four academic years of college work within the four years following matriculation. Slightly less than 60 percent of the students had received a terminal degree; almost half of the men, but only 34 percent of the women, held no

---

TABLE 10

Years of College Completed, Highest Degree Held, and
Persistence in College

(percentages)

ITEM	MEN	WOMEN
Years of college completed:		
Less than one term	1.9	2.3
Less than one year	1.9	2.3
One year	5.5	7.0
Two years	9.3	9.3
Three years	16.7	13.7
Four or more years	64.7	65.4
Highest degree held:		
None	46.5	34.3
Associate	3.4	2.5
Bachelor's	49.3	61.7
Master's	0.5	0.2
Other	0.2	1.4
Changed college or dropped out of college for any period of time since entering college of matriculation in 1961:		
Yes	44.0	44.6
No	56.0	55.4
Left first college:		
Because of unsatisfactory academic work	21.6	8.5
Because of disciplinary reasons	3.7	2.5
Voluntarily	74.7	89.0
Would have left first college even if greater financial resources had been available:		
Yes	57.9	66.0
No	26.9	20.0
Not sure	15.2	14.0
Attended any other colleges since 1961:		
Yes (3 or more)	2.2	2.2
Yes (2 other)	12.5	13.4
Yes (one other)	47.4	48.9
No	37.8	35.5

degree at the time of the followup study. More than 44 percent of the students in the population had changed colleges or dropped out of college since their matriculation in 1961.

The data shown in Table 10 indicate that extensive and complex migration between different colleges occurred among a substantial proportion of students during the first four years following matriculation. Thus, of the large proportion (44 percent) of students who left college before the traditional four-year period of residence was completed, nearly two-thirds enrolled at some other college. Nearly 15 percent of those students who left their first undergraduate college ended up attending *two or more* institutions during the first four years following matriculation at their first college. Extrapolating to the population of college students, it appears that nearly 7 percent of all entering college freshmen are exposed to the environments of at least three different collegiate institutions during the first four years after they leave high school. These generalizations appear to apply equally to men and women.

Of the students who changed institutions or dropped out of college for any period of time since 1961, 16 percent reported that they were asked to leave their first college because of unsatisfactory academic work, over 80 percent indicated that they left voluntarily, and 3 percent admitted that they were forced to leave for disciplinary reasons. Almost two-thirds of the students who left their college of matriculation said that they would have left even if they had had greater financial resources at their disposal; slightly more than 63 percent of these students had attended at least one other college since 1961. These data suggest that increased financial aid may not be the panacea, as some have suggested, for solving the problem of college student attrition.

Table 11 shows the importance assigned by the dropouts to each of several possible reasons for leaving college. Almost one-half of the students who left their first college indicated they were dissatisfied with the environment, a finding which suggests that, although great amounts of time and effort are expended annually by counselors, students, and parents in deciding on the "right" college, much more needs to be learned about the complex decision process involved in selecting a college. Over 40 percent reported that they dropped out of college because they had changed their career plans or wanted time to reconsider their interests and vocational goals. Almost 30 percent of the women said that marriage was a major reason for their decision to leave college, as compared with only 8 percent of the men.

The factors shown in Table 11 are, to be sure, the student's ex post facto explanations about why he dropped out of college, but they provide clues as to the types of items that should be included as input or control variables in studies of college student attrition. For example, the entering student's marital plans, his anxieties about college finances, and his degree of confi-

TABLE 11

Reasons for Leaving College of Matriculation

(percentages)

REASON	MEN		WOMEN	
	Major Reason	Minor Reason[a]	Major Reason	Minor Reason[a]
Changed career plans	22.1	15.4	20.7	13.6
Dissatisfied with college environment	26.7	22.3	27.0	19.7
Scholarship terminated	2.8	3.1	1.4	2.5
Wanted time to reconsider interests and goals	26.4	22.4	17.7	16.2
Marriage	7.8	3.1	29.0	6.1
Pregnancy	1.1	0.6	8.2	1.4
Tired of being a student	11.3	16.3	6.0	14.0
Could not afford cost	23.6	15.6	17.8	12.7
Academic record unsatisfactory	15.5	20.8	5.8	11.1
Drafted	1.4	0.9	0.0	0.1

[a] A third alternative, "unrelated to my decision," is not shown.

dence in his expressed interests and career plans may all prove to be predictors of attrition.

Undergraduate Achievements

Data on college grades are shown in Table 12. The modal (36 percent) overall college grade average as reported by the Class of 1965 was B− or C+. Over 12 percent had a B+ or better overall grade average, and 22 percent had a C overall grade average in their major field of study. These data clearly show that women tend to make much higher grades, both overall and in their major subjects, than do men. This trend has been found repeatedly in studies at both the undergraduate and the secondary school level. The grade level that seems to separate the sexes most distinctly is B or better: 46 percent of the women, as compared with less than 30 percent of the men, achieve this level in their overall college grade averages.

That 4 percent of the women reported averages of less than C during the undergraduate years is consistent with the fact that approximately 4 percent of the woman were asked to leave their first college for academic reasons.[2] Among the men, however, only 8 percent reported undergraduate grade point averages of less than C, even though 9 percent of the men said they had been asked to leave their first college for academic reasons. The reason for this discrepancy may be that those men who leave their first college for academic reasons are able to improve their performance more often in their second college than are the women who leave their first college for academic reasons. Of course, it is possible that women who leave because of poor academic performance are less likely to enter a second college than are men who leave for similar reasons.

Table 13 shows the students' responses to a question asking them about 12 academic and extracurricular achievements during college. (See also

TABLE 12
Overall College and Major Field Grade Average
(percentages)

	MEN		WOMEN	
GRADE AVERAGE		Major		Major
	Overall	Subject	Overall	Subject
3.75–4.00 (A or A+)	1.4	7.1	2.3	9.9
3.25–3.74 (A– or B+)	8.1	20.2	14.3	29.7
2.75–3.24 (B)	19.6	33.5	29.8	34.7
2.25–2.74 (B– or C+)	36.9	24.6	33.8	17.5
1.75–2.24 (C)	26.3	12.2	15.4	6.7
1.25–1.74 (C– or D+)	6.6	1.9	3.7	1.1
Less than 1.25 (D or less)	1.1	0.5	0.7	0.5

Table 17, which deals with their achievements during the senior year only.) Slightly more than 30 percent had initiated an independent research study during college, and 17 percent had participated in departmental or general honors programs during college. Table 13 also shows that more than one-third of the men, but only one-fifth of the women, had been placed on academic probation since entering college in 1961. Except for this and other indications that the women were superior in academic performance and that the men more frequently had achievements in science, the pattern of extra-curricular achievements was remarkably similar for the two sexes.

Educational and Vocational Plans

At the time of the followup survey, only 23 percent of the students reported that the bachelor's degree was the highest academic degree they planned to obtain; 70 percent said they hoped to take a postbaccalaureate

TABLE 13
Academic and Extracurricular Achievements During the Undergraduate Years
(percentages)

ACHIEVEMENT	MEN	WOMEN
Participated in the Undergraduate Research Program of National Science Foundation	2.1	2.0
(Was placed on academic probation)[a]	(36.7)	(20.9)
Assisted on research project	18.3	16.5
Independent research project	31.9	30.6
Elected to "Who's Who in American Colleges"	2.8	3.9
Elected to Phi Beta Kappa	8.0	9.5
Graduated with honors	10.7	14.1
Worked as laboratory assistant	12.4	8.1
Participated in departmental honors program	11.5	13.0
Participated in general honors program	9.5	12.7
Published a scientific article	2.4	1.1
Published other article	5.6	5.8

[a] Though not considered an achievement, this item was included for comparative purposes. See question 46 of the following questionnaire, Appendix B.

degree, and 26 percent of these students hoped to go on to the doctoral level. The degree plans of the Class of 1965 are shown in Table 14.

Even though 32 percent of the students acknowledged that they were not sure when they would obtain the highest degree to which they aspired, the data shown in Table 14 suggest that the Class of 1965 has somewhat unrealistic aspirations. A similar trend was noted in a recent study by Davis (1964), who found that more than three-fourths of a large sample of graduating college seniors expressed an interest in pursuing postgraduate training. If we can infer from these data that such a trend is general in higher education, it would seem that the articulation between undergraduate and graduate institutions must be much more carefully planned and evaluated.

TABLE 14

Level of Educational Aspiration

(percentages)

ITEM	MEN	WOMEN
Highest degree planned:		
None	2.2	5.8
Associate (or equivalent) (A.A., A.S., etc.)	2.6	3.0
Bachelor's degree (A.B., B.A., B.S., etc.)	21.7	25.3
Master's degree (M.A., M.S., etc.)	37.8	54.7
Ph.D. or Ed.D.	18.0	8.1
M.D., D.D.S., or D.V.M.	6.4	0.7
LL.B. or J.D.	8.4	0.5
B.D.	0.9	0.1
Other	2.0	1.8
Expected date of attainment:		
Degree already received	5.2	12.3
1965	1.9	1.9
1966	11.6	9.3
1967	10.9	8.9
1968	14.4	8.5
1969	14.9	7.3
Later than 1969	16.6	9.1
Not sure	24.6	42.7

The differences between men and women with respect to educational plans are indeed striking. Even though nearly equal proportions of the two sexes said that they would obtain some sort of graduate degree, nearly twice as many women as men were not sure when they would actually receive it. The sexes differed also in the level of graduate degree they planned to obtain, with one-third of the men, as compared with less than 10 percent of the women, aspiring to doctoral-level or professional degrees (Ph.D. or Ed.D., medical degrees, law degrees, etc.). Women were much more likely to be pursuing the master's degree, a trend which in part reflects their much higher concentration in the field of education.

Perhaps the most significant aspect of these data is that the percentages of either sex who had abandoned all hope of obtaining some college-level degree were very small. Since more than one-third of the students had completed no more than three years of undergraduate training at the time of the survey, these results indicate that the American student's desire for a full college education dies hard.

Detailed data on the specific career choices of the Class of 1965, and an analysis of the college environmental factors affecting these choices, are presented in Chapter 4. In this section, we shall summarize the students' responses to items concerning the general characteristics of their anticipated future jobs and job environments. The data in Table 15 show that, although more than 15 percent indicated that their first employment would be in a Federal, state, or local government job, less than 10 percent chose the government as a career employer. Business (private company) and education were chosen most consistently both as first employers and as career employers. Within the field of education, however, there occurred some very interesting major shifts from first employer to career employer. Many students of both

TABLE 15
Career Expectations
(percentages)

EMPLOYER	MEN		WOMEN	
	First Employer	Career Employer	First Employer	Career Employer
Government:				
Federal	15.2	8.2	4.9	5.1
State/local	4.2	1.6	5.2	3.2
Education:				
Elementary/secondary	13.7	5.9	44.2	34.8
Higher education	7.6	13.6	4.8	12.7
Other Nonprofit:				
Hospital/clinic	3.9	1.4	9.6	7.9
Social welfare	0.6	0.5	2.8	4.2
Church	1.5	1.6	1.2	1.2
Other	0.5	0.4	1.6	1.4
Business and Services:				
Self-employed	5.2	18.0	1.5	3.9
Private company	37.7	32.2	18.6	17.4
Partnership	4.5	10.4	0.6	1.3
Research	2.8	3.9	2.1	2.3
Other	2.8	2.3	2.9	4.6

WORK ACTIVITY	MEN			WOMEN		
	Little or None	Moderate Amount	Major Amount	Little or None	Moderate Amount	Major Amount
Teaching	52.5	29.4	22.6	28.8	24.1	47.1
Research and development	39.4	42.6	18.0	54.3	36.6	9.1
Administration	21.0	35.2	43.8	57.9	31.9	10.2
Science	42.3	23.0	34.7	46.7	23.3	30.0

sexes who intended to begin their careers working in elementary or secondary education planned to switch to some other career employer after a time. In contrast, higher education as a career employer stands to gain a considerable proportion of students from different first employers. These two trends were counterbalanced sufficiently so that the total proportion of students intending to work within the field of education changed only slightly from anticipated first employer to career employer.

Table 15 also shows that twice as many men as women planned to devote a major amount of their career activity to research and development, that more than 40 percent of the men but only 10 percent of the women saw administrative activities as forming a major part of their future careers, and that more than twice as many women as men felt that teaching would be their primary career activity.

EXTRACURRICULAR ACTIVITIES

In this section, we discuss some of the typical activities and achievements of those members of the Class of 1965 who were enrolled as students during the academic year 1964–65. Table 16 shows the students' membership status in a number of formal college organizations. About 30 percent were members of a national or local social fraternity or sorority, although one in five of these considered himself inactive. Nearly 10 percent of the class were members of a college choir, glee club, or marching band, and one-fourth participated in extracurricular activities as members of honorary (subject matter) societies.

TABLE 16

Membership Status in Campus Organizations

(percentages)

| | MEN | | WOMEN | |
ORGANIZATION	Active Member	Inactive Member[a]	Active Member	Inactive Member[a]
National social fraternity or sorority	28.0	7.2	21.8	6.6
Local social fraternity or sorority	8.6	1.7	7.9	2.1
Intramural athletic team	40.8	4.0	11.2	2.0
College athletic team	12.4	0.9	3.1	0.7
Choir or glee club	5.8	0.7	11.4	1.1
Marching band	2.4	0.2	1.3	0.4
Honorary (subject matter) fraternity	20.4	4.0	22.4	4.6

[a] A third alternative, "not a member," is not shown.

The largest differences between men and women with respect to organizational membership occurred in the area of sports. For both intramural athletic teams and college athletic teams, the proportion of men who participated was nearly four times as great as the proportion of women. The only organization shown in Table 16 in which substantially larger percentages of women participated is the choir or glee club, where proportionally they outnumbered the men two to one.

Those students who had remained in the same college since first matriculating in the fall of 1961 were asked a series of questions about their activities and experiences during the academic year 1964–65 (presumably their senior year in college). These questions involved two different types of activities: those which would normally occur only once for a given student during a single year (e.g., got married), and those which might be engaged in repeatedly (e.g., had a blind date). Data for the first type are shown in Table 17. Relatively high percentages of both men (34.0) and women (43.2) reported that they fell in love during their senior year; this finding is consistent with the fact that about one student in five reported getting married during the senior year. About one student in ten changed his major field during the senior year, and about one in four changed his long-term career plans; apparently for many undergraduate students, the question of career choice is still largely unsettled, even during the last year in college. These findings suggest further that additional changes in career choices are to be expected even after these students have completed college and entered graduate or professional schools.

TABLE 17
Senior Year Experiences
(percentages)

EXPERIENCE	MEN	WOMEN
Elected to a student office	22.8	29.1
Played on a varsity athletic team	11.6	2.5
Changed long-term career plans	28.2	26.4
Flunked a course	16.4	6.6
Changed major field	13.9	9.2
Fell in love	34.0	43.2
Got married	18.5	21.9
Had a lead in a college play	2.4	3.1
Wrote an article for the school paper or magazine	14.7	14.0

Except in the case of athletic achievement ("played on a varsity athletic team"), the proportions of men and women who reported performing the various extracurricular achievements listed in Table 17 were very similar. Thus, approximately one in four reported being elected to a student office, approximately one in seven reported having written an article for the school paper or magazine, and approximately 3 percent reported having had a lead in a college play during their senior year. These findings are consistent with the data shown earlier in Table 13.

The second group of items, those that concern the frequency of various activities during the senior year, are shown in Table 18. This heterogeneous

TABLE 18
Senior Year Activities
(percentages)

Activity	Men		Women	
	Occasionally	Frequently[a]	Occasionally	Frequently[a]
Stayed up all night	54.9	6.3	50.8	6.5
Came late to class	62.3	5.1	62.0	5.2
Prayed (not including grace before meals)	42.4	29.2	35.1	49.7
Listened to New Orleans (Dixieland) Jazz	52.8	5.1	50.6	5.1
Gambled with cards or dice	35.4	4.8	11.2	0.7
Lost privileges for infraction of college rules	2.9	0.2	7.9	0.2
Played a musical instrument	19.1	12.4	34.4	16.9
Took a nap or rest during the day	57.3	32.5	55.3	38.2
Drove a car	27.0	67.8	33.7	52.2
Discussed sex with friends	62.5	33.9	65.5	30.6
Drank beer	44.1	39.1	42.5	22.2
Voted in a student election	39.7	45.6	34.8	52.5
Studied in the library	48.2	45.1	44.5	50.4
Attended a ballet performance	12.5	1.1	23.4	3.5
Overslept and missed a class or appointment	47.0	4.3	37.9	2.7
Had a blind date	39.0	2.4	38.2	2.6
Drank in a bar or club	53.4	26.7	50.9	18.8
Attended church	38.9	37.4	34.3	51.8
Participated in informal group singing	46.6	13.1	49.9	28.5
Cheated on examinations	15.0	0.2	9.3	0.2
Became intoxicated	49.7	5.0	31.0	1.5
Drank wine	42.8	3.2	50.3	5.7
Went to the movies	65.5	31.2	62.1	35.0
Discussed how to make money with other students	64.6	24.5	61.6	13.6
Listened to folk music	60.8	20.4	57.1	37.0
Attended a public recital or concert	53.4	14.4	58.5	25.0
Made wisecracks in class	41.4	3.2	29.6	2.5
Arranged a date for another student	50.9	6.4	51.8	7.9
Went to an overnight or weekend party	33.5	4.4	28.5	4.2
Took weight-reducing or dietary formula	8.8	1.3	21.2	6.1
Argued with other students	71.8	16.5	72.1	9.6
Was interviewed as a client in the college counseling center	18.5	3.2	16.3	2.2
Called a teacher by his first name	29.9	6.6	20.4	4.9
Checked out a book or journal from the college library	41.3	54.4	22.5	75.3
Tried on clothes in a store without buying anything	45.0	3.6	68.3	19.9
Asked questions in class	48.9	49.6	51.3	45.7

[a] A third alternative, "not at all," is not shown.

pool represents behavioral "stimuli" that were identified in a recent study of college environments (Astin, 1968a). Those activities engaged in by nearly all the students (more than 95 percent) of both sexes during their senior year included discussing sex with friends, going to the movies, asking questions in class, and checking out a book or journal from the college library. Very high percentages of both men and women (85–95 percent) also reported that they studied in the library, voted in a student election, took a nap or rest during the day, and regularly drove a car during their senior year. Activities engaged in by less than 30 percent of both sexes included attending a ballet performance, taking weight-reducing or dietary formula, and cheating on examinations. Although very low proportions (less than 10 percent) of the students reported losing privileges for infractions of the college rules, it is interesting to note that the percentage of women who were so penalized (8.1) was substantially larger than the percentage of men (3.1). Since the rate of drinking, getting drunk, and cheating on examinations is higher among men than among women, the difference between the sexes with respect to lost privileges substantiates the notion that colleges perpetuate the double standard.

IMPRESSIONS AND EVALUATIONS OF THE COLLEGE

The students attending college during 1964–65 were also asked to rate their institution with respect to their satisfaction with the overall college experience and with a number of its specific features. These data are shown in Table 19.

Surely the most significant data in the table concern the students' overall evaluation of their undergraduate colleges. More than 80 percent of both sexes reported that they were either "satisfied" or "very satisfied" with their college. Approximately 10 percent reported that they were "on the fence," and only about six percent reported that they were either "dissatisfied" or "very dissatisfied" with their college experience. Thus, in spite of the severe criticism that many student groups have leveled recently at American higher education, the vast majority of students evaluate their colleges favorably. Two caveats should be observed in interpreting these results, however. First of all, the "dissatisfied customers" are probably much more likely to be found among students who drop out of their first college; these students were not included in the tabulation shown in Table 19. Second, in the four-year interval between the followup study and the publication of this report, student criticism of American colleges and universities has increased considerably, or at least so the mass media would suggest. Nevertheless, it should be noted that these data were collected approximately one year *after* the first major student protests began at the Berkeley campus of the University of California in the fall of 1964.

As Table 19 indicates, men and women graduates were almost perfectly agreed in their evaluations of specific aspects of the college. Thus, students appeared to be best satisfied with the number of personal contacts they had with classmates, with their freedom in course selection, and with the number

TABLE 19
Impressions of the College
(percentages)

SPECIFIC ASPECT	MEN		WOMEN	
	Too Much or Too Many	Just About the Right Amount[a]	Too Much or Too Many	Just About the Right Amount[a]
Freedom in course selection	3.6	81.1	2.4	77.2
Social life	7.1	71.1	4.2	73.2
Personal contacts with classmates	2.4	81.7	2.3	80.6
Work required in courses	11.7	75.4	14.8	75.3
Outlets for creative activities	1.8	58.0	1.6	57.1
Sleep	3.9	62.7	1.9	54.7
Exercise	1.2	48.5	1.1	46.0
Personal contacts with faculty	0.7	58.6	1.5	60.5
Personal contacts with family	4.8	73.4	3.7	78.1
Advice and guidance from faculty and staff	1.0	60.9	1.8	64.0

OVERALL EVALUATION	MEN	WOMEN
Very satisfied	40.0	41.3
Satisfied	43.8	42.2
On the fence	10.1	10.1
Dissatisfied	4.8	4.5
Very dissatisfied	1.2	1.3

[a] A third alternative, "not enough," is not shown.

of personal contacts they had with their families in their senior year. They were least satisfied with the number of outlets for creative activities and the amount of exercise that they had during their senior year. Except in the case of the item dealing with required course work, where the dissatisfied students were about equally divided between having too much and too little, those students who were dissatisfied most often indicate that they have had "too little or too few" of a particular item. For instance, they indicated that they would have preferred more personal contacts with the faculty, more social life, more advice and guidance from faculty and staff, and so forth.

Table 20 shows the students' rating of the college "image" and of its psychological "climate" or atmosphere. Over 50 percent of the students felt that there was a great deal of pressure to get high grades, that most of their fellow students were of a high caliber academically, that there was keen competition among students for high grades, and that being in college built poise and maturity. The pressure to get high grades was felt more by men (55 percent) than by women (49 percent). Over one-third of the students said that they felt "lost" when they first came to the campus, and almost as many (31 percent) felt that most students on the campus were like "numbers in a book." Over two-thirds of the students said that the labels "social," "practical," "warm," "realistic," and "liberal" were very descriptive of their college. Only 20 percent thought that "intellectual" was highly descriptive of the college atmosphere, and 16 percent said that the label did not apply at all.

TABLE 20
The College Image
(percentages)

DESCRIPTIVE LABEL	MEN		WOMEN	
	Very Descriptive	In Between[a]	Very Descriptive	In Between[a]
Intellectual	16.5	66.7	21.4	64.9
Snobbish	5.7	31.1	5.0	34.7
Social	36.6	52.6	35.9	52.8
Victorian	6.1	26.6	5.9	25.2
Practical-minded	34.8	57.3	31.9	59.6
Warm	36.5	51.9	48.6	43.0
Realistic	39.7	53.3	38.5	54.5
Liberal	32.0	53.3	34.2	51.8

ITEM	MEN	WOMEN
The students are under a great deal of pressure to get high grades	54.7	48.6
The student body is apathetic and has little "school spirit"	50.1	43.9
Most of the students are of a very high calibre academically	50.2	52.7
There is keen competition among most of the students for high grades	61.0	53.8
Freshmen have to take orders from upperclassmen for a period of time	21.3	27.7
There isn't much to do except go to class and study	21.7	21.0
I felt "lost" when I first came to the campus	33.5	33.2
Being in this college builds poise and maturity	74.6	75.3
Athletics are overemphasized	15.2	13.2
The classes are usually run in a very informal manner	62.5	62.6
Most students are like "numbers in a book"	33.0	27.6

[a] A third alternative, "not at all descriptive," is not shown.

The data in Table 20 once again support the contention that most members of the Class of 1965 were relatively well satisfied with their undergraduate college. Thus, the majority of students felt that being in college had increased their poise and maturity, and only a few felt that athletics were overemphasized, that there was not much to do except go to class and study, or that most of the students were like "numbers in a book." Similarly, a relatively small number of students felt that their college was "snobbish" or "Victorian."

SUMMARY

In this chapter, we have presented descriptive information about the backgrounds, achievements, activities, and plans of the Class of 1965. We have also reported detailed information concerning their perceptions of the college environment and their satisfaction with the undergraduate experience. All of the data were differentially weighted so as to represent the entire population of students entering four-year accredited colleges and universities in the fall of 1961. The major findings were as follows:

1. Although the students as a group tended to come from relatively well-educated and affluent families, all levels of income and family educational

background were represented in the student population. In terms of the expected base rate in the total population of college-age students, those entering college in 1961 included a relatively high percentage of Jews and a relatively low percentage of Negroes, in particular Negro men.

2. The bulk of the student's undergraduate college expenses was carried by the parents, although student employment was frequently a substantial source of support during college. Scholarships and loans were a major source of support for only a small minority of students.

3. Although most students began their college years living in dormitories, many shifted to apartments during the undergraduate years. The shift was much greater for men, however, than for women. The percentage of students who lived with their parents and commuted to college (approximately one-fifth) remained relatively constant throughout the undergraduate years.

4. Nearly two-thirds of the students had completed four or more years of college during the four years following matriculation. Only about half of the men and approximately 62 percent of the women, however, had obtained a bachelor's degree in that time period. Although 44 percent of the students left their first college before the end of the four years, most of them transferred to another institution rather than dropping out of college completely. The majority of those students who did drop out reported that having additional funds would not have changed their decision. The reasons most frequently given for leaving college were dissatisfaction with the college environment, changes in career plans, and the need to reconsider career interests. Among the women, marriage was the most frequently cited major reason for dropping out of the first college.

5. More than 10 percent of the students who completed their undergraduate training during the four-year period graduated with honors, although high grades and academic honors were more common among the women than among the men. Men, on the other hand, were more likely to take part in scientific and athletic activities during the undergraduate years.

6. Nearly three-fourths of the total group of students reported that they intended to obtain a graduate degree, even though many of them had not yet completed even their undergraduate work. Men intending to do graduate work were about equally divided between those planning to get the master's degree and those planning doctoral-level or professional degrees, whereas the vast majority of women planning graduate work aspired to the master's degree only. The men were much more sure about the specific date when they would complete their graduate degree. Most of the students felt that, after completing their education, they would begin work for a private company, an educational institution, or the Federal government. Later on, however, many of them, particularly the men, expect either to be self-employed or to be working in a partnership of some kind.

7. Although some students expressed dissatisfaction with certain aspects

of their undergraduate experience, the large majority were favorable in their judgments and seemed relatively well satisfied with most aspects of their experience during the four years in college.

In the chapters that follow, we shall explore some of the personal and environmental factors that affect the student's achievement and plans during these undergraduate years.

REFERENCES

1. It will be recalled that the number of students to whom the 1965 followup questionnaire was sent was slightly less than half of the number who furnished input information in 1961.

2. These percentages were obtained from Table 10 by multiplying the percentage of students who leave their first college (44.0 for men and 44.6 for women) by the percentage of dropouts (21.6 and 8.5 respectively) who indicate that they were asked to leave their college for academic reasons. In other words, these percentages are based on the total sample of students, rather than on just those who left their initial college.

3

Determinants of Educational Attainment and Educational Plans

THIS CHAPTER is concerned with the personal and environmental factors that affect the student's educational achievement and educational plans. We shall present the results of our analyses for these specific outcomes:

1. Attrition during the undergraduate years.
2. Attainment of the baccalaureate degree
3. Highest level of academic degree planned
4. Performance on the Area Tests of the Graduate Record Examination (GRE)

The first three sections deal with the influence of student input characteristics, of within-institution environmental characteristics, and of between-institution environmental characteristics, respectively. The particular outcomes considered in each are attrition, attainment of the baccalaureate, and plans for graduate study. The fourth section examines traditional notions about the effect of institutional "excellence" on student achievement, as measured by scores on the Graduate Record Examination; it is presented in a somewhat different manner from the first three sections because the data were obtained after the earlier analyses had been completed. Finally, the findings about influences on educational attainment and plans are summarized.

THE INFLUENCE OF STUDENT INPUT CHARACTERISTICS

In this section we shall present the findings from the analyses in which student input characteristics were used to predict the various educational outcomes. Results will be presented separately for each of the first three measures of educational progress and plans.

College Student Attrition[1]

For the purposes of this analysis, the student's criterion status (dropout or nondropout) was defined as follows: a *nondropout* was any student who reported in 1965 that he had completed four or more academic years of college credit work, whether or not he had received a baccalaureate degree or its equivalent. All other students were considered to be *dropouts*, even if they were enrolled in college at the time of the followup study.[2] Because some of the students classified as dropouts in this analysis will eventually graduate and some of those classified as nondropouts will never receive a terminal degree, this analysis may be regarded as an examination of the personal and environmental factors associated with completing four academic years of college work within the four years following matriculation.[3] The results of the multiple regression analysis predicting persistence in college from freshman input data are shown in Table 21.

In brief, Table 21 indicates that the college student who was most likely not to complete four years of college within the four years following matriculation was one who had relatively low grades in high school, who came from a relatively low socioeconomic background, and whose racial background was either American Indian or "other."[4] In addition, the dropout was relatively more likely than was the nondropout to have declared secretary, businessman, or engineer as a career choice at the time of entrance to college, to have been married before starting college, and to have participated in high school plays. Finally, women were more likely to drop out than were men.

Although sex was not significantly related to dropping out in the zero-order correlation matrix ($r[phi] = -.002$), it did enter into the stepwise multiple regression analysis. This result is somewhat surprising since, as Summerskill (1962, p. 631) has pointed out, "studies over the years . . . have either shown little sex difference in attrition rates . . . or somewhat less attrition among women at certain colleges." An examination of each step in the regression analysis reveals that the largest adjustments in the partial correlation between sex and the dropout criterion, prior to the entry of sex into the regression analysis, occurred after the entry of high school grades. Thus, the explanation seems to be that, among entering college freshmen, women usually have better academic records than do the men; when this advantage has been controlled, however, we find that men are more likely to remain in college than were women. In short, given a man and a woman with the same high school grade average, the woman is the more likely to drop out of college.

Clearly, our ability to predict whether or not a student will drop out of college is limited. Indeed, even though this analysis dealt with a national sample of college students and a large and diverse pool of input measures, the best linear combination of input variables accounted for only 9 percent of the variance in the criterion.

Attainment of the Baccalaureate

On the followup questionnaire, the students indicated the highest academic degree they held at the time of the survey. The notion that the traditional four-year period of residence required to obtain the bachelor's degree is not a relevant time span for all students is supported by the finding that 35 percent of the sample had not completed at least four academic years of college in the four years following matriculation and that 40 percent had not received a bachelor's degree (see Chapter 2, Table 10). On the other hand, almost 60 percent of the students *had* obtained a bachelor's degree after four

TABLE 21

The Prediction of Persistence in College (Completion of Four Years of College by 1965) from Freshman Input Data (1961)

(N = 3,821 students)

STEP	STUDENT INPUT VARIABLE ENTERING EQUATION AT DESIGNATED STEP	SIGN	R	R^2	F-VALUE* To Enter Equation	F-VALUE* In Final Equation
1	Average grade in high school—C	−	.153	.023	91.2	101.6
2	Average grade in high school—C+	−	.191	.036	52.4	53.7
3	Average grade in high school—A	+	.215	.046	39.0	23.3
4	Career choice—Secretary	−	.231	.054	29.2	22.5
5	Father's education—Postgraduate	+	.244	.059	23.3	13.8
6	Average grade in high school—B −	−	.252	.064	17.8	22.9
7	Married before college matriculation	−	.259	.067	13.2	13.0
8	Career choice—Businessman	−	.264	.070	12.2	17.7
9	Sex—Female	−	.270	.073	12.5	20.1
10	High school—Elected to student office	+	.275	.076	12.2	13.9
11	Religious background—Jewish	+	.280	.078	9.2	7.7
12	Career choice—Engineer	−	.283	.080	8.4	10.7
13	Highest degree planned—Master's	+	.287	.082	9.0	8.8
14	Race—White	+	.291	.084	8.7	15.8
15	High school—Participated in school plays	−	.294	.086	7.8	8.4
16	Father's education—Grammar school	−	.296	.088	6.3	6.8
17	Average grade in high school—B	−	.298	.089	5.0	4.9
18	Race—Oriental	+	.300	.090	4.3	7.2
19	Race—Negro	+	.302	.091	5.4	5.4

* $F_{05} = 3.84$.

years of college, so that criterion remains a relevant and important one for most students and institutions.

For the purposes of this analysis, the criterion measure was scored "1" if the student indicated at the time of the followup that he held a bachelor's degree or higher, and "0" otherwise. The results of the multiple regression analysis predicting attainment of the bachelor's degree from freshman input data are shown in Table 22.

The most striking aspect of these results is the correspondence between the input variables that predicted attainment of the bachelor's degree and those that predicted persisting in college. Of the 19 input variables shown in Table 21, 15 also appear in Table 22, and the direction of the relationship for each is identical. This finding is not too surprising in view of the substantial correlation between completing four years of college and attaining the bachelor's degree (r [phi] = .72). However, since the correlation is far from perfect, it is surprising that the predictive patterning of the input variables was so similar for both outcomes. That 15 input variables from a pool of 90 should show the same pattern of relationships with both outcomes cannot be dismissed as an artifact.

Table 22 shows that high school grades carried the largest weight in predicting attainment of the bachelor's degree. Indeed, high school grade average in this (and in the previous) analysis accounted for nearly half of the predictable variance in the criterion. In light of this strong relation, the possibility suggests itself that the effects of academic ability were not adequately controlled in the regression analyses shown in Tables 21 and 22. But the introduction of additional information about the student's academic ability did not improve the prediction (see p. 54 of this chapter).

The most striking difference in the pattern of relationships shown in Table 22 and that shown in Table 21 is the effect of sex. As we have seen (Chapter 2, Table 10), less than half the men had obtained a bachelor's degree, compared with almost 62 percent of the women. This differential sex effect appeared in the significant zero-order correlation between being a woman and obtaining the bachelor's degree (r [phi] = .09) but not in the multiple regression analysis. Thus, although sex was predictive of dropping out of college, it was not predictive of obtaining the bachelor's degree when the effects of other variables were controlled. These results illustrate the usefulness of the multiple stepwise regression model and underscore the dangers inherent in attempting to interpret simple correlation coefficients. In short, on the basis of the zero-order correlations with sex, one would infer that being a woman is positively related to obtaining the bachelor's degree and that sex is unrelated to attrition. That such an interpretation would be misleading is apparent from the results of the regression analyses.

Educational Aspirations

At the time of initial matriculation in 1961, the students were asked to indicate the highest level of academic degree they planned to obtain; their

TABLE 22

The Prediction of Attainment of the Bachelor's Degree by 1965 from Freshman Input Data (1961)

(N = 3,821 students)

STEP	STUDENT INPUT VARIABLE ENTERING EQUATION AT DESIGNATED STEP	SIGN	R	R^2	F-VALUE* To Enter Equation	F-VALUE* In Final Equation
1	Average grade in high school—A	+	.154	.024	93.0	26.5
2	Average grade in high school—C	–	.207	.043	75.4	82.2
3	Average grade in high school—C+	–	.237	.056	54.7	58.0
4	Career choice—Engineer	–	.256	.066	39.0	47.9
5	Average grade in high school—B–	–	.270	.073	30.2	27.3
6	Mother's education	+	.281	.079	24.5	10.9
7	High school—Elected to a student office	+	.291	.084	22.3	22.6
8	Career choice—Secretary	–	.297	.088	16.6	17.0
9	Career choice—Pharmacist	–	.303	.092	14.4	15.8
10	Career choice—Nurse	–	.308	.095	13.2	14.5
11	Career choice—Businessman	–	.313	.098	13.8	16.4
12	Average grade in high school—B	–	.318	.101	11.8	9.1
13	Career choice—Architect	–	.322	.104	11.2	13.1
14	Career choice—Artist	–	.326	.106	10.1	10.3
15	Religious background—Jewish	+	.329	.108	10.3	7.2
16	Highest degree planned—Master's	+	.332	.110	8.4	8.2
17	Race—White	+	.335	.112	7.5	7.3
18	Father's education—Postgraduate	+	.337	.114	7.1	6.6
19	Career choice—No response	–	.340	.115	7.0	7.5
20	High school—Participated in school plays	–	.342	.117	5.8	5.6
21	Married before college matriculation	–	.343	.118	4.9	4.6
22	High school—Edited school paper	+	.345	.119	4.6	5.1
23	High school—Less than 50 students	–	.346	.120	4.0	4.0

* $F_{.05} = 3.84$.

responses were coded as follows:

1. Less than a bachelor's degree (none and associate)
2. Bachelor's (A.B., B.A., B.S., etc.)
3. Master's (M.A., M.S., etc.)
4. Doctorate (Ph.D. or Ed.D.)
5. Professional (M.D., D.D.S., D.V.M., LL.B., etc.)
6. Other

Because of limitations on the number of variables that could be used in our programs, numbers 5 and 6 above were excluded as input measures. (Note that the various professional degrees would presumably be redundant with the student's career choice.) Students were asked again in 1965 about their plans for obtaining an advanced degree, and from their responses we defined three dependent variables:

1. Plans to pursue graduate training (master's, doctorate, or professional)
2. Plans to obtain doctorate degree (Ph.D. or Ed.D.)
3. Plans to obtain professional degree (M.D., D.D.S., etc.)

The regression analysis for predicting plans to pursue graduate training from freshman input data is summarized in Table 23.

Table 23 shows that the student's plans to pursue graduate training after four years of college were a function of his initial level of educational aspiration, his high school grade average, and his socioeconomic background, with the first two variables carrying the largest weights. Substantial weights are also associated with several of the freshman career choices.

Although freshman plans to obtain only a bachelor's degree initially carried the largest weight (a negative one) in the analysis, it no longer contributed significantly to the prediction of plans for graduate work after step number 19 and was therefore removed from the regression equation. Thus, it would appear that any predictive information contained in this variable was redundant with information contained in variables 2–19 (e.g., choices of other degrees, academic ability, sex, career choice). The fact that being a woman had a substantial negative weight in the final equation suggests that during the undergraduate years, a man's interest in graduate training tends to increase more than does a woman's. As the results of the next two analyses indicate, this sex difference applies also to doctorate and professional degrees.

Table 24 shows the results of the analysis predicting plans to obtain the doctorate degree. The student's initial degree plans, high school grades, and sex (being male) carried the largest weights. Initial interest in science and mathematics and past achievement in science contests also carried substantial weights. In fact, all the career choices that were positively related to this criterion are careers for which the Ph.D. is the appropriate terminal degree, whereas for those careers which carried negative weights (businessman and accountant), the Ph.D. is neither demanded nor expected.

TABLE 23

The Prediction of Plans to Pursue Graduate Training (1965) from Freshman Input Data (1961)
(N = 3,281 students)

STEP	STUDENT INPUT VARIABLE ENTERING EQUATION AT DESIGNATED STEP	SIGN	R^2	R	F-VALUE* To Enter Equation	F-VALUE* In Final Equation
1	Highest degree planned—Bachelor's	—	.039	.197	154.2	(†)
2	Average grade in high school—C	—	.053	.230	57.6	50.6
3	Highest degree planned—Less than a B.A.	—	.066	.257	52.8	6.0
4	Career choice—Nurse	—	.072	.269	25.3	16.5
5	Career choice—Pharmacist	—	.077	.277	18.5	17.9
6	Sex (Female)	—	.081	.285	18.2	29.1
7	Average grade in high school—C+	—	.086	.294	21.8	13.4
8	Average grade in high school—A	+	.090	.300	15.1	8.7
9	High school—Elected to a student office	+	.093	.305	12.7	11.9
10	Career choice—Architect	—	.095	.309	10.8	8.4
11	Career choice—Secretary	—	.098	.313	10.5	7.7
12	Career choice—Artist	—	.100	.317	10.0	7.8
13	Highest degree planned—Doctorate	+	.103	.320	9.6	72.3
14	Father's education—Postgraduate	+	.105	.323	8.5	9.1
15	Parental family income	—	.107	.327	10.4	12.0
16	Father's occupation—Laborer	+	.109	.330	7.5	8.3
17	Average grade in high school—A+	+	.110	.332	7.1	6.1
18	Highest degree planned—Master's	+	.112	.335	6.9	71.8
19	Career choice—Physician	+	.115	.339	12.9	30.7
20	Highest degree planned—Bachelor's	(†)	.114	.338	2.5	(†)
21	Career choice—Lawyer	+	.117	.342	10.9	10.6
22	High school class—Less than 50 students	—	.118	.344	6.4	6.4
23	Mother's education	+	.120	.346	5.0	5.0
24	Career choice—Teacher	+	.121	.347	4.6	4.6
25	High school—Published original work	+	.122	.349	4.2	4.2

* $F_{.05} = 3.84$.
† Note that this variable was removed from the regression equation at step number 20.

TABLE 24

The Prediction of Plans to Obtain the Doctorate (1965) from Freshman Input Data (1961)

($N = 3,281$ students)

Step	Student Input Variable Entering Equation at Designated Step	Sign	R	R^2	F-value* To Enter Equation	F-value* In Final Equation
1	Highest degree planned—Doctorate	+	.310	.096	404.7	237.9
2	Highest degree planned—Master's	+	.334	.111	66.7	40.1
3	Average grade in high school—A	+	.347	.120	38.1	41.9
4	Sex—Female	−	.360	.129	40.7	53.5
5	Major field—Physical Science	+	.366	.134	19.1	9.2
6	Average grade in high school—A−	+	.370	.137	15.2	10.2
7	High school—Edited school paper	+	.373	.139	8.8	9.4
8	Career choice—Mathematician	+	.376	.141	9.0	9.1
9	High school—Won award in regional science contest	+	.378	.143	8.6	6.3
10	Career choice—Accountant	−	.381	.145	7.6	8.9
11	Career choice—Biological scientist	+	.383	.146	6.9	6.5
12	Career choice—College professor	+	.384	.148	6.2	6.1
13	Mother's education	+	.386	.149	5.5	6.2
14	Career choice—Businessman	−	.388	.150	5.5	6.0
15	Career choice—Physicist	+	.389	.151	4.7	4.1
16	High school class—More than 500 students	+	.390	.152	4.7	4.8
17	Career choice—Undecided or no response	−	.392	.153	3.9	3.9

* $F_{.05} = 3.84$.

The results of the analysis predicting plans to obtain a postgraduate professional degree are shown in Table 25. Although the student's initial career choice in one of the professional fields and sex (being male) carried by far the largest weights, their contribution to the prediction would undoubtedly have been smaller if the analysis had included as an input variable the student's statement of his initial plans to obtain a professional degree.

The magnitude of the multiple correlation coefficients shown in Tables 21 through 25 indicates that the student's persistence in college and his final level of educational aspiration cannot be predicted very accurately, given our pool of student input variables and the linear regression model. Although one might argue that this result is attributable to inadequate or irrelevant input measures, it is difficult to imagine that a dramatic improvement in prediction would result if additional student input information were introduced. The pool of 90 input variables used in this analysis included basic biographical and demographic variables (race, religion, sex, parental income, parents' level of education, father's occupation, and so forth) and other background data (size of high school graduating class, high school grade average, high school achievements, initial major field of study, initial career choice, initial level of educational aspiration, and marital status at college entry); these would seem to cover most of the relevant input information.

The control of relevant input variables appears to have been quite adequate in the case of educational aspiration four years after matriculation (Tables 23–25), for which we had available a "pretest" (i.e., the student's initial degree plans) that accounted for more than half the predictable variance in the final equations. The other predictors that entered these regression equations with positive weights can be regarded as input variables that are associated either with maintaining an initially high level of aspiration or with changing to a higher level during the four years. Similarly, predictors carrying negative weights can be regarded as indicative of personal traits characteristic of students who maintained an initially low level of aspiration or who lowered their aspirations during the four years. In other words, these additional input variables predicted stability and change in the student's level of educational aspiration.

For instance, the student's sex carried a substantial negative weight in predicting final educational plans. In particular, women were relatively more likely than were men both to have an initially low level of aspiration and to change to a lower level during the four years. This result suggests that the sex difference in academic performance which exists at the entering freshman level may be even more extreme at the graduate level, since those undergraduate women who go on to graduate work are more highly screened than are the undergraduate men. The factors associated with this loss of talented "womanpower" from the potential pool of graduate students constitutes an intriguing and potentially important topic for future research.

The student's academic ability also carried substantial weights in pre-

TABLE 25

The Prediction of Plans to Obtain a Professional Degree (1965) from Freshman Input Data (1961)

(N = 3,821 students)

Step	Student Input Variable Entering Equation at Designated Step	Sign	R	R^2	F-value* To Enter Equation	F-value* In Final Equation
1	Career choice—Physician	+	.330	.109	466.4	427.5
2	Sex—Female	−	.388	.150	184.8	125.9
3	Career choice—Lawyer	+	.422	.178	130.3	134.0
4	Career choice—Clergyman	+	.430	.185	32.3	43.1
5	Religious background—Jewish	+	.436	.191	25.9	20.0
6	Career choice—No response	+	.442	.195	21.3	23.2
7	Career choice—Dentist	+	.446	.199	20.1	20.8
8	Highest degree planned—Doctorate	+	.450	.202	15.3	7.8
9	Career choice—Foreign service	−	.453	.205	12.8	10.2
10	Average grade in high school—C	−	.456	.208	12.2	14.9
11	Career choice—Veterinarian	+	.458	.210	10.2	10.1
12	Average grade in high school—C+	−	.460	.212	10.3	10.8
13	Career choice—Engineer	−	.462	.214	9.8	9.8
14	Parental family income	+	.464	.216	9.4	11.5
15	Father's occupation—Business manager	−	.466	.217	6.0	6.0
16	High school—Elected to a student office	+	.467	.218	5.0	5.0

* $F_{05} = 3.84$.

dicting stability and change in educational plans. Students with relatively superior academic records, as reflected by their grade average in high school, were more likely to maintain an initially high level of educational aspiration or to switch from a lower to a higher level. Conversely, students with poorer academic records were relatively more likely to maintain, or to change to, a lower level in their degree plans. Moreover, students with superior academic records were more likely to plan to obtain a Ph.D. or Ed.D. degree rather than a professional degree.

Students from different socioeconomic backgrounds differed in their plans to obtain a graduate degree (of any type) as opposed to a professional degree. For instance, the higher the parents' educational level, the more likely the student was to plan on graduate study, although there was no such relationship in the case of plans to attain a professional degree. Somewhat surprisingly, high parental family income was negatively related to plans to attain a graduate degree and positively related to plans to attain a professional degree. That the largest proportion of students who planned to pursue a graduate degree had the master's degree in mind probably explains these seemingly contradictory results. Thus, students from affluent families were more likely to maintain an initial desire to obtain a professional degree or to raise their level of aspiration to a professional degree during the four college years, whereas students from less affluent families tended to gravitate more toward the master's degree. It is interesting to note that the student whose father was a laborer tended to maintain, or change to, plans to pursue graduate training (the master's degree). These results suggest that the various postgraduate degrees have different values as social status symbols for persons of different social classes.

The student's initial career choice was related systematically to changes in his level of educational aspiration. Except for the choice of physician, all the initial choices that tended to be associated with declining interest in graduate training also decreased in popularity during the four-year interval. That is, fewer students chose these careers four years after entering college than at the time of matriculation. (An analysis of the relative percentage change for each career choice is given in Chapter 4; see Table 44.) On the other hand, career choices that were positively related to upward swings in level of educational aspiration increased in popularity during the four years.

Several high school extracurricular achievements were also significantly related to maintaining an initially high level of educational aspiration or changing to a higher level during the four years. In general, students who, in high school, had achieved in such nonacademic areas as being elected to a student office, receiving an award in a regional or state science contest, and editing the school paper tended to raise the level of their educational aspirations during their undergraduate years more than did students without such achievements.

The students' racial and religious backgrounds were not related to their final levels of aspiration, with the exception that those whose parents were Jewish were more likely to maintain, or to switch to, plans to obtain a professional degree. This result probably reflects the tendency for students whose religious background is Jewish to choose careers as lawyers or physicians (see Chapter 4).

THE INFLUENCE OF WITHIN-COLLEGE ENVIRONMENTAL CHARACTERISTICS

As was mentioned in Chapter 1, information concerning the student's within-college environmental experiences (i.e., experiences to which all students at a given institution are not exposed) included measures of how he financed his undergraduate education, where he lived during his freshman year, whether he got married after entering college, and whether he received vocational counseling as an undergraduate. To reduce project costs, we decided to examine the effects of these within-college variables on the subsample of 1,590 students for whom scores on the five subtests of the National Merit Scholarship Qualifying Test (NMSQT) were available. This subsample was used to determine whether the input variables included in our analyses had adequately controlled the effects of initial academic ability and to examine the effects of the within-college variables.

Part correlations between the five subtests of the NMSQT and each of the five residual criterion scores are shown in Table 26. Although all the coefficients were relatively small, several of the residual criteria showed statistically significant ($p = <.05$) correlations with at least one of the NMSQT subtests. Consequently, we decided to partial out the effects of the five NMSQT subtests from the residual criterion scores. Thus, our analyses are based on the partial correlations between the within-college variables and the residual criteria after the student input variables, along with academic ability as measured by the five NMSQT subtests, were controlled.

TABLE 26

Educational Attainment and Plans: Correlations of Residual Criterion Scores[a] with Scores on the National Merit Scholarship Qualifying Test

($N=1,590$ students)

RESIDUAL CRITERION	NMSQT SCORE				
	English	Mathematics	Social Science Reading	Natural Science Reading	Word Usage
Completed four years of college					
Obtained the bachelor's degree				−.05*	
Planning graduate study					
Planning Ph.D.	.06*	.06*	.07*	.06*	.09**
Planning professional degree			.06*		.05*

[a] Residual scores on each criterion (from analyses shown in Tables 21–25) were correlated with each NMSQT scale. Coefficients shown are actually "part" correlations.
 * $p < .05$.   ** $p < .01$.

TABLE 27

Effects of Marital Status and Source of Financial Support on
Educational Attainment and Plans

($N = 1,590$ students)

ENVIRONMENTAL VARIABLE	PART CORRELATION[a] WITH				
	Completed Four Years of College	Obtained Bachelor's Degree	Planning Graduate Study	Planning Ph.D.	Planning Professional Degree
Got married after entering college	−.14***	−.07**	−.11***		
Financial support:					
Parents (50% or more)	.09***				
Scholarship	.05*				

[a] Correlation between environmental variable and residual criterion score (i.e., after control of input variables shown in tables 21 through 25 and NMSQT score).
* $p < .05$.   ** $p < .01$.   *** $p < .001$.

Of the several possible within-college influences considered, only type of financial support during the undergraduate years and marital status during college had any pattern of significant relationships with the residual criteria. Table 27 shows the statistically significant partial correlations of these measures with persistence in college and with final level of educational aspiration. As Table 21 indicated, students who were already married when they entered college were more likely not to complete four years of college within the four years after matriculation than were unmarried entering freshmen. Table 27 shows that students who got married during college were more likely than were other students both to drop out of college and to lower their initial level of aspiration. These findings are consistent with Bayer's recent longitudinal study (1968), which showed that getting married was one of the principal determinants of dropping out of college among the students from the Project Talent sample. Students who received a major amount of financial support (50 percent or more) from their parents were more likely than were other students to complete four or more academic years of college during the four-year period. Similarly, students who received scholarships were more likely than were other students to remain in school during the four years.

Although the findings shown in Table 27 are statistically significant, their substantive significance is questionable because of the relatively small size of the coefficients. Given the large number of coefficients that were computed, it is possible that the few statistically significant correlations shown in Table 27 were chance occurrences. With these qualifications in mind, it is clear that the pattern of relationships makes sense: One would expect that the student who receives support from his parents or scholarship aid would be better able to remain in school than the student who has to obtain his funds from other sources. Similarly, it is not surprising that many students who get married during college give up plans for future education.

It is somewhat remarkable that the effects observed in these analyses were not more pronounced, since students vary greatly in their within-college environmental experiences. In particular, one might suppose that the student's living arrangements during his freshman year would be related to some of these educational outcomes—but they were not. It is also interesting to note that, even though most dropouts indicated that they would have left college even if they had had more money (see Chapter 2, Table 10), the type of financial support received during the undergraduate years was significantly related to completing four or more years.

THE INFLUENCE OF BETWEEN-COLLEGE ENVIRONMENTAL CHARACTERISTICS

Table 28 shows how the 246 institutions were ranged with respect to their actual and residual criterion scores on each of the five criteria of educational attainment and educational plans. The first three columns of percentages indicate the spread of the actual scores. For example, the observed (actual) percentage of students at a given institution who had completed four years of college by the time of our followup varied from a low of 36 percent to a high of 93 percent. The variation among institutions in the percentage of 1961 entering students who completed the bachelor's degree by 1965 was even more remarkable: from a low of 15 percent to a high of 91 percent. It should be kept in mind when interpreting these percentages that they are based on the *unweighted* data. The most likely effect of response bias would be to *reduce* the variation among colleges with respect to outcomes such as completing four years of college and obtaining the bachelor's degree. In short, the variation is probably even greater in reality.

The mean actual score for each of the criteria (fourth column of data in Table 28) corresponds very closely to the median score shown in the second column of data, although the large size of the standard deviations relative to the means of two of the criteria (planning to attain the Ph.D. degree and planning to attain a professional degree) suggests that these distributions are positively skewed. In other words, most institutions had relatively low scores on these two outcomes; just a few had very high scores.

The residual scores shown in the next five columns of data in Table 28 indicate the extent to which the actual and the expected percentages varied. For example, the actual percentage of students who completed four years of college during the four-year interval at one of the institutions was 30 percent less than the expected percentage estimated on the basis of the characteristics of the entering students. The institution with the highest residual score, on the other hand, exceeded the expected figure by 16 percent. The median percentage for this and the other four criteria shown in Table 28 was very close to zero. The most extreme variation in residual scores once again occurred in the percentage obtaining the bachelor's degree, with one institution falling fully 60 percent short of the expected figure.

The large discrepancies at some institutions between the expected and actual percentages of students who completed four years of college or who

TABLE 28

Distribution of Actual and Residual Scores on Five Criteria of Educational Attainment and Plans
(N = 246 institutions)

CRITERION	ACTUAL SCORES					RESIDUAL SCORES[a]					PROPORTIONATE REDUCTION IN VARIANCE[b]
	Lowest Institution %	Median Institution %	Highest Institution %	Mean	S.D.	Lowest Institution %	Median Institution %	Highest Institution %	Mean	S.D.	
Completed four years of college	36	71	93	70.1	11.6	−30	01	16	−0.6	7.9	−.546
Obtained bachelor's degree	15	63	91	61.9	15.0	−60	02	22	−0.3	10.9	−.471
Planning graduate study	36	65	92	65.7	11.6	−30	−02	06	−2.2	6.9	−.646
Planning Ph.D.	2	14	69	15.4	8.8	−10	−01	17	−0.4	4.3	−.761
Planning professional degree	0	7	43	9.4	8.2	−13	00	17	−0.1	3.8	−.785

[a] Difference between the actual percentage at the institution and the expected percentage based on student input characteristics (i.e., Actual percent minus Expected percent).
[b] Ratio between (1 minus SD^2) of residual scores and SD^2 of actual scores.

obtained the bachelor's degree during the four years following their initial matriculation are somewhat startling. In these extreme cases, however, the discrepancies can be explained by the existence of special programs at the institutions, a good indication that our extensive data and complex data processing procedures were valid. For example, on the residual score for completing four years of college, there was a gap of 12 percent between the lowest-ranked institution and the next lowest-ranked institution. It turned out that the lowest-ranked institution was a college where a high proportion of students interrupt their education at some time during the traditional four-year period to spend a year in missionary work. Similarly, there was a 33 percent gap between the lowest-ranked and the next lowest-ranked institution on the criterion of obtaining the bachelor's degree. In this case, the lowest-ranked institution proved to be a four-year college that maintains a five-year program to obtain the bachelor's degree. This particular college requires that its students spend one year working in the field in a job related to their major; during this time they receive degree credit but are not expected to obtain their bachelor's degree within the four years following their initial matriculation. Even if these two institutions were excluded however, the range in discrepancies between actual and expected percents remains extensive: from −27 to +22 for obtaining the bachelor's degree, and from −18 to +16 for completing four or more years of college.

The last column of data in Table 28 shows the extent to which the institutional variance in actual outcome scores was reduced when the expected outcome scores based on student input data were subtracted. (This value was obtained by subtracting the ratio between the squares of the two standard deviations shown in the table from 1.) Approximately half of the variance in the percentages of students who completed four years of college and who obtained the bachelor's degree can be accounted for in terms of expected outputs based on student inputs. The output variance in degree plans is even more dependent on input: nearly two-thirds of the variance in the percentage planning graduate study and more than three-fourths of the variance in both the percentage planning Ph.D. degrees and the percentage planning professional degrees can be attributed to differential student inputs. It seems likely that the relatively smaller reductions in variance on the first two criteria resulted in part from certain specialized institutional practices, such as five-year work-study programs, which are not covered in our student input measures.

The next step was to determine whether the residual criterion scores for the 246 institutions were related to any of the college characteristics described in Chapter 1. Accordingly, a stepwise linear multiple regression analysis was performed, in which the residual criterion score was used as the dependent variable and the 72 college characteristics in Chapter 1 were used as independent variables. These 72 measures of the college environment were permitted to enter into the regression equation until no further environmental variable was capable of producing a reduction in the residual sums of squares exceeding $p = .05$.

Table 29 summarizes the results of these analyses for each of the five criteria of educational attainment and educational plans. Both the multiple correlation coefficient (second column, Table 29) and the squared multiple correlation coefficient (third column, Table 29) indicate that a substantial proportion—roughly half—of the residual criterion variance can be explained in terms of the 72 college characteristics. The prediction of differential college effects was especially successful in the case of the criterion of obtaining the bachelor's degree ($R^2 = .62$).

The college characteristics that entered into the regression analyses involving the residual criteria of completing four years of college and of obtaining the bachelor's degree are shown in Table 30. The first column of figures gives the F-ratios that were associated with each college characteristic in the final multiple regression equation. The F-ratio of each reflects its relative contribution in accounting for the differential effects of colleges on their students' completing four years of college and obtaining the bachelor's degree within four years after matriculation. The sign indicates whether the effect was positive or negative.

It is of some interest to note that the zero-order correlations of both selectivity and cohesiveness (defined mainly by the number of close friendships among the students) had zero-order correlations with the mean residual scores (second column of figures in Table 30) which were substantially smaller than the zero-order correlations of several other college characteristics with these criteria; yet these two environmental variables ended up having relatively large weights in the final multiple regression equation. This apparent inconsistency is easily explained when one realizes that the two measures—selectivity and cohesiveness—have a substantial negative correlation ($r = -.48$) with one another. In other words, institutions with highly cohesive peer environments tend to be relatively unselective in admissions policies. Consequently, the joint contribution of the two variables in predicting educational attainment was masked by the negative correlation between them. Considered singly, the importance of these two variables appeared to be relatively small, but considered jointly, they were more important than most of the other measurable characteristics of the college. This masking phenomenon, which occurred in the prediction of many other of the criteria throughout this book, underscores the necessity of viewing the college environment as being composed of many different characteristics rather than as being unidimensional.

The pattern of environmental effects shown in Table 30 indicates that students were more likely to complete four years of college and to obtain the bachelor's degree during the four years following matriculation if they attended relatively selective institutions that have cohesive peer environments and that are located in regions other than the West and Southwest.

TABLE 29

Educational Attainment and Plans:
Multiple Correlations of Residual Criterion Scores with College Characteristics
(N = 246 institutions)

RESIDUAL CRITERION SCORE[a]	All 72 College Characteristics			STEPWISE MULTIPLE REGRESSION USING: 21 Dichotomous Characteristics Only		
	Number of Variables Entering[b]	R	R^2	Number of Variables Entering[b]	R	R^2
Completed four years of college	12	.747	.558	6	.550	.303
Obtained bachelor's degree	12	.786	.618	7	.593	.352
Planning graduate study	11	.670	.449	5	.563	.317
Planning Ph.D.	8	.610	.482	6	.482	.232
Planning professional degree	13	.688	.473	5	.528	.279

[a] Difference between the actual percentage and the expected percentage based on student input characteristics (i.e., Actual percent minus Expected percent).
[b] College variables were entered into the multiple regression equation until no additional variable was capable of producing a reduction in the residual sum of squares exceeding $p = .05$.

TABLE 30

Effects of Various College Characteristics on Educational Attainment

(N = 246 institutions)

College Characteristic	Completing Four Years of College			Obtaining the Bachelor's Degree		
	Sign	F-ratio* in Final Regression Equation	r† with Mean Residual Score	Sign	F-ratio* in Final Regression Equation	r† with Mean Residual Score
Selectivity	+	63.9	.26	+	23.8	.20
Cohesiveness (ICA)	+	40.0	.17	+	28.2	.25
West-and-Southwest location	−	22.5	−.27	−	7.0	−.31
Familiarity with the Instructor	+	15.1	n.s.	−	—	.13
Career Indecision (ICA)	−	14.6	n.s.	−	15.3	−.21
Regularity of Sleeping Habits (ICA)	+	13.2	n.s.	+	19.3	n.s.
Verbal Aggressiveness (ICA)	+	12.3	.32	+	13.0	.33
Realistic orientation (EAT)	−	10.1	−.39	−	9.0	−.34
Percent males in student body	−	9.2	−.14		—	n.s.
Liberal arts college	+	6.2	.36		—	.31
Enterprising orientation (EAT)	+	5.5	.28		—	.23
Student Employment (ICA)	−	3.6	−.27	−	37.5	−.35
Private (vs. public) control		—	.38	+	31.0	.41
Northeastern location		—	.29	+	12.7	.34
Leisure Time (ICA)		—	n.s.	+	11.4	n.s.
Organization in the Classroom (ICA)		—	.16	+	7.1	.19

* Only those college characteristics with statistically significant ($p < .05$) weights in the final regression equation are shown.

† n.s. = zero-order correlation between the mean residual criterion score and the college characteristic was not significant ($p > .05$).

Selectivity and cohesiveness have the greatest facilitative effect on completion of four years of college, whereas student employment was relatively more important in its (negative) effect on attainment of the bachelor's degree. Apparently, the student's chances of getting the baccalaureate four years after matriculation were reduced if he attended a college where a relatively large number of the other students were employed and where, presumably, he himself is more likely to be employed. This finding accords with our earlier observation that the institution with the largest negative residual score on the outcome had a work-study program in which five years were normally required to attain the baccalaureate degree.

As Table 30 also shows, the patterning of environmental effects on the two criteria of educational attainment were quite similar; to underscore this point, it should be recalled that the patterns of student input variables that predict these two outcomes were also very much alike. The major difference in the patterns of environmental effects, other than those already noted, is that private colleges located in the Northeast had a greater facilitative effect on obtaining the bachelor's degree than they had on completing four years of college.

The finding that staying in college is positively affected by the institution's selectivity and negatively affected by the percentage of men in the student body is consistent with the results of an earlier study of highly able students (Astin, 1964).

The college characteristics that entered into the regression analyses for the three criteria of students' educational plans are shown in Table 31. It is clear that different combinations of environmental variables were related to aspirations for different types of degrees. Thus, colleges which facilitated the students' plans to pursue graduate education of any type were more likely to be relatively selective private colleges located in the Northeast, whereas the student's interest in obtaining the doctorate was increased if he attended a private liberal arts college that had relatively high expenditures per student for educational and general purposes. Students were more likely to want to obtain a professional degree if they attended universities located in a large city or men's colleges. The latter relationship is consistent with the finding— to be discussed in the next chapter—that men's colleges had a facilitative effect on the student's interest in becoming a lawyer. Moreover, it is relevant to earlier research (Astin, 1962c, 1963a), which suggested that Northeastern colleges for men have a negative impact on the student's interest in pursuing the Ph.D. degree. The mean residual scores of all seven such colleges in the current study (Amherst, Bowdoin, Colgate, Dartmouth, Hamilton, Trinity, Williams, and Yale) were all negative for this outcome, whereas their mean residual scores on the outcome of pursuing a professional degree were all markedly positive. All these findings suggest that such institutions channel students away from careers requiring the Ph.D. and into careers requiring a professional degree, particuarly law (see Chapter 4).

TABLE 31
Effects of Various College Characteristics on Educational Plans
($N = 246$ institutions)

CRITERION: COLLEGE CHARACTERISTIC	SIGN	F-RATIO* IN FINAL REGRESSION EQUATION	r† WITH MEAN RESIDUAL SCORE
Planning graduate study:			
Selectivity	+	28.9	.32
Private (vs. public) control	+	25.8	.37
Northeastern location	+	24.8	.39
Social orientation (EAT)	+	11.1	n.s.
Enterprising orientation (EAT)	+	9.7	.21
Teachers college	+	8.2	n.s.
North Central location	+	6.8	n.s.
Predominantly Negro	+	6.7	n.s.
Flexibility of the Curriculum (ICA)	−	6.7	−.23
Planning Ph.D. degree:			
Organized Dating (ICA)	−	33.9	−.26
University	−	28.2	−.29
Permissiveness (ICA)	−	21.9	−.23
Northeastern location	+	13.0	.22
Expenditures per student	+	12.1	n.s.
Private (*vs.* public) control	+	11.0	.31
Career Indecision (ICA)	+	8.4	.13
Planning professional degree:			
Men's college	+	58.0	.29
Drinking *vs.* Religiousness (ICA)	−	35.5	n.s.
Technical institution	−	18.3	−.29
University	+	17.3	n.s.
Enterprising orientation (EAT)	+	14.2	.37
Snobbishness (ICA)	+	11.6	.27
Academic Competitiveness (ICA)	+	10.1	.19
Located in a large city	+	7.9	n.s.

* Only those college characteristics with statistically significant ($p < .05$) weights in the final regression equation are shown.
† n.s. = zero-order correlation between the mean residual criterion score and the college characteristic was not significant ($p > .05$).

The apparently contradictory finding that a Northeastern location increased the student's interest in pursuing the Ph.D. (see Table 31) results from the fact that the institutions *other than men's colleges* located in this region had relatively high positive mean residual scores on the criterion.

Earlier studies of college effects had also suggested that the student's interest in attaining the Ph.D. is increased by his attending either a technological institution or a selective, coeducational liberal arts college. All five such liberal arts colleges in our sample (Antioch, Carleton, Grinnell, Oberlin, and Reed) had positive mean residual scores (ranging from +2.1 to +12.7 percent) on plans to pursue the Ph.D. Although one of the seven technological institutions has a substantial *negative* mean residual score (−8.8 percent), three others (Brooklyn, Caltech, and MIT) were among the six top-ranked institutions in our sample with respect to this outcome; their mean residual scores ranged from +6.4 to +14.6 percent.

These findings are consistent in certain respects with earlier studies of differential college influence on the student's plans to attain the Ph.D. In one study of highly able students (Astin, 1963a), such plans were found to be negatively related to size—the larger the institution, the less likelihood of the student's aspiring to the doctorate—and by the dominance of the Social orientation in the environment (see Chapter 1, p. 12). Attendance at a liberal arts college, on the other hand, increased the chances of the student's aspiring to the Ph.D. However, the earlier finding that public institutions are more likely than are private institutions to be overproductive of Ph.D.'s (Astin, 1962c) was contradicted by the present study, in which private institutions had a pronounced facilitative effect on the student's interest in attaining the Ph.D. This discrepancy may have occurred in part because the earlier study employed a highly biased sample of institutions.

Evidence (Astin and Holland, 1961, Table 2) indicates that the environmental measures which Thistlethwaite (1966) found to have a positive effect on the student's level of aspiration (e.g., high press for Humanism and for Reflectiveness) are similar to our Selectivity measure, which, as Table 31 shows, had a positive effect on the student's interest in going to graduate school. However, the fact that such different patterns of environmental variables were found for the two outcomes—aspiring to the Ph.D. and aspiring to a professional degree—suggests that important information may be lost if such qualitatively different degrees are lumped together in a single measure of "level of aspiration."

One interesting environmental effect shown in Table 31 is that predominantly Negro colleges tended to facilitate the desire to go on to graduate study. In several recent studies (Astin, Panos, and Creager, 1967b; Panos, Astin, and Creager, 1967; Creager, Astin, Boruch, and Bayer, 1968), it has been shown that entering freshmen at predominantly Negro institutions often have educational aspirations that are not only higher than those of other entering college freshmen but also higher than would be expected in view of their own academic preparation in high school. Apparently, students are likely to maintain this high level of educational aspiration if they attend predominantly Negro colleges.

Three college characteristics with relatively large negative weights in the analysis deserve attention. Somewhat surprisingly, students who attended a university were less likely than other students to aspire to a Ph.D. In addition, students were less likely to seek a Ph.D. if they attended colleges where there was a good deal of formal dating among the students and where the faculty was relatively permissive.

The results of the analyses of college effects shown in Table 28 through 31 support the notion that educational outcomes are determined both by the students' personal characteristics and by the environmental context. Although a substantial proportion of the residual criterion variance was accounted for in these analyses, it is of considerable interest that the environmental effects were not more pronounced, since the 246 institutions in the sample were extremely diverse in their characteristics. From half to three-fourths of the observed variance in the five educational criteria was attributable to differential student inputs (last column in Table 28), and only about half of the *remaining* variance was attributable to institutional variables (last column of Table 29). Thus, with respect to the problem of the interaction between the individual and his environment, these findings suggest that the large observed differences among institutions in educational outcomes are more a function of differences in their entering students than of differences in measurable characteristics of their environments.[5]

Relative Importance of Different Types of College Characteristics

Six additional regression analyses were performed with each of the mean residual outcome measures in order to determine the relative importance of various types of environmental variables. In each analysis, only one of the six subsets of college characteristics (e.g., the 36 ICA factors) were permitted to enter in a stepwise fashion until no additional variable within the subset was capable of contributing significantly ($p < .05$) to the prediction of the outcome. The results of these analyses are shown in Tables 32 and 33. The values shown in Table 32 indicate the percentage of common variance between a given outcome and a particular subset of institutional characteristics. The values shown in Table 33, which were obtained by subtracting selected proportions in Table 32, indicate the percentage of variance which is *uniquely* attributable to a particular subset. For example, the percentage of variance in completing four years of college that is uniquely attributable to the eight

TABLE 32

Mean Residual Variance[a] Accounted for by Different Types of Environmental Measures

(percentages)

($N = 246$ institutions)

ENVIRONMENTAL MEASURE	Completed Four Years of College	MEAN RESIDUAL EDUCATIONAL OUTCOME Obtained Bachelor's Degree	Graduate Degree	Planning: Ph.D.	Professional Degree
8 EAT measures	26.4	22.0	19.1	10.7	20.5
28 ICA Stimulus[b] factors	39.4	50.7	26.3	25.7	12.2
12 ICA Image[b] factors	29.0	33.2	19.7	18.7	19.7
All 36 ICA factors	43.0	49.5	28.0	29.7	34.6
All 44 "trait" measures	49.8	56.3	31.1	29.7	41.5
21 "type" characteristics	30.3	35.2	31.7	23.2	27.9
All 72 college variables[c]	55.8	61.8	44.9	37.2	47.3

[a] $R^2 \times 100$ (as determined by separate stepwise multiple regression analyses, each of which was terminated at $p \geqq .05$).

[b] The four factors from the administrative environment were included among both the stimulus and the image factors. Also an unlabeled factor (see Chapter 1, p. 11) was included in these analyses, bringing the total number of ICA factors to 36.

[c] Includes 8 EAT measures, 36 ICA factors, 21 type characteristics, 5 student input factors (Astin, 1965d), percentage of men in the student body, and per student expenditures for educational and general purposes.

TABLE 33

Educational Attainment and Plans:
Amount of Mean Residual Variance Uniquely Attributable to Different
Types of Environmental Variables

($N=246$ institutions)

MEAN RESIDUAL EDUCATIONAL OUTCOME	PERCENTAGES OF VARIANCE UNIQUELY ATTRIBUTABLE TO:					
	"Trait" Variables *vs.*	"Type" Variables	EAT Measures *vs.*	ICA Factors	ICA Stimulus Factors *vs.*	ICA Image Factors
Completed four years of college	25.5	6.8	6.8	23.4	14.0	3.6
Obtained bachelor's degree	26.5	5.5	6.8	34.3	17.5	0.0
Planning graduate study	13.2	13.8	3.1	12.0	8.3	1.7
Planning Ph.D.	14.0	7.5	0.0	19.0	11.0	4.0
Planning professional degree	19.4	5.8	6.9	21.0	12.0	19.7

EAT measures (6.8) equals the variance accounted for by all 44 "trait" measures (49.8) minus the variance accounted for by the 36 ICA factors (43.0). Conversely, we find that the percentage of variance in completing four years of college uniquely attributable to the 36 ICA factors is 49.8 minus 26.4, or 23.4. Although the percentage of variance which is *jointly* attributable to the two sets of characteristics is not shown in the two tables, it can easily be obtained by subtracting the two unique percentages (6.8 plus 23.4, or 30.2) from the total percentage (49.8 minus 30.2, or 19.6). Jointly attributable variance reflects overlap or redundancy in the two sets of college characteristics that are being compared.

The results in Table 32 show that the 21 administrative "type" characteristics (e.g., public versus private, religious versus nonsectarian) accounted for substantially less of the differential institutional influence on the five educational outcomes than did the entire set of 72 institutional characteristics: almost twice as much of the variation could be accounted for when the entire set of characteristics was used. It is clear that potentially important information about institutional environments is lost when colleges are considered only in terms of the traditional administrative typologies. The type characteristics do, of course, contribute some unique information, particularly in accounting for differential institutional effects on plans to pursue graduate study. (This latter finding is probably a reflection of the positive effects of private colleges and teachers colleges; see Table 31.)

Other comparisons in Table 33 indicate that the eight EAT measures contribute very little unique information relative to the contribution made by 36 ICA factors. Moreover, the ICA stimulus factors are of greater import than the ICA image factors in predicting educational outcomes, the one notable exception being the outcome of pursuing a professional degree, which has substantial positive relationships with two ICA image factors: Snobbishness and Academic Competitiveness (see Table 31).

College Effects: The Institution As the Unit of Analysis

As was pointed out in Chapter 1, we performed another series of college effects analyses using the institution rather than the student as the unit of analysis in controlling differential student inputs. Our purpose was to determine whether any of the 72 measures of the college environment showed effects which were independent of the types of students entering the institutions. In these analyses, each institution's mean score on each student input characteristic (e.g., percentage of men) was computed. The mean actual scores on each of the criteria of educational attainment and aspiration served as the dependent variables in a series of two-stage stepwise regression analyses. In the first stage, the mean scores on the student input measures were allowed to enter into the regression equation until no additional input variable was capable of producing a reduction in the residual sum of squares exceeding $p = .05$. In the second stage, the environmental characteristics were permitted to enter the regression equation after the student input variables from the previous analysis had been forced into the equation until the same criterion of $p = .05$ was reached. The results of using the institution as the unit of analysis in controlling differential inputs for the criteria of educational achievement are shown in Table 34.

TABLE 34
The Prediction of Educational Attainment and Plans Using
the Institution as the Unit of Analysis
($N = 246$ institutions)

CRITERION	STEPWISE CONTROL OF STUDENT INPUT VARIABLES			ADDITIONAL CONTRIBUTION OF ENVIRONMENTAL VARIABLES		
	Number Entering* Equation	R	R^2	Number Entering† Equation	Final R	Increase in R^2
Completed four years of college	14	.855	.731	8	.903	.085
Obtained bachelor's degree	18	.843	.711	14	.923	.140
Planning graduate study	20	.910	.829	4	.921	.020
Planning Ph.D.	19	.926	.858	5	.939	.024
Planning professional degree	14	.946	.894	3	.950	.008

* $p < .05$.   † After control of student input variables.

The multiple correlation coefficients (R) shown in the second column of Table 34 indicate that a highly accurate estimate of the relative position of each institution on each outcome can be obtained using only the input information provided by the students at the time they entered college. Only very modest gains in accuracy of prediction can be achieved from a knowledge of environmental variables (last column of Table 34). In our earlier discussion of this alternative method of analysis (Chapter 1), we indicated that using the institution as the unit of analysis in the control of differential student inputs provides a very conservative test of environmental influence, since this particular method is likely to partial out the effects of those environmental variables that depend on characteristics of the students who are selectively recruited into the institution. Thus, while the results shown in Table 34 cannot be regarded as revealing the relative importance of student inputs and environmental characteristics in determining educational outcomes, they do show clearly that *substantial environmental effects, if they exist, are probably mediated by environmental characteristics that are dependent on the student input.*

For the most part, the more conservative analyses of environmental effects summarized in Table 34 were consistent with the results shown in Tables 30 and 31. As would be expected, the number of environmental variables that seem to influence the five criteria of educational achievement was reduced when the institution was used as the unit of analysis, although in practically no case did the results contradict the results shown in Tables 30 and 31. For example, in 57 of those 58 instances where a particular environmental variable and a particular outcome were significantly correlated in both analyses, following the control of differential student inputs, the signs of the coefficients were the same. Similarly, the signs of the coefficients matched in all 18 instances where a given environmental variable actually entered the equation for the same outcome in both analyses. In other words, when we controlled student inputs using the *institution* as the unit of analysis, fewer significant environmental effects appeared, but there were no reversals in sign or otherwise contradictory effects. Nevertheless, when the college environment is viewed independent of the characteristics of the student body, its effects appear to be trivial, a finding which suggests that the diverse environmental measures employed in this study were largely dependent on initial student input.

ENVIRONMENTAL EFFECTS ON EDUCATIONAL ACHIEVEMENT[6]

Although the American system of higher education is noted for its diversity, most of its institutions pursue a common quest for quality or "excellence." Among the attributes generally regarded as indices of excellence are a select student body, a highly trained faculty, an institutional emphasis on scholarship, a large library, a high faculty-student ratio, and a vigorous program of research. Perhaps the most important benefit presumed to derive from these attributes concerns the intellectual development of the student. In the folklore of higher education, it is assumed that the student's learning and intellectual development will be enhanced if he attends a "high-quality" institution. The principal goal of our analyses of the student's performance on the Graduate Record Examination (GRE) was to test this assumption empirically.

Student Input Measures

As we indicated earlier in Chapter 1, the traditional grade point average is not an appropriate measure for these purposes, since grades are not comparable from college to college. Thus, even though the GRE Area Test Scores were available for only a biased and relatively small sample of 669 subjects at 38 of our 246 institutions, we considered these scores a more valid means for assessing comparative institutional effects on the student's academic achievement. Scores on the National Merit Scholarship Qualifying Test (NMSQT), which the students had taken prior to their college entrance, were also available for this sample.[7] Some of the input characteristics of the 669 students are summarized in Table 35. The sample included approximately equal numbers of men and women majoring in a variety of undergraduate fields. Several items in Table 35 suggest that this group of students was generally superior: Nearly one-third of them had obtained average grades of A− or better in high school, and their mean scores on the subtests of the NMSQT were somewhat above the mean for college students in general (approximately 23). Nevertheless, the group manifested considerable *variation* in academic potential: Nearly 15 percent had obtained grades of C+ or lower in high school, and their standard deviations on the NMSQT subtests were comparable to those of college students in general. Their means and standard deviations on the Area Tests of the GRE (the output measures) compared favorably with the population mean of 500 and standard deviation of 100, indicating that the performance of our sample of students is reasonably representative of the over-all achievement level of seniors at institutions where this particular battery of tests is administered.

TABLE 35

Some Characteristics of Students for Whom Input Data and Scores on the GRE Area Tests Were Available

($N = 669$ students)

CHARACTERISTIC	PERCENT OR MEAN	STANDARD DEVIATION
Percentage of men in sample	51.1	
Percentage initially majoring in:		
social sciences	13.0	
education	11.1	
arts and humanities	16.1	
natural sciences	29.1	
other fields	12.9	
undecided	17.8	
Percentage with average high school grade of:		
A− to A+	31.8	
B− to B+	53.4	
C+ or lower	14.8	
National Merit Scholarship Qualifying Test		
English Usage	20.7	4.0
Mathematics	22.7	4.9
Social Science Reading	23.5	4.5
Natural Science Reading	23.5	5.4
Word Usage	23.8	4.7
Composite	22.8	3.8
Graduate Record Examination Area Test		
Social Science	511.3	102.9
Humanities	516.1	91.3
Natural Science	523.1	88.1

Environmental Measures

Measures of institutional quality. In a recent factor analysis of character-istics of colleges and universities (Astin, 1962*a*), it was found that most of the traditional indices of institutional "quality" were highly interrelated. Insti-tutions with relatively large expenditures per student for general operating expenses, for example, also tended to have a relatively high income per student for research and relatively high endowments, capital income, and scholarship funds. Furthermore, these wealthier institutions tended to recruit highly able student bodies and to have large libraries and high faculty-student ratios. The statistical factor identified with this complex of closely intercorrelated institutional characteristics was labeled "affluence" in the earlier study, although such terms as "quality" and "prestige" would be equally appropriate. The two best indicators of institutional affluence turned out to be the average academic ability of the entering student body and the per-student expenditures for "educational and general" purposes (meaning, primarily, salaries for faculty and staff). These two measures constituted the principal indices of institutional excellence used in the study.

1. Selectivity (an estimate of the average academic ability of the entering students) (Astin, 1965*d*).

2. Per-student expenditures for educational and general purposes (Cartter, 1964).

Within the total population of four-year institutions, the *absolute* degree of variation with respect to these (and related) measures of quality is con-siderable. The thirty most affluent institutions in the United States, for example, spend more than *four times* as many dollars per student for educa-tional and general purposes as the thirty least affluent do. Similarly, it has been estimated that the 25 most selective institutions recruit half or more of their entering students from among the top 3 percent in academic ability. On the other hand, fully 15 percent of the population (nearly 200 institutions) enroll virtually *no* students from this select 3 percent. That our measure of selectivity conforms to common-sense notions about which are the "quality" institutions can be seen by listing the ten most selective institutions in the country: Caltech, Radcliffe, MIT, Swarthmore, Rice, Harvard, Stanford, Reed, Amherst, and Pomona (Astin, 1965*a*.) As might be expected, selec-tivity is also highly correlated ($r = .69$) with the over-all quality of the insti-tution's graduate program, as revealed in Cartter's study (1966).

Five additional measures of affluence, which are also generally consid-ered to be indicative of institutional quality, were used:

3. Number of books in the library
4. Number of books in the library per student
5. Faculty-student ratio
6. Percentage of faculty with Ph.D.'s
7. Total affluence (average based on measures 2–6)

Our final measure of institutional quality was included to test the assumption that the student's intellectual achievement is increased if he is exposed to an environment where the competititon for intellectual rewards is very great. Although one would expect that the intelligence level of the student's peers (environmental measure #1, above) affects the amount of competition at an institution, we used a more direct measure derived from the recent study of college environments (Astin, 1968a) described earlier in Chapter 1:

8. Academic competitiveness (the degree of competition for grades as perceived by the student body)

Other environmental measures. In addition to the eight variables listed above, we included 61 of our other measures of institutional characteristics for exploratory purposes.

Some of the characteristics of our sample of 38 institutions are summarized in Table 36. The mean of 48.8 and standard deviation of 9.0 for selectivity were very close to the population values of 50 and 10, indicating that, in its general level and diversity of selectivity, our sample was reasonably representative of the total population of accredited four-year institutions. The fact that 32 of our 38 institutions were liberal arts colleges (the other six being five universities and one teachers college) is reflected in the relatively small mean and standard deviation for enrollment size. This over-representation of liberal arts colleges is characteristic of the total group of institutions participating in the Institutional Research Program of the Educational Testing Service (ETS).

The 38 institutions in our sample spent a median of $1,170 per student for educational and general purposes, with a range from $660 to $4,280. These figures, together with the data shown in Table 36, indicate that the sample was reasonably diverse with respect to quality, the principal independent variable of concern in the analysis.

TABLE 36
Characteristics of the 38 Institutions
Attended by the 669 Students

CHARACTERISTIC[a]	MEAN	STANDARD DEVIATION
Selectivity	48.8	9.0
Size of Student Body	45.8	7.4
Characteristics of Entering Classes:		
Intellectualism	50.1	8.7
Estheticism	46.4	9.2
Status	52.0	9.2
Pragmatism	51.6	6.5
Masculinity	50.6	8.2

[a] Population ($N = 1,015$) means and standard deviations on each characteristic have been set at 50 and 10, respectively (Astin, 1965d).

The distribution of the 669 students among the 38 institutions was fairly uniform. There were no more than 49 students from any one instituion, and the median number of students per institution, which was 16, was very close to the mean number per institution, which was 17.6.[8]

Interaction Measures

Some of the folklore concerning institutional excellence deals with the *interaction* between student and institutional quality, rather than simply with independent effects of institutional quality. More specifically, many educators assume that the greater the academic ability of the student, the more intellectual benefit he will derive from exposure to an institution of high quality. This assumed benefit is frequently used to justify the highly selective admissions policies of many institutions. Although many such interaction terms between specific student and environmental characteristics can be calculated, the following seem best to represent this expected positive interaction:

1. The product of the individual student's academic ability (as measured by his composite score on the NMSQT) and the average ability of all undergraduate students at his institution (Selectivity)
2. The product of the student's academic ability and the institution's per-student expenditures for educational and general purposes

Prior to the computation of these terms, all variances were equated in order to balance the contribution of student and of institutional quality to each term.

Testing of Hypotheses

Stated in positive terms, the general hypotheses tested in this analysis were as follows:

1. The academic excellence of the undergraduate institution—as defined by the level of ability of the student body, the level of the institution's financial resources, and the degree of academic competitiveness in the college environment—has a positive effect on the undergraduate student's intellectual achievement.
2. The extent of the positive effect of institutional quality on intellectual achievement is proportional to the student's academic ability.

In conventional statistical terminology, the first hypothesis is concerned with the *main* effects of institutional excellence on intellectual achievement, whereas the second is concerned with the *interaction* effects of institutional quality and student ability on intellectual achievement.

The statistical design used for testing the hypotheses was a three-stage stepwise linear regression analysis, in which the dependent variable was the student's score on one of the Area Tests of the GRE. During each stage of the analysis, a different subset of independent variables was entered into the regression equation in a stepwise fashion until no additional variable from that subset was capable of producing a reduction in the residual sum of squares in the GRE test exceeding $p = .05$. During the first stage in each analysis, the 103 student input (control) variables were permitted to enter into the equation. During the second stage, the 69 college environmental variables, including the measures of institutional excellence, were permitted to enter. The final stage of the analysis permitted the two interaction terms to enter the equation. Three such three-stage analyses were performed, one for each of the GRE Area Tests.

Note that, at the end of the first stage in each analysis, the student's residual score on the particular Area Test was linearly independent of his characteristics at the time of entrance to college. Presumably, this residual variation in performance is attributable either to differential environmental experiences since entering college (including effects of the college environment) or to errors of measurement.[9] In short, the purpose of the first stage was to equate statistically the students entering each institution in order to minimize bias in the interpretation of relationships between institutional characteristics and student achievement.

Results

Table 37 shows the results of the tests of our two major hypotheses. The first three columns of data give the correlations between the three achievement measures and each measure of institutional quality prior to control of differential student inputs. All 30 of the coefficients were positive, and 27 of them were statistically significant. Thus, there was clearly a positive relationship between the college senior's intellectual achievement and the quality of his institution. More simply: Students in higher quality institutions tended to perform better than students in institutions of lesser quality. The estimated *effects* of institutional quality on student achievement are shown in the last three columns of data in Table 37. The size of virtually all the coefficients was greatly diminished as a consequence of controlling differential inputs, and nearly half of the signs became negative. More important, only seven of these partial coefficients were statistically significant, and, of these, five were *negative* in sign.[10]

These findings offer little support for either of our general hypotheses concerning the effects of institutional quality on student achievement. Significant positive relationships with measures of quality were found only in the case of achievement in social science, whereas the significant partial correlations involving achievement in humanities and natural sciences were all negative. All of these coefficients, however, were trivial in size, and no single measure of institutional quality seemed to have a consistent effect—positive or negative—on achievement in even two of the three areas.

The results of the stepwise linear regression analyses are summarized in Tables 38–40. Of the student's characteristics at the time he enters college, the most important single determinant of his level of achievement as a college

TABLE 37

The Effects of Institutional "Quality" on Student Achievement

(N=669 students; 38 institutions)

INDEX OF QUALITY OR EXCELLENCE	CORRELATIONS WITH SCORES ON AREA TESTS OF THE GRE					
	Before Control of Input Measures			After Control of Input Measures		
	Social Science	Humanities	Natural Science	Social Science	Humanities	Natural Science
Selectivity	.20**	.17**	.09*	.00	−.07	−.08*
Expenditures (educational and general) per student	.21**	.11**	.13**	.04	−.08*	−.05
Number of books in the library	.24**	.11**	.16**	.12**	.03	.03
Number of books per student	.10**	.02	.08*	.03	.02	−.06
Faculty-student ratio	.17**	.09*	.05	.07	.02	−.08
Percentage of faculty with Ph.D.'s	.20**	.09*	.18**	.06	.05	.00
Total affluence	.27**	.13**	.15**	.12**	.05	−.05
Academic competitiveness	.11**	.15**	.05	.01	.04	−.09*
Interaction between student aptitude and						
Selectivity	.46**	.45**	.32**	.02	−.06	−.08*
Expenditures (educational and general) per student	.52**	.47**	.39**	.05	−.07	−.06

* $p < .05$.   ** $p < .01$.

TABLE 38

The Prediction of Undergraduate Achievement in Social Science
(N = 669 students; 38 institutions)

Step Number	Independent Variable Entering Equation	Sign	Increase in R^2	R	To Enter Equation	F-value* In Final Equation
	Student Input Characteristics:					
1	Academic aptitude (NMSQT Composite)	+	.318	.564	310.9	179.5
2	Sex—(Male)	+	.062	.616	66.1	33.2
3	Major in history or political science	+	.023	.634	25.2	15.2
4	English aptitude (NMSQT)	−	.013	.644	14.2	30.4
5	Major in economics, psychology, or sociology	+	.009	.651	10.4	14.7
6	Father's occupation—Skilled worker	−	.007	.656	8.3	3.1
7	Mathematical aptitude (NMSQT)	−	.005	.660	6.1	18.5
8	Major in mathematics	+	.006	.665	6.9	10.2
9	Major in education	+	.006	.669	6.8	5.8
10	Career choice of politician or diplomat	+	.005	.673	6.0	6.8
11	Won leadership award in high school	+	.006	.677	6.9	9.7
12	High school grade average	+	.008	.683	9.6	14.0
13	Career choice of businessman	+	.005	.686	6.1	6.9
14	Career choice of nurse	−	.004	.689	4.3	0.4
15	Career choice of college professor	−	.004	.691	4.4	5.2
16	Father's educational level	+	.004	.694	4.5	2.0
	College Environmental Characteristics:					
17	Severity of Administrative Policy against Heterosexual Activity (ICA)	−	.013	.703	16.1	6.4
18	College located in suburban area	−	.010	.710	12.6	17.8
19	Student Employment (ICA)	+	.008	.715	9.9	10.7
20	Predominantly Negro	−	.004	.718	5.1	5.1

* $F_{05} = 3.88$; $F_{01} = 6.75$; $F_{001} = 11.11$.

TABLE 39
The Prediction of Undergraduate Achievement in Humanities
(N = 669 students; 38 institutions)

STEP NUMBER	INDEPENDENT VARIABLE ENTERING EQUATION	SIGN	R	INCREASE IN R^2	F-VALUE* To Enter Equation	F-VALUE* In Final Equation
	Student Input Characteristics:					
1	Word Usage aptitude (NMSQT)	+	.593	.351	361.0	122.7
2	English aptitude (NMSQT)	+	.624	.039	42.2	14.6
3	High school grade average	+	.637	.016		
4	Natural Science Reading aptitude (NMSQT)	+	.642	.006	6.8	6.5
5	Major in business	−	.646	.006	6.8	5.0
6	Major in fine arts or music	+	.650	.005	6.0	6.1
7	Planning a Ph.D.	+	.653	.004	4.5	3.0
8	Father a college professor	+	.656	.004	4.0	5.0
	College Environmental Characteristics:					
9	Verbal Aggressiveness (ICA)	−	.678	.029	35.4	38.2
10	Familiarity with the Instructor (ICA)	+	.688	.014	17.6	13.2
11	Private-Nonsectarian	+	.692	.005	6.3	7.9
12	Expenditures (educational and general) per student	−	.695	.005	5.7	9.5
13	Total affluence	+	.697	.004	4.7	4.7

*$F_{05} = 3.88$; $F_{01} = 6.75$; $F_{001} = 11.11$.

TABLE 40

The Prediction of Undergraduate Achievement in Natural Science

($N = 669$ students; 38 institutions)

Step Number	Independent Variable Entering Equation	Sign	Increase in R^2	R	F-value To Enter Equation	F-value In Final Equation
	Student Input Characteristics:					
1	Mathematical aptitude (NMSQT)	+	.222	.471	190.1	18.9
2	Sex—(Male)	+	.062	.532	57.9	112.0
3	Natural Science Reading aptitude (NMSQT)	+	.050	.578	50.3	14.3
4	Major in physical science	+	.036	.609	38.0	34.2
5	Major in biological science	+	.037	.638	40.8	28.7
6	High school grade average	+	.013	.648	14.6	22.1
7	Word Usage aptitude (NMSQT)	+	.011	.656	12.7	18.8
8	Career choice of lawyer	−	.010	.664	11.8	11.6
9	Major in accounting	−	.007	.669	8.7	14.9
10	Career choice of businessman	−	.006	.674	7.7	9.6
11	Major in English	−	.006	.679	7.6	3.1
12	Major in philosophy or religion	−	.006	.683	7.2	7.3
13	Career choice of biological scientist	+	.005	.687	6.3	9.2
14	Won award in high school debate contest	−	.005	.690	6.4	7.9
15	Father's occupation—farmer	+	.005	.694	5.8	4.8
16	Edited high school paper or magazine	+	.004	.697	4.8	5.6
17	Career choice of dentist	−	.004	.699	5.1	6.4
18	Elected to student office in high school	−	.004	.702	4.7	3.8
19	Major in agriculture	+	.003	.704	4.2	3.8
	College Environmental Characteristics:					
20	Student Employment (ICA)	+	.011	.712	14.9	10.2
21	Private-Nonsectarian	+	.008	.718	10.4	21.3
22	Severity of Administrative Policy against Drinking (ICA)	+	.005	.721	6.9	9.2
23	Emphasis on Athletics (ICA)	−	.003	.724	4.3	10.1
24	Extraversion of the Instructor (ICA)	−	.003	.726	4.3	8.2
25	Rate of Cheating in the Classroom (ICA)	+	.003	.728	4.5	4.5

* $F_{.05} = 3.88$; $F_{.01} = 6.75$; $F_{.001} = 11.11$.

senior was his academic ability as measured during high school. As might be expected, the student's mathematical aptitude was most important in predicting his subsequent level of achievement in natural science, whereas his aptitudes in word usage and in English were most important in predicting achievement in humanities. Overall academic ability (as measured by the NMSQT Composite score) was the best single predictor of undergraduate achievement in social sciences. Being male carried substantial positive weights in predicting achievement in both natural and social science, although sex did not enter into the prediction of achievement in humanities.

Next to academic ability and sex, the most important predictors of undergraduate achievement were the student's intended field of study and his career choice at the time he entered college. For the most part, the fields of study and careeer choices that carried significant weights in each analysis were appropriate to the particular Area Test under consideration. The student's level of achievement in natural science, for example, was relatively high in his senior year if he had initially intended to major in physical science, biological science, or agriculture, and relatively low if his initial major had been in accounting, English, or philosophy. Similarly, students tended to perform well on the Area Test in social science if they had initially planned to major in history, political science, economics, psychology, sociology, education, or (rather surprisingly) mathematics. Students performed relatively well on the humanities test if they had initially planned to major in fine arts or music and relatively badly if they had initially planned to major in business. A similar predictive pattern was found when the student's initial career choice was considered. (There is, of course, some redundancy in career choices and fields of study.)

Since the student's initial study plans had these effects, even though his initial achievement level as measured by the NMSQT was controlled, it seems safe to conclude that scores on the GRE Area Tests reflect the differential learning that occurred as a result of the student's particular undergraduate course of study.

The only other input variable consistently related to performance on the Area Tests was the student's average grade in high school, which, not surprisingly, carried a positive weight in predicting achievement in all three areas.

The college environmental characteristics that entered into the regression equation during the second stage of the analysis (after the control of student input characteristics) are listed in the bottom part of Tables 38–40. Measures of institutional excellence or quality entered into only one of the three analyses, that of achievement in the humanities. In this instance, the educational and general expenditures per student entered in with a negative weight, after which the total affluence measure entered in with a positive weight. (Until this last step, total affluence showed no relationship to achievement in humanities.) These findings once again contradict the folklore concerning institutional excellence.

TABLE 41

Environmental Characteristics Having Similar Effects on All Three
Measures of Achievement

($N = 669$ students; 38 institutions)

ENVIRONMENTAL VARIABLES	PARTIAL CORRELATION, AFTER CONTROL OF STUDENT INPUT VARIABLES, WITH ACHIEVEMENT IN:		
	Social Science	Humanities	Natural Science
Peer Environment (ICA Factors):			
Use of Automobile	.08*	.13**	.15**
Career Indecision	.08*	.11**	.10**
Verbal Aggressiveness	−.07	−.23**	−.14**
Independence	−.02	−.08*	−.12**
Administrative Environment (ICA Factors):			
Flexibility of the Curriculum	.09*	.16**	.04
Severity of Administrative Policy against Cheating	−.09	−.14**	−.11**
Severity of Administrative Policy against Heterosexual Activity	−.16**	−.10*	−.02
Realistic (technical) emphasis in the curriculum	.10*	.08*	.08*
Total enrollment	.07	.08*	.10*
Roman Catholic	−.14**	−.12**	−.08*

* $p < .05$.   ** $p < .01$.

This second stage in our three analyses failed to reveal any clear-cut pattern of institutional characteristics which either fosters or inhibits student achievement. However, in order to explore further the possibility that there might be certain consistent patterns which are obscured by the large number of partially redundant college variables, we examined the partial correlations between the three achievement measures and each of the 69 measures of environmental characteristics immediately following the first stage of the analysis (the control of student input variables). Several environmental characteristics which, at this stage in the analysis, had consistent partial correlations with all three achievement measures are listed in Table 41. The criteria for inclusion in this list were that the sign of the partial correlation be the same for all three measures and that at least two of the partial correlations be statistically significant ($p < .05$). Somewhat surprisingly, the peer environments of those institutions where the students' level of achievement exceeded the level predicted from their freshman input characteristics had several distinct characteristics: students tended to make frequent use of automobiles, to be undecided about their careers, and to manifest little independence or verbal aggressiveness in the classroom. Moreover, at institutions which had relatively flexible curricula (that is, few required courses) and relatively permissive policies concerning cheating and heterosexual activity, students tended to achieve above the expected level. Students attending relatively large institutions with a fairly strong technical emphasis in the curriculum tended to perform somewhat better than expected, whereas students attending Roman Catholic institutions tended to perform below expectation.

At first glance, these patterns of environmental characteristics seem contrary to common-sense notions about the environmental influences that facilitate student achievement. One obvious explanation for the apparently negative effect that severe policies against cheating have on achievement is that students find it easier to "improve" their scores when the GRE is administered in an environment where cheating is tolerated.

Our findings concerning environmental effects on student attrition, discussed earlier in the chapter, may help elucidate this total pattern of relationships. All the environmental characteristics listed in Table 41 except one (Severity of Administrative Policy Against Heterosexual Activity) showed statistically significant effects on the student's chances of dropping out, as measured both by his completing four years of college and by his obtaining the bachelor's degree (see Table 30 and Appendix F); in every case, the direction of the effect was the *opposite* of the direction shown in Table 41. In other words, the same environmental characteristics which increase the chances that some students will drop out seem to have a favorable effect on the achievement of other students during the senior year. Perhaps those institutions with relatively high dropout rates facilitate student achievement because they encourage the less motivated and less able students to drop out before they reach the senior year. Consequently, those students who survive the four undergraduate years have endured a more stringent screening procedure. Conversely, institutions with relatively low dropout rates may have a negative effect on student achievement in that they encourage students who might otherwise drop out because of low motivation to stay through the four years. These students, in turn, would tend to perform below expectation on the GRE.

Relative Importance of Student Input and Environmental Variables

Although our analyses failed to confirm the folklore concerning the presumed educational benefits of institutional quality, they provided some evidence that the student's achievement is affected by institutional characteristics other than the traditional measures of quality. But these effects appear to be relatively small compared with the effects of student input characteristics. In order to test more directly the relative importance of these two classes of effects, we performed a second series of analyses similar to those summarized in Tables 38–40. In these additional analyses, however, the 69 college characteristics were permitted to enter the regression equations *before* any of the student input measures were permitted to enter (i.e., the first two stages in the earlier analyses were reversed).

The results of both sets of analyses are compared in Table 42. Each of the coefficients (R^2) in the table represents the proportion of common variance or overlap between one of the achievement measures and a particular subset of independent variables. The first row of the table, for example, shows what proportion of variance in each of the three achievement measures is attributable to the combined effects of student input and college environmental char-

TABLE 42

The Relative Contributions of Student Input and College
Environmental Variables to Achievement

($N = 669$ students; 38 institutions)

PROPORTION OF VARIANCE* ATTRIBUTABLE TO:	GRE ACHIEVEMENT MEASURE		
	Social Science	Humanities	Natural Science
Joint contribution of student input and college environment	.515	.486	.530
Student input alone	.482	.430	.496
College environment alone	.198	.106	.104
Input independent of environment	.317	.381	.426
Environment independent of input	.034	.056	.023

* R^2.

acteristics. (These values are simply the squares of the final multiple correlation coefficients shown in Tables 38–40.) The second row of coefficients was taken from the last step in the first stage of the three-stage analyses shown in Tables 38–40 (i.e., after the control of student input characteristics). The third row of coefficients shows the comparable proportions of variance that were obtained when the 69 environmental variables were entered into the regression equation first. The fourth and fifth rows of coefficients were obtained by subtracting the third and second rows, respectively, from the first row.

In brief, these results show clearly that variations in achievement during the senior year in college were much more dependent upon differences in student characteristics that existed prior to matriculation than they were upon the characteristics of the colleges attended. Even when the bias resulting from differential student inputs was not controlled, college characteristics accounted for only about 20 percent of the variance in social science achievement and only about 10 percent of the variance in achievement in humanities and natural science. When student input differences were controlled, the contribution of college characteristics shrank to only about 5 percent of the variance in achievement. The substantial contribution of student input, on the other hand, was only moderately reduced when college characteristics were first controlled.

These results tend to confirm earlier studies of differential college influence, in which variations in student performance on the GRE aptitude tests were found to be primarily dependent upon variations in student inputs (Astin, 1965c; Nichols, 1964). It must be kept in mind, however, that our analysis accounted for only about half of the observed variation in student achievement during the senior year. A large proportion of this residual variation is undoubtedly attributable to errors in our measuring instruments, although it is also possible that we have so far failed to identify other important environmental factors.

The results of these analyses suggest that it may be wise to reexamine some of our traditional notions about institutional excellence, particularly as it relates to the intellectual development of the student.

SUMMARY

In this chapter, we have presented an analysis of the personal and environmental factors that influence students' persistence in college, educational achievement, and educational aspirations during the undergraduate years. The major conclusions to be drawn from this analysis are as follows:

1. In general, our ability to predict whether a student will drop out of college and what his final level of educational aspiration will be is limited. Although we may have failed to include all relevant input variables in our analyses, it seems unlikely that additional input controls would result in dramatic improvements in prediction.

2. Students are more likely to complete four years of college and to obtain the bachelor's degree within the four years following their initial matriculation if they have relatively superior academic records in high school and come from a relatively high socioeconomic background.

3. Although a greater proportion of women than of men obtain the baccalaureate within four years after entering college, equal proportions of men and women complete four years of college credit during that period. When women's initially superior academic records are taken into account, however, we find that women are more likely than are men to drop out of college.

4. The best single predictor of the student's final level of educational aspiration is his initial statement of educational plans. Men are relatively more likely than are women both to have an initially high level of aspiration or to raise their aspirations during the four years. Students with superior academic records in high school are more likely to raise their educational aspirations after entering college than are students with poorer academic records.

5. Getting married after entering college appears to increase the student's chances of dropping out and to lessen interest in graduate education.

6. Students who receive a major proportion of financial support from their parents or who receive scholarship support are more likely than are other students to complete four years of college within the four years following matriculation.

7. The 246 institutions vary markedly in the actual percentages of their students who plan further education, complete four years of college, or obtain the bachelor's degree. Although the range in these outcomes is somewhat reduced when differential student inputs are controlled, the variations among institutions remain extensive.

8. A relatively small proportion of the variation in institutional influence on the student's educational progress and plans can be accounted for when the college environment is considered only in terms of administrative typologies. Nearly twice as much of the variation is accounted for when the college environment is viewed in terms of the more sophisticated environmental measures derived from previous research.

9. Students are more likely to complete four years of college and to obtain the bachelor's degree during the four years following matriculation if they attend relatively selective institutions where the peer environment is cohesive and where the number of students who are employed is relatively low. The negative effects of student employment seem to result in part from work-study programs which normally require five years to attain the baccalaureate.

10. The student's interest in pursuing graduate training appears to be increased by attendance at selective, private colleges located in the Northeast, particularly if these institutions have relatively high budgets in terms of expenditures per student for educational and general purposes and if the academic work is fairly demanding. The student is more likely to want to obtain a professional degree if he attends a men's college or a university located in a large city.

11. The large observed differences among institutions in educational outcomes appear to be more a function of differences in their entering students than of differences in the measurable characteristics of their environments.

12. Analyses of college effects which use the institution as the unit of analysis in controlling differential student inputs indicate that the different effects of colleges are mediated by environmental variables which are almost wholly dependent on the characteristics of the entering students, who are differentially recruited into the various institutions.

13. A special analysis of educational achievement as measured by student performance on the Area Tests of the Graduate Record Examination reveals variations in student achievement are almost completely a function of differences in students' characteristics that existed prior to matriculation; student achievement is little affected by the characteristics of the college environment, including those characteristics traditionally associated with institutional quality or "excellence."

REFERENCES

1. Portions of this section also appear in R. J. Panos & A. W. Astin, "Attrition Among College Students," *American Educational Research Journal*, 1968, 5, 57–72.

2. Note that the expected criterion score (a weighted linear regression composite) and hence, the residual criterion score, are both continuous variables, whereas the actual dichotomously scored criterion measure can assume only one of two discrete values. Although it would have been possible to perform a series of multiple discriminant analyses for each of the dichotomously scored criterion measures in this study instead of the multiple point-biserial regression analyses actually used, the two methods yield sets of weights that are proportional (Michael and Perry, 1956). The regression approach we have used is similar to the "reduced model" as described by Bottenberg and Ward (1963).

3. The need for an unambiguous (even though necessarily arbitrary) definition of *dropout* is apparent from the equivocal nature of the term. For example, as was shown in Chapter 2 (table 2), although 65 percent of the population had completed four or more years of college, only 50 percent of the men and 62 percent of the women had re-

ceived a bachelor-level degree. Thus, despite the high correlation (.72) between completing four or more years and attaining the bachelor's degree, these are, in fact, different phenomena. It is important to note that the results of many attrition studies are not comparable because they deal with different phenomena.

4. As was pointed out in Chapter 1, because of arbitrary limits on the number of input variables in our regression analysis program, we did not include the dichotomously scored race variables "American Indian" and "Other" in this analysis. Since the other three race variables entered into the stepwise solution with positive weights (see Table 21), at least one of the remaining race variables is negatively related to the criterion.

5. This conclusion must be tempered by recognizing (1) that some of the differential environmental effects may have been confounded with differential student inputs and therefore removed when these input variables were controlled, and (2) that the proportion of variance in the residual output scores is probably substantial.

6. Portions of this section also appear in A. W. Astin, "Undergraduate Achievement and Institutional 'Excellence'," *Science*, 1968 *161*, 661–68.

7. The substantial loss of subjects was caused primarily by random subsampling within colleges, dropouts, transfers, and the requirement that NMSQT scores be available. NMSQT scores, rather than scores on either the Scholastic Aptitude Test or the American College Test, were selected, in order to avoid regression artifacts that might result from the use of the SAT and ACT in college admissions.

8. Slightly more of the students in the sample were in the more selective institutions, so that the mean Selectivity score (52.5) using the *student* as the unit of analysis was slightly higher than the mean Selectivity score (48.8) using the *institution* as the unit of analysis (Table 36). Student means on other institutional characteristics, however, tended to be very close to the institutional means.

9. It is always possible, of course, that the residual GRE scores were not independent of certain potentially biasing student input characteristics that were inadvertently left out of our analysis. The principal objective in this and similar "natural experiments" is to measure and statistically control as many potentially biasing student input characteristics as possible.

10. According to classical test theory, our method of analysis would not produce residual scores on the dependent variable which are independent of the student's "true" input scores, as long as there are random errors in the measurement of the input variables. Such errors have the effect of flattening the slope of the observed regression of the dependent variable on the independent variables. The appropriate procedure to adjust for this source of bias is to compute the intercorrelations of the variables using the variances of the "true" input scores rather than the variances in the observed input scores. We were not able to conduct our entire analysis using these "true" variances, because of the difficulty in estimating the reliability (i.e., the ratio between "true" and observed variances) of the many qualitative input variables (e.g., the student's initial field of study). However, the availability of reliability estimates for our key input variables—the NMSQT scores—enabled us to run two additional analyses: one using the observed variances in the NMSQT scores, and the other using their estimated true variances. In both analyses, the NMSQT scores were first entered into regression, and then the partial correlations between GRE achievement and the various measures of institutional quality were examined. Using the true rather than the observed variances altered the partial correlations only slightly, but in every instance the shifts were in the negative direction (i.e., contrary to the two hypotheses).

4
Determinants of Career Choice
and Field of Study

IN THIS CHAPTER, we shall examine some of the personal and environmental factors affecting the student's career choice during the undergraduate years and, closely associated with career choice, his eventual undergraduate major field. The general plan of this chapter is similar to that of the preceding one, except that here we are concerned with a larger number of different possible outcomes: careers and fields of study.

The first of the four sections of the chapter is devoted to a descriptive analysis of changes in students' career preferences and fields of study during the undergraduate years, with special emphasis on systematic patterns of changes occurring among different careers and fields. The second section deals with the prediction of the student's eventual career choice and final field of study, on the basis of his characteristics as an entering freshman. The last two sections are concerned, respectively, with the effects of within-college and of between-college environmental characteristics.

CHANGES IN CAREER CHOICE AND FIELD OF STUDY DURING THE UNDERGRADUATE YEARS

The student's career preference and field of study, both at the time he entered college and four years later at the time of the followup, were assessed through two open-ended items, which were subsequently coded. The classification system for careers comprised 49 possible categories, and the system for field of study comprised 54 categories. Since several of these categories turned out to contain only a small number of students, the 49 careers and 54 fields of study were subsequently reduced to 40 and 44 categories, respectively, by collapsing some of the original categories. The original coding scheme and the later revision are shown in Appendix G.

Table 43 ranks the 40 career choices on the basis of their stability—that is, their "holding power," their success in retaining the students initially attracted to them—during the four years following matriculation. These data show clearly that the student's choice of a career at the time he enters college typically changes by the time of graduation: Only two of the careers, nurse and schoolteacher, managed to hold as many as half the students initially choosing them. Although there is no obvious relationship between

85

TABLE 43
Stability of Different Career Choices
($N = 36,405$ students)

1961 CHOICE	PERCENT STILL CHOOSING SAME CAREER IN 1965[a]
Nurse	57.1
Teacher (elementary or secondary school)	56.3
Clergyman	43.0
Lawyer	39.0
Architect	37.4
Engineer	36.1
Therapist (physical or occupational)	35.6
Actor; Entertainer	33.3
Pharmacist	33.2
Social worker	33.1
Housewife	32.5
Farmer	32.0
Accountant	29.5
Dietitian; Home economist	29.4
Physician	28.5
Artist	27.2
Business executive	27.0
College professor	25.3
Military serviceman	24.7
Musician	24.5
Clerk; Secretary	24.5
Veterinarian	23.3
Dentist	21.7
Journalist; Writer	20.6
Chemist	20.0
Salesman	19.5
Physicist	18.1
Interior decorator; Designer	16.4
Laboratory assistant or technician	14.3
Biological scientist	14.1
No response	12.9
Undecided	12.0
Other occupation	11.9
Advertising man; Public relations man	10.9
Psychologist	10.7
Businessman (unspecified)	9.5
Mathematician	9.2
Government service worker	5.5
Diplomat; Foreign service worker; Politician	5.2
Housewife and occupation	4.5

[a] Data have been differentially weighted to approximate national norms for all students entering four-year accredited institutions in the fall of 1961.

type of career and degree of stability, the more popular careers (those that were initially chosen by a relatively large proportion of students) tended to be more stable over time than did the less popular. Exceptions to this trend are the careers of architect, actor or entertainer, and pharmacist, which were chosen by very small proportions of students but which had relatively high rates of stability during the four years.

TABLE 44

Distribution of Career Choices in 1961 and in 1965

($N = 36{,}405$ students)

CAREER CHOICE	PERCENT OF TOTAL SAMPLE[a] CHOOSING IN		RELATIVE PERCENTAGE CHANGE[a] BETWEEN
	1961	1965	1961 AND 1965
Housewife	.5	2.4	+433
College professor	.6	3.3	+416
Business executive	1.8	5.1	+178
Housewife and occupation	.3	.9	+175
Salesman	.9	2.0	+116
Military serviceman	.5	.9	+94
Advertising man; Public relations man	.4	.8	+83
Businessman (unspecified)	1.7	2.9	+75
Actor; Entertainer	.3	.6	+70
Social worker	1.4	2.4	+69
Lawyer	3.0	3.8	+28
Other	7.1	8.8	+23
Government service worker	.6	.7	+22
Musician	.3	.3	+14
Psychologist	1.0	1.2	+11
Accountant	2.0	2.1	+10
Teacher (elementary or secondary school)	23.6	24.9	+6
Therapist (physical or occupational)	.9	.9	−5
Undecided	6.8	6.3	−6
Clergyman	.9	.8	−8
Artist	.6	.5	−8
Dietitian; Home economist	.4	.4	−10
Nurse	2.1	1.7	−16
Biological scientist	.8	.6	−20
Journalist; Writer	1.1	.8	−21
Clerk; Secretary	1.3	1.0	−22
Farmer	1.4	1.1	−24
Architect	.9	.7	−28
No response	14.7	9.9	−33
Pharmacist	.9	.6	−34
Dentist	1.2	.8	−36
Engineer	7.9	4.7	−41
Chemist	1.7	1.0	−42
Designer; Interior decorator	.4	.3	−42
Mathematician	.9	.5	−42
Physician	5.0	2.6	−48
Veterinarian	.5	.2	−51
Laboratory assistant or technician	1.3	.6	−52
Physicist	1.0	.5	−54
Diplomat; Foreign service worker; Politician	1.3	.3	−74

[a] Data have been differentially weighted to approximate national norms for all students entering four-year accredited institutions in the fall of 1961.

Table 44 compares the distributions of career choices in 1961 and in 1965; Table 45 does the same for fields of study. The last column of both tables shows the relative percentage change for each field during the four-year interval, with careers and fields being listed in descending order from the biggest "gainer" to the biggest "loser." By "relative" change, we mean simply that the number of students initially choosing the career or major in 1961 was used as the base for computing the percentage of change. Note

TABLE 45

Distribution of Major Fields in 1961 and in 1965

($N = 36,405$ undergraduates)

Major Field	Percent of Total Sample[a] Choosing in		Relative Percentage[a] Change between
	1961	1965	1961 and 1965
Economics	.6	2.6	+302
Philosophy	.2	.6	+259
Zoology	.3	.9	+245
Social sciences	.7	1.7	+146
Sociology	1.2	2.8	+129
Geology	.2	.4	+114
Political science	1.6	3.0	+94
English	3.4	6.6	+93
Accounting	1.3	2.4	+88
History	2.5	4.7	+85
Speech	.7	1.2	+73
Psychology	2.1	3.4	+62
Advertising (marketing)	.3	.4	+58
Fine Arts	1.1	1.7	+48
Business administration	6.1	8.9	+45
Physical education	1.4	2.0	+45
Industrial arts and trade	.5	.7	+36
Music	1.1	1.5	+33
Biology	2.6	3.4	+32
Animal husbandry	.2	.3	+31
Foreign languages	2.3	2.9	+30
Mixed majors and others	5.9	6.8	+16
Agriculture	.8	.8	+13
Social work	.2	.2	+10
Nursing	1.8	1.8	00
Home economics	1.9	1.8	−05
Mathematics	4.0	3.7	−08
Chemistry	2.8	2.5	−11
Journalism	.6	.5	−15
Religious education	.2	.2	−16
Education	10.7	8.7	−18
Architecture	.8	.6	−26
Foreign service	.3	.2	−26
Pharmacy	.8	.6	−28
Humanities, other	1.4	1.0	−28
Theology	.3	.2	−30
Physics	1.3	.9	−31
Engineering	8.6	5.7	−34
No response	15.1	8.8	−42
Health technology	.8	.4	−45
Natural sciences	2.2	1.1	−50
Forestry	.7	.2	−75
Preprofessional	5.3	1.2	−78
Undecided	3.4	.2	−95

[a] Data have been differentially weighted to approximate national norms for all students entering four-year accredited institutions in fall 1961.

that the percentage change for each category is dependent on two factors: the number of *defectors* (those who initially chose the career or field but changed to some other) and the number of *recruits* (those who moved into

TABLE 46

Changes in the Distribution of Career Choices and Major Fields[a]
between 1961 and 1965

($N = 36,405$ undergraduates)

CHOICE	PERCENT OF TOTAL SAMPLE[b] CHOOSING IN		RELATIVE PERCENTAGE CHANGE[b] BETWEEN
	1961	1965	1961 AND 1965
Career:			
College professor	.6	3.3	+416
Housewife	.8	3.3	+328
Businessman	6.8	13.0	+90
Lawyer	3.0	3.8	+28
Other	17.3	18.5	+07
Teacher (elementary or secondary school)	23.6	24.9	+06
Performing artist or writer	2.3	2.3	+01
Undecided	6.8	6.3	−06
Health professional (non-M.D.)	5.5	4.0	−27
No response	14.7	9.9	−33
Natural scientist	4.4	2.6	−41
Engineer	7.9	4.7	−41
Physician or Dentist	6.3	3.4	−46
Major Field of Study:			
Social sciences	6.2	13.5	+117
Business	7.7	11.8	+53
Arts and humanities	15.3	21.3	+39
Other	10.0	10.3	+03
Education	12.2	10.9	−11
Biological sciences	11.1	9.1	−17
Physical sciences	10.5	8.6	−18
Engineering	8.6	5.7	−34
No response	15.1	8.8	−42
Undecided	3.4	.2	−95

[a] Broad categories derived from Tables 44 and 45.

[b] Data have been differentially weighted to approximate national norms for all students entering four-year accredited institutions in the fall of 1961.

the category from some other category). If defectors outnumbered recruits, the category shows a negative percentage change; if recruits outnumbered defectors, the change is positive. Generally, the most extreme changes occurred for careers that were relatively unpopular in 1961. Two exceptions to this trend were the careers of engineer and physician, which were chosen by relatively large percentages (7.9 and 5.0, respectively) in 1961 and which suffered relatively large losses by 1965.

In order to facilitate discussion of changes in students' preferred careers and fields of study during college, the data in Tables 44 and 45 were recast into a small number of more general careers and fields (see Table 46). College professor, housewife, and businessman were the careers manifesting the largest net gains over time. It is especially interesting to note that the largest net losses occurred in the three career categories that are most closely allied with science and mathematics: physician or dentist, engineer, and natural scientist. Indeed, if undecided students and nonresponding students are excluded, *all* career choices which registered net losses during the undergraduate years were science related.

The trends for major field (second part of Table 46) were generally consistent with the trends for career choice. The social sciences and business enjoyed the greatest net gains during the undergraduate years, whereas the largest losses (excluding the "no response" and "undecided" categories) occurred in engineering and in the physical and biological sciences.

In a recent review of the literature in this general area, H. S. Astin (1967b) noted that several studies of secondary school and undergraduate college students (H. S. Astin, 1967a; Davis, 1965; Flanagan and Cooley, 1966) revealed similar trends. Davis (1965), whose study bears the greatest resemblance to the present one, analyzed changes in career choices during the undergraduate years for a national sample of students who were graduating college seniors in 1961. Since our study and Davis's will be compared at several points later on, it is essential to mention certain important methodological differences between the two. First, Davis's target population consisted of graduating seniors rather than entering college freshmen. His data on changes in careers, therefore, are relevant only to those entering freshmen who survived through graduation, including students who transferred from other institutions. Dropouts were not included in his tabulations. A second difference between the two studies—and a more important one from a methodological point of view—is that Davis's data concerning the student's freshman choices of field and career were obtained retrospectively at the time of graduation rather than at the time of matriculation. Since such retrospective reports are frequently inaccurate (Astin, 1962b), some of the discrepancies between the two studies may be attributable to systematic errors in retrospective reporting of initial choices. A third difference is that Davis used a precoded scheme for recording the students' choices, as contrasted with our open-ended responses which were postcoded. Finally, Davis's data were collected in the spring of 1961, while the students were still in college, whereas our followup data were collected in the summer of 1965, after most of the sample had finished college.

One of the most striking discrepancies between the results of the current study and those of Davis's study is in the percentages of students who changed careers during the undergraduate years. All but two of the 40 specific career choice categories had retention rates of less than 50 percent in our study, compared with an *average* rate of change of 50 percent as reported by Davis's students. The highest rate of defection from a specific career field in Davis's data was only 64 percent (social science), a rate exceeded by 32 of the 40 career fields in the present study (see Table 43).

There are several possible explanations for this discrepancy. One is that dropouts (who were excluded from Davis's study but included in the present one) are probably more likely to change their career choices in the four years following matriculation than are those students who stay through until graduation. Another possibility is that, because of errors in the retrospective reports of Davis's subjects, the actual percentages of change are underestimates, an explanation supported by earlier evidence (Astin, 1962b) showing that those students who report earlier plans incorrectly are likely to err in the direction of their current plans. Also, because graduation from college may for many students be a time for making major changes in their career plans, our data—which were collected in the summer after the senior year—may reflect such changes. Whatever the correct explanation, the present study shows clearly that the great majority of entering college students change their initial career choices during the ensuing four years.[1]

The current study and Davis's are in much greater agreement with respect to the *relative* stability of the various fields. If we compare only those five categories of career choice that are the same in the two studies—schoolteacher, businessman, lawyer, engineer, and physician—the rank orderings on the basis of stability during the undergraduate years are identical (see Table 43 in this chapter and Davis's Table 2.4 on page 15). The relative ranking of careers and fields of study with respect to net gains or losses are also highly similar (see Table 46 in the current chapter and Davis's Table 2.6 on page 24). The principal discrepancy in the two sets of data is that Davis's "education" category showed the greatest net gain of all his nine fields, whereas our career category of teacher and our major field category of education showed relatively little net gain or loss during the four years. A partial explanation of this discrepancy is that Davis's category of education included college professor, a career which in our data had the largest relative percentage increase during the undergraduate years. Combining this career with our teacher category raises the percentage of increase for teacher somewhat, but the percentage increase for our businessman category is still much higher. Moreover, our major field category of education actually showed a small relative decrease.

The very large relative increase in the number of students who chose the career of college professor is of special interest. This change may reflect the student's growing familiarity with the role of the college professor as he progresses through college. A closer inspection of the patterns of change (see pp. 92–95 of this chapter) suggests that this increase occurred in part because many students who originally gave "scientist" as a career choice changed it to college professor. Perhaps many undergraduates learn that college professors have unusual opportunities for pursuing scientific interests.

For persons concerned with maintaining adequate supplies of scientific manpower, the heavy loss of students from scientific fields during the undergraduate years may be cause for alarm. While it could be argued that such losses are a natural consequence of the high academic standards that exist in these fields, the patterns of data in Table 46 suggest that certain rigidities in the curricula may be in part to blame. Note that those career fields which registered the greatest net losses—physician or dentist, engineer, and natural scientist—typically prescribe a large number of specific introductory and prerequisite courses for admission to each higher level of study. By contrast, those fields showing the largest gains in students during the undergraduate years—businessman and lawyer—often accept students for advanced work without requiring that they have an elaborate background of related courses. Consequently, while courses in science and mathematics do not necessarily handicap the student who wishes to become a businessman or a lawyer, courses other than science or mathematics are of little use to the student who wishes to become a doctor, an engineer, or a scientist. It seems likely that these science-oriented career fields would fare better in the competition for students if the number of prerequisite courses at each stage were reduced to a minimum and if measures were instituted to accelerate the "catching-up" phase for late recruits.

Patterns of Change in Careers and Major Fields

Do the defectors from a field change to a related field? Do the recruits into a field come from similar or related fields? Are the patterns of defecting and recruiting the same? Or are changes in major field and career choice random and haphazard? To explore these questions and to discover what systematic patterns of change—if any—operate, we must examine the specific paths followed by students who change their career choices and major fields.

A casual inspection of these paths suggests that changers gravitated toward fields that were relatively popular initially—principally education and business.[2] However, closer examination reveals clearly that the field finally chosen by the changer depended to some extent on his initial field. In other words, two defectors from different initial fields were not equally likely to pick a given final field. The student who defected from an initial choice of salesman, for example, was much more likely to pick "business executive" four years later than was the student who defected from an initial choice of teacher.

The same was true of the recruits into the different fields. Most of them tended to come from the fields that were initially more popular, simply because there were a large number of students (and thereby a large number of potential changers) in these fields. When the actual patterns of changes are examined, one finds that two recruits into different fields were not always equally likely to come from a given initial field. The student who changed his choice to physician, for example, was much more likely to have initially chosen the career of psychologist than was the student who changed his choice to engineer.

To explore these patterns of change in more detail, we examined the defectors from the five most popular career fields to see what careers they changed to, and we examined the recruits into these same five fields to see what their initial career choices were. However desirable it might have been to analyze each of the 40 career fields in this way, our analyses had to be confined to the five most popular fields if we were to have numbers large enough to obtain reliable estimates of the rates of change.

The major purpose of these analyses was to identify the career choices that were most similar and those that were least similar to each of the five popular fields. A specific career field was considered to be "most similar" if it met the following two conditions: (1) that a greater-than-chance ($p < .01$) proportion of those who defected from the popular career field changed into the specific field; and (2) that a greater-than-chance proportion of those who were recruited into the popular career field come from the specific field.[3] Conversely, a career field was considered to be "least similar" to a popular career if it met the following conditions: (1) that a less-than-chance proportion of those who defected from the popular career field ended up choosing the specific field; and (2) that a less-than-chance proportion of those who were recruited into the popular career field initially chose the other field.

The results of these analyses are shown in Table 47. The relatively large numbers of specific careers that satisfied our criteria of similarity or dissimilarity to one of the popular career choices provide ample evidence that changes in career plans during the undergraduate years are not random; distinct patterns exist. Moreover, these patterns are usually symmetrical, with changes between related fields occurring in both directions.

In general, the most similar occupations proved to be those which common sense tells us resemble the corresponding popular career choice. For example, the four careers that turned out to be most similar to the popular choice of business executive all involve manipulating money. Similarly, each of the six careers that were most similar to the popular choice of physician is concerned either with a medicine-related science or with one of the healing professions.

Equally interesting trends in patterns of career change during the undergraduate years are revealed in the lists of least similar choices, which are shown in the last column of Table 47. For example, the first four popular careers—business executive, engineer, lawyer, and physician—had in common many of the same least similar careers. That these careers tend to be stereotypic feminine occupations reflects perhaps the traditionally masculine nature of the four corresponding popular career choices. (The sex-linked aspects of career change are dealt with in more detail in the next section.) One of these careers, dietitian or home economist, was among the least similar to all four of the corresponding popular careers. Five others— clerk or secretary, housewife, musician, nurse, and therapist—appeared in the "least similar" column of three of the first four popular career fields. The exceptions to this pattern were usually consistent with the nature of the career: Clerk or secretary was not among the careers that are least similar to

TABLE 47
Similarity of Five Popular Career Choices to Other Choices, as Determined by Patterns of Changes between 1961 and 1965

POPULAR CAREER CHOICE	MOST SIMILAR CHOICES[a]	LEAST SIMILAR CHOICES[b]
Business executive	Accountant Advertising man; Public relations man Businessman (unspecified) Salesman	Actor; Entertainer Dietitian; Home economist Housewife Housewife and occupation Musician Nurse Therapist
Engineer	Chemist Mathematician Military officer Physicist	Artist Clerk; Secretary Designer; Interior decorator Dietitian; Home economist Diplomat; Politician Musician Nurse Therapist
Lawyer	Business executive Businessman (unspecified) Diplomat; Politician Government service worker (unspecified)	Biological scientist Clerk; Secretary Designer; Interior decorator Dietitian; Home economist Laboratory technician Housewife Musician Nurse Therapist
Physician	Biological scientist Chemist Dentist Laboratory technician Pharmacist Psychologist	Architect Artist Clerk; Secretary Dietitian; Home economist Housewife
Teacher (elementary or secondary school)	College professor Dietitian; Home economist Housewife and occupation Musician No response Other Social worker Psychologist	Architect Dentist Engineer Pharmacist Physician Veterinarian

[a] Greater-than-chance proportions of those (a) who were recruited into the corresponding popular field initially chose this field, and (b) who defected from the corresponding popular field changed to this field.

[b] Less-than-chance proportions of those (a) who were recruited into the corresponding popular field initially chose this field, and (b) who defected from the corresponding popular field changed to this field.

business executive, and both nurse and therapist were missing from the "least similar" column for the popular career choice of physician.

Another interesting pattern occurred with the popular choice of schoolteacher. With the exception of architect, all the least similar careers relate to some phase of natural science. Thus, it seems clear that defectors from teaching avoid careers involving natural science and that very rarely do recruits into teaching express an initial preference for careers connected with natural science.

These results are relevant to current theory and research in the area of career choice and development. Most noteworthy, it appears that the occupational groupings that result from empirical data on the relative frequency of exchange of students among various categories strongly resemble some of the groupings that have been developed on the basis of psychological theory (Holland, 1966a; Roe, 1956). In particular, the groupings shown in Table 47 resemble some of the six occupational groupings developed by Holland (1966b) on the basis of common personality characteristics of persons in different careers. The careers of business executive and lawyer, for example, both of which Holland classifies as Enterprising personality types, have in common many of the "most similar" and "least similar" careers. The major difference between them is that the career of business executive is slightly more similar to occupations directly concerned with money, whereas the career of lawyer is slightly more similar to occupations directly concerned with power and status.

Holland's classification of schoolteacher as a prototypic Social personality type is also supported by our data, since most of the career choices that were most similar to schoolteacher are also, according to Holland, at least partially of the Social type. This conclusion is further supported by the fact that the careers that bore the *least* similarity to teacher, as shown in Table 47, are all concerned with science. Holland's theory holds that the Scientific[4] and Social types are antithetical in many of their personal characteristics.

One possible discrepancy between these data and Holland's occupational classification is suggested by the pattern of similar and dissimilar careers for the popular choice of physician. Although Holland considers the physician to be at least partially similar to the Social type, only one of the six most similar careers, psychologist, resembles Holland's Social type in the slightest degree. The five other most similar careers are either purely or partially of the Scientific type. The implication that the career of physician should probably not be regarded as a Social personality type is supported by two additional lines of evidence: (1) Two of the careers *least* similar to physician were of the Social type; and (2) physician was listed among the least similar careers for teacher, a pure Social type. The physician's scientific inclinations would seem to disqualify him from being classified as a strongly Social type.

In brief, the results of our analyses indicate that meaningful groupings of occupations can be developed from purely empirical data concerning the exchange of persons among different careers over time.

THE INFLUENCE OF STUDENT INPUT CHARACTERISTICS

To examine the influence of personal and environmental factors on career choice and study plans, it was necessary first to sort the dependent variables (the student's choices of a career and of a major field in 1965) into a set of meaningful categories. Although for some purposes it might have been desirable to use all 40 career choices and all 44 fields of study, several considerations led us to decide not to do so. First, empirical results for such a large number of dependent variables are difficult to synthesize meaningfully. Second, some of these categories were chosen so infrequently by the students in the followup survey that the results of any statistical analyses would be highly unreliable. Finally, using such a large number of dependent variables would greatly increase the cost of the data analyses.

The classification of choices into a smaller number of dichotomous criterion groups was based on the following guidelines:

1. Choices that proved to be similar in the analyses of change patterns (see Table 47) should be grouped together, if possible.

2. Choices that proved to be maximally dissimilar should not be grouped together.

3. Groupings should be pertinent to the manpower policy concerns of the governmental agencies that contributed to the support of the project.

4. No criterion category should comprise less than 1 percent of the sample of students.

On the basis of these four considerations, a total of 21 dichotomous criterion (dependent) variables were developed from the career choices and major fields of study reported by the students in the 1965 followup survey. These variables are listed in Table 48. Approximately 70 percent of the students' final career choices could be classified as belonging to one of 14 career categories. (The remaining 30 percent included unclassifiable choices, undecided responses, and nonresponses.) It should be noted that these 14 career categories are not mutually exclusive: career choice #13 (scientist or engineer, all fields) and #14 (professional, all fields) are, of course, simply additive combinations of several of the first 12 categories. Even the first 12, however, are not always mutually exclusive: the category of college professor (#4) overlaps somewhat with three other categories: biological scientist, physical scientist, and social scientist. Here, we assumed that a student who chose college professor as his career four years after matriculation and, at the same time, had his final college major in a scientific field, can be considered to have chosen a career both as a scientist and as a college professor. This assumption is based on the recognition, noted earlier in the chapter, that students who originally aspired to careers as scientists tended to change their choice to college professor during the undergraduate years.

Approximately 82 percent of the students' final choices of major field could be classified in one of seven categories (see second part of Table 48). Note that these seven categories, unlike the career choice categories, are mutually exclusive; that is, no student can be classified simultaneously in

TABLE 48

Criteria of Career Choice and of Major Field Choice

1965 Criterion	Percent of Students in Sample[a] ($N = 3,821$) Choosing	1961 Categories[b]
Career choice:		
1. Biological scientist	1.2	Biological scientist; College professor (major in biological science)
2. Businessman	12.2	Accountant; Advertising man; Public relations man; Business executive; Businessman (unspecified); Salesman
3. Clergyman	1.2	Clergy; Missionary
4. College professor	5.2	College professor
5. Engineer	4.3	Engineer
6. Health professional (non-M.D.)	5.9	Laboratory assistant or technician; Nurse; Pharmacist; Social worker; Therapist (physical or occupational); Veterinarian
7. Lawyer	4.1	Lawyer
8. Performing artist	1.5	Actor or Entertainer; Artist; Journalist; Writer; Musician
9. Physical scientist	4.5	Chemist; Physicist; College professor (major in physical science)
10. Physician or Dentist	4.5	Physician; Dentist
11. Social scientist	2.4	Anthropologist; Psychologist; Sociologist; College professor (major in social science)
12. Teacher (elementary or secondary school)	26.1	Teacher
13. Scientist or Engineer (all fields)	11.3	Numbers 1, 5, 9, 11 (above)
14. Professional (all fields)	14.7	Numbers 6, 7, 10 (above)
Final major field of study:		
1. Arts and humanities	27.5	Architecture; English; Fine arts; History; Journalism; Language; Library Science; Music; Philosophy; Prelaw; Speech; Theology; Humanities (other)
2. Biological sciences	8.4	Agriculture; Animal husbandry; Biology; Forestry; Medicine; Preveterinary; Zoology; Health technology; Nursing; Pharmacy; Predentistry
3. Business	7.9	Accounting; Advertising; Business administration; Public administration
4. Education	9.4	Education; Physical education; Religious education
5. Engineering	5.1	Engineering
6. Physical sciences	11.8	Biochemistry; Chemistry; Geology; Mathematics; Physics; Natural science (other)
7. Social sciences	12.1	Anthropology; Economics; Geography; Political science; Psychology; Sociology; Social science (other)

[a] Unweighted percentages.
[b] See Tables 44 and 45.

more than one category. We chose not to analyze as a separate category, called "other," the remaining 18 percent of the choices, because such an analysis would have been redundant with the analyses of the other seven categories.[5]

Multiple Regression Analyses: Overall Results

Table 49 summarizes the results of the multiple regression analyses[6] for the first 12 career choice categories.[7] The rather small sizes of the multiple correlation coefficients shown next to each of the 12 criteria indicate that the student's final career choice could be predicted with only low to moderate accuracy using this statistical model and the particular set of student input variables that were collected at the time of matriculation. The accuracy of the prediction varied considerably from one career field to another, however, with clergyman ($R = .523$) and engineer ($R = .530$) being the easiest and biological scientist ($R = .201$) and social scientist ($R = .202$) being the most difficult to predict, over the four-year interval. Although it could be argued that the relative success of prediction is a statistical artifact of the percentage of students choosing the career,[8] the data are not entirely consistent with such an interpretation. Clergyman, for example, which was the easiest career choice to predict, was named by fewer of the students (1.2 percent) than all but one other career. The choices of businessman and schoolteacher, on the other hand, which could be predicted with only average accuracy, were named by far greater percentages of students (12.2 percent and 26.1 percent, respectively) than any of the other ten careers. Although the number of input predictors entering into the stepwise regression analysis varied from as few as five (clergyman) to as many as 17 (physician or dentist), no systematic relationship was observed between the number of variables in the regression equation and the accuracy of the prediction.

In every case, the student's chosen career at the time he first entered college proved to be an important and accurate predictor of his career choice four years later; in fact, this variable carried the largest weight in seven of the equations and the second largest weight in the other five. Thus, there was some consistency in the student's career choices over a relatively long period of time, although the degree of consistency differed from field to field and was always far from perfect.

The student's intended major field of study at the time of matriculation also contributed to the prediction of his career choice four years later. In almost all cases, the major fields that carried significant weights were either identical with or closely related to the career field being predicted. Indeed, for some careers (biological scientist, engineer, and physical scientist), the relevant major field of study carried more weight in prediction than even the initial career choice, perhaps because additional students whose final majors were in the corresponding fields (i.e., biology, engineering, physics or chemistry) were included in these three career choice groups if their final career choice was college professor.

Results for final major field of study are given in Table 50. The multiple correlation coefficients indicate that, except in the case of the social sciences, moderately accurate predictions of the students' final fields of study were possible from the types of data collected at the time of matriculation. The

TABLE 49

The Prediction of Career Choice (1965) from Freshman Input Data (1961)

($N = 3,821$ students)

Career Choice (Criterion)	R	Total Number of Predictors ($p < .05$) Entering Stepwise Regression	Predictors with Largest ($p < .01$) Weights in Final Regression Equation	Sign	F-ratio* in Final Equation
Biological scientist	.201	10	Biological science (major field)	+	38.0
			Biological scientist (career choice)	+	25.5
			Dentist (career choice)	+	19.6
			Physical science (major field)	+	10.4
Businessman	.372	12	Male (sex)	+	102.0
			Business man (career choice)	+	85.7
			Business (major field)	+	36.3
			Accountant (career choice)	+	32.8
			Parents' income	+	37.9
			Undecided (career choice)	+	13.6
			High school grades	−	7.8
Clergyman	.523	5	Clergyman (career choice)	+	977.6
			Philosophy (major field)	+	57.4
			Clergyman (father's occupation)	+	24.1
			Male (sex)	+	11.9
College professor	.250	15	Highest degree sought	+	38.1
			College professor (career choice)	+	32.1
			High school grades	+	30.5
			Mathematician (career choice)	+	19.1
			Physician (career choice)	−	14.5
			Schoolteacher (career choice)	+	9.6
			Education (major field)	−	9.3
			Size of high school	+	8.8
Engineer	.530	12	Engineering (major field)	+	164.1
			Engineer (career choice)	+	148.1
			Male (sex)	+	11.0
			Parents' income	−	8.0
Health professional (non-M.D.)	.477	14	Nurse (career choice)	+	131.3
			Health technology (major field)	+	103.8
			Therapist (career choice)	+	63.4
			Pharmacist (career choice)	+	37.6
			Male (sex)	−	25.0
			Social worker (career choice)	+	22.4
			Social science (major field)	+	17.5
			Negro	+	16.2
			Philosophy (major field)	+	14.6
			Undecided (major field)	+	11.8
			Highest degree sought	−	10.2
			Laboratory technician (career choice)	+	10.0
			Biological science (major field)	+	9.5

TABLE 49—Continued

Career Choice (Criterion)	R	Total Number of Predictors ($p < .05$) Entering Stepwise Regression	Predictors with Largest ($p < .01$) Weights in Final Regression Equation	Sign	F-ratio* in Final Equation
			Lawyer (career choice)	+	282.0
			Male (sex)	+	81.8
			Jewish (parents' religion)	+	28.2
			Parents' income	+	26.0
Lawyer	.373	16	High school grades	+	24.3
			Engineer (career choice)	−	13.4
			Diplomat; Politician (career choice)	+	11.6
			Lawyer (father's occupation)	+	7.8
			Undecided (career choice)	+	6.9
			Actor; Entertainer (career choice)	+	135.1
			Artist (career choice)	+	79.1
			Fine arts (major field)	+	37.3
Performing artist	.298	8	Undecided (career choice)	+	12.0
			Business executive (father's occupation)	−	9.0
			Architect (career choice)	+	7.8
			Physical science (major field)	+	95.7
			Mathematician (career choice)	+	64.7
			Mathematics (major field)	+	45.8
			Physicist (career choice)	+	31.9
Physical scientist	.383	15	Chemist (career choice)	+	27.7
			High school grades	+	23.9
			Male (sex)	+	19.3
			College professor (career choice)	+	18.9
			Mother's educational level	+	9.9
			Physician (career choice)	−	9.8
			Physician (career choice)	+	374.9
			Male (sex)	+	37.8
			Dentist (career choice)	+	34.4
			High school grades	+	32.8
			Award in state music contest	+	16.1
			Jewish (parents' religion)	+	16.0
			Highest degree sought	+	13.5
Physician or dentist	.485	17	Laboratory technician (career choice)	+	13.2
			Edited high school paper	−	12.3
			Caucasian	−	11.6
			Mathematics (major field)	−	10.2
			Biological science (major field)	+	9.3
			Undecided (career choice)	+	7.8
			Negro	−	6.8
			Physician (father's occupation)	+	6.7
			Lawyer (career choice)	−	6.7
			Psychologist (career choice)	+	44.8
Social scientist	.202	10	Highest degree sought	+	32.8
			Social sciences (major field)	+	14.9
			History (major field)	+	7.1

TABLE 49—Continued

Career Choice (Criterion)	R	Total Number of Predictors ($p < .05$) Entering Stepwise Regression	Predictors with Largest ($p < .01$) Weights in Final Regression Equation	Sign	F-ratio* in Final Equation
			Teacher (career choice)	+	248.9
			Male (sex)	−	128.1
			Nurse (career choice)	−	16.4
Teacher			Parents' income	−	13.2
(elementary			Education (major field)	+	12.1
or secondary			Teacher (father's occupation)	+	9.0
school)	.444	13	Elected to student office	+	8.5
			Undecided (career choice)	+	8.1
			Philosophy (major field)	−	7.8
			High school grades	−	6.8

* Based on the proportion of variance in the criterion which is independently attributable to the variable ($F_{01} = 6.7$).

prediction of final major fields tended to be slightly more accurate and to involve a considerably larger number of variables (from a low of 12 to a high of 25) than the prediction of career choices. These larger numbers may have resulted from our having scored as separate dummy variables certain predictors—high school grades, father's educational level, highest degree sought—which were treated as single continuous variables in the prediction of career choice; another possible explanation is that the major field categories were broader and more complex than were the career choice categories.

The patterns of predictors which had substantial weights in the regression analyses involving major fields were very similar to those for career choice. Initial choice in the same major field carried the largest weight in each of the seven categories of final major field, and the appropriate initial career choice tended to carry a relatively large weight. As would be expected, the relative contributions of initial major and initial career choice were reversed in the two analyses, with initial career choice being the best predictor of final career choice, and initial major field the best predictor of final major field.

Since the student's initial career and study plans appear to have been adequately controlled in the analyses summarized in Tables 49 and 50, the other student input variables that entered into the regression equations can be regarded as indicative of personal traits associated with stability or change in the student's choices. Predictors that carried positive weights for a particular choice were associated both with maintaining that choice during the four years and with changing to that choice from some other initial choice. Similarly, predictors that carried negative weights tended to be characteristic of students who changed from that choice to a different one and of students who neither initially chose nor changed to that choice during the undergraduate years.

The patterns that emerged from these additional predictors of career and major field are discussed below.

TABLE 50
The Prediction of Final Major Field (1965) from Freshman Input Data (1961)
($N = 3,821$ students)

Final Major Field (Criterion)	R	Total Number of Predictors ($p < .05$) Entering Stepwise Regression	Predictors with Largest ($p < .01$) Weights in Final Regression Equation	Sign	F-ratio* in Final Equation
			English (major field)	+	178.1
			History (major field)	+	137.3
			Fine arts (major field)	+	121.2
			Languages (major field)	+	55.2
			Undecided (major field)	+	38.0
			Diplomat; Politician (career choice)	+	32.6
			Lawyer (career choice)	+	24.5
Arts and			Graduate degree (father's education)	+	15.5
humanities	.452	25	Seeking master's degree	+	13.8
			Nurse (career choice)	−	13.5
			Elected to student office	+	12.6
			Engineer (career choice)	−	10.2
			Won literary award	+	10.1
			Exhibited art outside of school	+	9.1
			Clergyman (career choice)	+	8.7
			Farmer (father's occupation)	−	8.4
			Male (sex)	−	7.8
			Biological sciences (major field)	+	112.4
			Laboratory technician (career choice)	+	101.2
			Physician (career choice)	+	68.3
			Physical sciences (major field)	+	34.4
			Veterinarian (career choice)	+	29.8
			Agriculture (major field)	+	24.7
Biological science	.425	18	Farmer (career choice)	+	16.9
			Award in regional science contest	+	13.6
			C average in high school	−	12.1
			Dentist (career choice)	+	10.0
			Undecided (major field)	+	9.6
			Biological scientist (career choice)	+	7.1
			C+ average in high school	−	6.7
			Business (major field)	+	446.5
			Male (sex)	+	58.0
			Clerk; Secretary (career choice)	+	45.6
Business	.444	12	Agriculture (major field)	+	14.8
			Accountant (career choice)	+	14.3
			Undecided (major field)	+	9.9
			A− average in high school	−	9.3
			A average in high school	−	8.7
			Education (major field)	+	401.4
			Male (sex)	−	45.0
			Teacher (career choice)	+	24.3
Education	.463	14	A average in high school	−	12.0
			Business (major field)	+	10.0
			President of high school class	+	9.7
			Catholic (parents' religion)	−	8.2

TABLE 50—Continued

Final Major Field (Criterion)	R	Total Number of Predictors ($p < .05$) Entering Stepwise Regression	Predictors with Largest ($p < .01$) Weights in Final Regression Equation	Sign	F-ratio* in Final Equation
			Engineering (major field)	+	516.2
			Engineer (career choice)	+	139.7
			Male (sex)	+	15.4
Engineering	.651	13	C average in high school	−	14.6
			Physical scientist (career choice)	+	8.9
			C+ average in high school	−	8.0
			High school class size > 500	+	7.7
			Mathematics (major field)	+	368.9
			Physical science (major field)	+	213.5
			A+ average in high school	+	32.3
			Biological science (major field)	+	31.6
Physical science;			Undecided (major field)	+	29.6
Mathematics	.495	18	Physicist (career choice)	+	23.0
			Chemist (career choice)	+	21.4
			Male (sex)	+	19.5
			Planning Ph.D. degree	+	11.3
			Pharmacist (career choice)	+	8.7
			A average in high school	+	7.1
			Social sciences (major field)	+	49.4
			Businessman (career choice)	+	18.8
			Negro	+	13.4
Social science	.254	15	Psychologist (career choice)	+	12.5
			President of high school class	−	12.3
			Parents' income	+	7.8
			Social worker (career choice)	+	7.4
			Health technology (major field)	−	6.7

* Based on the proportion of variance in the criterion which is independently attributable to the variable ($F_{01} = 6.7$).

Sex

The sex of the student entered into the prediction of more careers and more majors, and with generally larger weights, than did any other personal characteristic except initial choice of a career and of a major field. The most striking feature about the predictive role of sex was that being a man carried a positive weight in the prediction of "masculine" choices (i.e., careers and majors initially chosen by more men than women), and being a woman carried a positive weight in the prediction of "feminine" choices. Sex carried little or no weight in the prediction of those choices which were not markedly preferred initially by one of the sexes. Thus, of the entering college freshmen who initially planned one of the six masculine careers (businessman, clergyman, engineer, lawyer, physical scientist, or physician), the women were much more likely than were the men to switch to some other choice during the undergraduate years. In addition, women were less likely than were men to be recruited into one of these masculine fields from some other field. Men, on the other hand, were less likely during the undergraduate years to remain in or to be recruited into either one of the two feminine careers (the non-M.D. health professions and teaching).

Almost identical patterns of change by sex can be observed in the undergraduate major fields: Men were much more likely than were women to remain in or to be recruited into business, engineering, and physical sciences/mathematics majors, whereas women were much more likely to remain in or to be recruited into majors in the arts and humanities and in education.

The importance of the student's sex in mediating these career and major field changes is further illustrated by the relative probabilities of certain types of changes for men and women (see Appendix H). For example, a woman who started college planning a career in one of the six masculine choices mentioned above was less likely (($p = .23$) to end up pursuing such a career four years later than she was to switch to one of the two feminine careers ($p = .32$). By contrast, men who started college aspiring to masculine careers were much more likely ($p = .60$) to pursue a masculine career four years later than they were to switch to a feminine career ($p = .09$). Moreover, among those students who initially chose careers not dominated by one sex (e.g., biological scientist, college professor, performing artist, undecided), men were much more likely ($p = .41$) than were women ($p = .08$) to switch to a masculine career four years later, and women were much more likely ($p = .31$) than were men ($p = .08$) to switch to a feminine career.

These trends are reflected in the rise in the percentage of women among all students choosing feminine careers, from 71.3 percent in 1961 to 76.1 percent in 1965. The percentage of men among students choosing masculine occupations, however,[9] showed virtually no change (from 90.5 percent to 90.2 percent). This apparent paradox is the result of two phenomena: (1) the percentages of men among students who changed to masculine career choices from unclassifiable choices (86.8) was somewhat lower than the percentage of men among all students initially choosing masculine careers (90.5); and (2) the career choice of engineer suffered a substantial loss (41 percent) during the four years, and since this choice accounted for a much higher percentage of men (30.6) than of women (3.1) among those who initially aspired to masculine careers, the high net loss tended to reduce markedly the percentage of men among students choosing masculine careers four years later.

These differential changes are very similar to those observed in the earlier study by Davis (1965), who found that men tended to become increasingly concentrated in the more masculine occupations, and women in the more feminine occupations. Apparently, initial differences between the sexes in their preferences for various types of occupations become more marked throughout the undergraduate years. These trends may be attributable to social pressures, to the increased sharpening of sexual roles and of the identification that occurs with increased maturity, or to other factors;

further exploration of the possible influence of such factors would be an interesting and potentially important task for future research.

Academic Ability

The student's academic ability, as reflected in his average grade in high school, also carried a significant weight in predicting many of the career choices and final major fields of study, although the magnitude of this weight was usually smaller than that for sex. Students with superior academic records in high school were more likely than were average students to make stable choices of or to change their choices to college professor, lawyer, physical scientist, or physician. Some borderline findings ($.01 < p < .05$) (not shown in Table 50) suggest that high grades were positively related to the final career choice of engineer and negatively related to the final choice of businessman or of teacher.

The pattern of changes in major field as a function of the student's academic ability was almost identical with the pattern of changes in career choice. Students with better grades tended to remain in or to be recruited into the biological sciences, engineering, and the physical sciences and mathematics, whereas students with poorer grades tended to remain in or to be recruited into business and education.

These relationships are not entirely consistent with those reported earlier by Davis (1965). Both studies showed that the group of students choosing medicine, physical sciences, and law became more select academically over the four-year period and that the group choosing business became less select. Davis's reported increase in the academic ability level for the humanities and social sciences, however, was not observed in the present study. Furthermore, our data revealed that, over time, engineering tended to retain and to recruit the brighter students, whereas education tended to retain and to recruit the more mediocre ones. Davis found no changes over time in the relative ability levels of students in these two groups. More information is needed to explain these discrepancies fully, but it seems likely that some of the differences are attributable to Davis's excluding dropouts from his sample.

As Davis also noted, changes in the relative ability levels of students in different fields during the undergraduate years were partially obscured by the fact that the grades of college women tend to be higher than those of college men. For example, when the sexes are considered together, the average high school grades of all students who chose teaching at the entering freshmen level did not differ from those of all students who chose teaching four years later. The reason for this apparent lack of change is that relatively more women than men chose teaching in 1965 than in 1961. In other words, even though men and women who chose teaching four years after entering college were academically less able than men and women who chose teaching at the time of matriculation, these differences were masked by the increase in the proportion of women who made a final choice of teaching. Fortunately, this odd statistical phenomenon became visible in the linear multiple regression analysis, which successively controls the influences of the different variables. Thus, when the student's sex entered the stepwise regression equation for predicting the choice of teacher, the influence of grades was revealed. This phenomenon is similar to the one noted in Chapter 3 with respect to predicting attrition during the undergraduate years.

Socioeconomic Background

The level of education attained by the parents of the student had virtually no relationship to changes either in careers or in major fields during the undergraduate years. The father's educational level carried a small positive weight in predicting a final major field of study in arts and humanities, and the mother's educational level carried a small positive weight in predicting the final career choice of physical scientist.

The *income* of the student's parental family, on the other hand, had a substantial and consistent pattern of predictive relationships to final career choice. Students from wealthier families were more likely to stay in or to be recruited into careers as businessmen or lawyers than were students from less affluent family backgrounds, who were more likely to stay in or to be recruited into careers as engineers and schoolteachers. Parental income also carried a small positive weight in predicting a final major in physical science or mathematics.

Once again these patterns of change during the undergraduate years appear to perpetuate trends that were already observable at the time of matriculation. Thus, the income of the student's family showed significant positive correlations with freshman career choices of businessman ($r = .044$) lawyer ($r = .084$) and significant negative correlations with freshman career choices of engineer ($r = -.057$) and teacher ($r = -.106$). One notable exception to this trend was the career choice of physician. At the time of college entrance, choosing a career in medicine was positively correlated ($r = .090$) with the income of the student's parents. Parental income does not, however, appear to be related to changes toward or away from the career of physician, since it did not enter into the multiple regression equation.

The occupation of the student's father showed several small but highly systematic predictive relationships with the student's final career choice. If the father was a clergyman, a lawyer, a physician, or a teacher, there was a tendency for the student's final career choice to be the same. At least two explanations can be advanced to account for this tendency. The first, which might be called the "initial commitment" interpretation, argues that, of the freshmen who choose one of these occupations, the student whose father is employed in the occupation has a somewhat greater degree of commitment to the career than do other students. Such an explanation assumes, of course, that these motivational differences were too subtle to be detected by our other student input measures (major field of study, level of aspiration, high school grades, nonacademic achievements, socioeconomic level, race, religion, and so forth). The second explanation treats the father's occupation as a kind of environmental variable. A father who is himself a physician, for example, probably exerts more pressure on his son to remain in a premedical curriculum or to change to such a curriculum during the undergraduate years than does a father who is not a physician. The difference between these two interpretations is essentially a matter of timing, since even the "initial commitment" interpretation implicitly assumes the existence of environmental effects—family pressures—earlier in life. The initial commitment hypothesis, of course, also raises the possibility of genetic factors which may operate to increase the correlation between the father's and son's careers.

These alternative explanations of the role played by the father's occupation could be tested empirically by using more elaborate measures of the student's commitment to his initial choice. If the addition of such variables to the regression equations did not substantially change the contribution of the father's occupation to the student's final choice, then the "environmental effect" interpretation of this relationship would gain support. In the absence of such additional evidence, however, the relative plausibility of the two interpretations depends on one's judgment as to whether the controls on students' initial motivation used in the regression analyses were adequate.

Race and Religion

The student's race had only a few scattered relationships to his final major field of study and final career choice. The Negro student was somewhat more likely than were others to choose a career in the health professions or, as Davis (1965) also found, to have a final major field in the social sciences. Somewhat surprisingly, being *either* a Caucasian or a Negro carried a negative weight in predicting the career choice of physician. Since "Oriental," the only other dichotomous measure of race used in the analysis, did not enter into the regression equation at all, it must be concluded that the omitted category, "other," which included about 1.5 percent of the sample used in the regression analysis, would have entered in with a fairly sizable positive weight if it had been used in the analysis.[10] In these circumstances, the negative weights for Caucasian and Negro would either disappear or be reduced substantially. The "other" category presumably includes Puerto Ricans, Mexican Americans, American Indians, and mixed racial types, as well as students who chose not to report their race. Why the students in this small, heterogeneous category should be more inclined than other students to remain in or be recruited into careers as physicians during the undergraduate years is open to speculation.

The religion of the student's parents entered into only three of the 19 regression analyses, but in two of these instances, the associated regression weights were substantial: Students were more likely to remain in or to be recruited into careers as either lawyers or physicians if their parents were Jewish. Similar findings were reported earlier by Davis (1965). Once again, it is possible that we are observing either an "initial commitment" or an "environmental" effect: Students from Jewish homes, as compared with other students, are either (1) more committed to careers in medicine or law when they first enter college, or (2) subjected to greater parental pressure during the undergraduate years to pursue careers in one of these two professions. It is possible, of course, that both interpretations are valid, since they are not necessarily incompatible.

The religion of the parents entered into only one other regression analysis: Students whose parents were Catholic showed a slight tendency to change out of and to avoid switching into the field of education during the undergraduate years.

THE INFLUENCE OF WITHIN-COLLEGE ENVIRONMENTAL CHARACTERISTICS

The effects of the within-college environmental variables were examined, using the subsample of 1,590 students for whom scores on the National Merit Scholarship Qualifying Test (NMSQT) were available. Table 51 shows the part correlations between the five subtests of the NMSQT and the 21 residual criterion scores (14 career choices, 7 final major fields) for this subsample. Of the 21 residual criteria, 16 had small but statistically significant ($p < .05$) correlations with at least one of the NMSQT subtests, a finding which indicates that the effects of academic ability on final career choice and final major field were not entirely controlled in the regression analyses shown in Tables 49 and 50.

Correlations between the within-college environmental variables and each of the 21 criteria were computed after the effects of the five NMSQT subtests had been partialed out from the residual criterion scores, a procedure which presumably controlled more adequately for academic ability. Of the various within-college influences considered, only the type of financing produced any pattern of significant relationships with final career choice and final major field. Table 52 shows the statistically significant part correlations between four different sources of financial support (scored dichotomously) and the 21 residual criteria of career choice and final field of study. (By "residual criteria," it is understood that the input variables shown in Tables 49 and 50 and the NMSQT scores shown in Table 51 have been controlled.) Students who received half or more of their college finances from their parents were more likely than other students to end up choosing careers either in medicine or in other (non-M.D.) health professions and less likely to end up majoring in business or pursuing a career as a businessman. Simi-

TABLE 51
Career Choice and Major Field:
Correlations of Residual Criterion Scores[a] with Scores on the
National Merit Scholarship Qualifying Test
($N = 1,590$ students)

CRITERION	English	Mathematics	NMSQT SCORE Social Science Reading	Natural Science Reading	Word Usage
Career Choice:					
Biological scientist					
Businessman	.06*				−.06*
Clergyman	−.06*				
College professor					.05*
Engineer					
Health professional			.05*		
Lawyer			.06*		
Performing artist			−.07**		
Physical scientist		.07**			
Physician or Dentist				.05*	
Social scientist					
Teacher		−.05*			
Scientist or engineer (all fields)		.06*			
Professional (all fields)					
Final Major Field:					
Arts and humanities		−.05*			.09**
Biological sciences			−.09**	.06*	
Business	.07**				
Education					
Engineering				.05	
Physical sciences		.14***			
Social sciences					

[a] Residual scores on each criterion (from analyses shown in Tables 49 and 50) were correlated with each NMSQT scale. Coefficients are actually "part" correlations.
* $p < .05$. ** $p < .01$. *** $p < .001$

larly, students who received scholarships were more likely than were others to end up pursuing careers as physicians and less likely to end up majoring in business. Students who financed part of their education by means of a college loan were less likely than other students to report their final career choice as being either engineer or physical scientist and more likely to choose the career of social scientist.

Although these relationships are small and difficult to interpret, they nevertheless indicate that type of financial support for undergraduate education may affect the eventual distribution of college-trained persons in various career fields. This conclusion is supported by those findings from Chapter 3 which suggested that the student's persistence in college and his chances of eventually completing his undergraduate training may depend in part on the type and amount of financing available to him.

Marital status after entrance to college and residence during the freshman year showed virtually no relationships to the 21 residual criteria of career

TABLE 52

Effects of Different Types of Financial Support on Career Choice
and Final Major Field[a]

($N = 1,590$ students)

CRITERION	SOURCE OF FINANCIAL SUPPORT			
	Parents (50% or more)	Scholarship (any amount)	Work During School Year	Loan from the College
Career Choice:				
Biological scientist				
Businessman	$-.06*$			
Clergyman				
College professor				
Engineer				$-.08*$
Health professional	$.07**$		$-.06*$	
Lawyer				
Performing artist				
Physical scientist				
Physician or dentist	$.06*$	$.07**$		
Social scientist				$.05*$
Teacher				
Scientist and Engineer (all fields)				$-.07**$
Professional (all fields)	$.09***$	$.06*$		
Final Major Field:				
Arts and Humanities				
Biological sciences				
Business	$-.07**$	$-.05*$		
Education				
Engineering				
Physical Sciences				$-.10***$
Social Sciences				

[a] Only significant ($p < .05$) coefficients are shown. Part correlations are between the source (scored dichotomously) and the residual criterion scores (i.e., after control of input variables shown in Tables 49 and 50 and NMSQT scores as shown in Table 51).
* $p < .05$.   ** $p < .01$.   *** $p < .001$.

choice and final field of study. Getting married was negatively correlated ($-.08$; $p < .01$) with pursuing a career in the health professions (non-M.D.). The student who lived at home, in a fraternity house, or in a dormitory during the freshman year appeared less likely than other students to pursue a career as a schoolteacher ($-.05$; $p < .05$). Because of the large number of correlations that were computed (21 criteria $\times$ 4 types of living arrangements = 84 coefficients), these four statistically significant correlations may well be chance occurrences.

THE INFLUENCE OF BETWEEN-COLLEGE ENVIRONMENTAL CHARACTERISTICS

Having discovered that academic ability was not entirely controlled in our initial regression analyses, we were faced with the problem of deciding whether to apply additional statistical controls using the NMSQT scores of the special sample. Would the disadvantages of the costs of data analysis and of the use of a smaller and more biased sample be balanced by gains in the accuracy of the results? Preliminary analysis (see Appendix E) revealed that these additional controls for academic ability had virtually no effect on observed relationships between college characteristics and the residual criterion scores; therefore, we decided against instituting them.

Table 53 shows the distributions of actual and residual criterion scores for the 246 institutions on each of the 21 criteria of career choice and final major field. The first three numbers in each row show the range of scores (rounded to the nearest whole percent) among the 246 institutions. For example, the percentage of students at a given institution who, four years after matriculation, intended to become biological scientists varied from a low of zero percent to a high of 5 percent. At the typical (median) institution, 1 percent of the students reported their career choice as biological scientist four years after matriculation. In general, each median and its corresponding mean percentage were very similar to the percentages shown previously in Table 48. The reader should bear in mind that the variation among the 246 institutions may have been reduced somewhat by response bias, although the degree of attenuation was probably much smaller than it was for the criteria of educational attainment and educational aspiration (see Chapter 3), since these criteria were more highly related to response to the followup questionnaire than was the choice of any single career or major field.

It is interesting that for each career, except that of schoolteacher, there was at least one institution in which virtually no students (less than half of 1 percent of the total sample) aspired to the career. The same generalization holds true for each final major field of study, except arts and humanities.

The institutional variations in actual percentages indicate the degree of diversity in the sources of supply for various manpower fields. Careers with relatively small percentage variations (e.g., biological scientist) receive their supplies from a great many diverse sources, whereas careers with wide percentage variations and skewed distributions (e.g., engineer) receive their supplies from a much more limited number of (presumably) homogeneous sources.

Residual criterion scores are shown in the second five columns of data in Table 53. It will be recalled that the residual score for a given choice of career or major field was computed by subtracting, from the actual percentage of students with that choice, the expected percentage as estimated from students' input characteristics. A positive residual indicates that the percentage of students making that particular choice four years after matriculation was greater than expected; a negative residual indicates that the actual percentage was smaller than expected. The range of these scores (from lowest to highest) for any career indicates the degree to which the institution attended made a difference in the percentage of students who aspired to that career four years after entering college. Although in some cases the range is only a few percentage points, the practical importance of

TABLE 53
Distribution of Actual and Residual Scores on 21 Criteria of Career Choice and Final Major Field
(N = 246 institutions)

CRITERION	ACTUAL SCORES					RESIDUAL SCORES[a]					REDUCTION IN VARIANCE IN ACTUAL SCORES[b]
	Lowest Institution %	Median Institution %	Highest Institution %	MEAN	SD	Lowest Institution %	Median Institution %	Highest Institution %	MEAN	SD	
Career Choice:											
Biological scientist	00	01	05	1.1	1.2	−02	00	04	0.0	1.1	−.160
Businessman	00	11	34	11.1	6.0	−10	−01	08	−1.4	3.4	−.679
Clergyman	00	01	09	1.2	1.6	−05	00	04	−0.1	1.0	−.609
College professor	00	03	20	4.1	3.3	−05	−01	09	−0.5	2.2	−.556
Engineer	00	02	45	3.8	6.7	−04	00	16	0.0	2.6	−.849
Health professional	00	05	33	6.1	4.8	−08	00	13	0.0	2.5	−.729
Lawyer	00	03	27	3.8	4.3	−06	00	11	0.1	2.2	−.738
Performing artist	00	01	09	1.3	1.3	−03	00	06	−0.2	1.1	−.284
Physical scientist	00	03	37	3.5	3.3	−05	−01	16	−0.4	2.1	−.595
Physician or dentist	00	03	22	3.9	3.5	−06	00	07	−0.3	2.0	−.673
Social scientist	00	02	10	2.0	1.8	−03	−01	07	−0.2	1.5	−.306
Teacher	03	25	69	26.8	12.9	−15	−01	16	−0.4	5.5	−.818
Scientist or Engineer (all fields)	00	09	67	6.9	6.8	−09	−01	32	−0.4	3.2	−.779
Professional (all fields)	01	13	35	14.0	7.4	−13	00	19	−0.2	4.1	−.693
Final Major Field:											
Arts and humanities	02	25	64	27.3	12.6	−16	−01	18	−0.2	7.3	−.664
Biological sciences	00	07	25	7.4	4.2	−08	−01	11	−0.6	3.2	−.409
Business	00	08	44	8.4	6.7	−08	00	13	−0.1	4.0	−.644
Education	00	09	43	10.4	9.2	−11	00	17	0.1	4.9	−.716
Engineering	00	01	53	4.3	8.5	−08	00	20	−0.1	3.2	−.858
Physical sciences	00	10	54	10.5	5.4	−09	00	12	−0.3	3.6	−.556
Social sciences	00	10	29	11.3	6.4	−14	−02	15	−1.0	5.1	−.365

[a] Difference between the actual percentage at the institution in 1965 and the expected percentage based on the student input characteristics (i.e., Actual percent minus Expected percent).
[b] Ratio between (1 minus SD²) of residual scores and SD² of actual scores.

these variations in residual scores must be evaluated in relation to the median and mean actual scores shown to the left in the table. To illustrate, while the residual institutional variation of from -2 percent to $+4$ percent for the career of biological scientist may at first seem trivial, it takes on considerable practical significance when one notes that only 1 percent of the students at the typical (median) institution chose this type of career four years after entering college. Of course, since these percentages were based on relatively small numbers of students (approximately 140 at each institution) it is possible that the smaller variations reflect chance differences rather than true differential effects of the institutions.[11]

The largest institutional deviations from expectation occurred in the case of the career choice of teacher, where the actual number of students who planned careers as teachers four years after entering was 15 percent lower than expected at one institution and 16 percent higher than expected at another. In general, the range in residual scores appears to be positively correlated with the median actual score. That is, the more popular a career or major field (with respect to the proportion of students who choose it), the wider the variation in institutional effects on that choice. Engineering—both as a major field and as a career choice—was an exception to this generalization: The median actual scores were quite small, and the range of residual scores relatively large. The explanation here is that the distribution of actual scores was highly skewed; because a few institutions had very high actual scores, large positive deviations from expectation were possible.

The last column in Table 53 indicates the proportion of variance in the actual criterion scores that was eliminated by taking into account the expected scores derived from the student input variables. For 16 of the 21 outcome measures, more than half the institutional variation in actual output is attributable to differential student inputs. Those career choices which seem to be most highly dependent on student input include engineer (-85 percent), health professional (-73 percent), lawyer (-74 percent), and teacher (-78 percent); the major fields include education (-72 percent) and engineering (-86 percent). Those outcomes which appear to be least dependent on student input characteristics include the careers of biological scientist (-16 percent), performing artist (-28 percent), and social scientist (-31 percent), and the major fields of biological science (-41 percent) and social science (-37 percent). Since these last five outcomes are among the lowest in terms of variation in actual scores, it seems likely the relatively small reduction in their actual variances is attributable in part to their relatively low reliability (see footnote 11). In fact, if we were to take into account the lack of perfect reliability in our actual and expected scores for each of the 21 outcomes, the variance attributable to differential student inputs would be substantially higher. In other words, the last column of data in Table 53 can be regarded as a conservative estimate of the importance of student inputs in determining differential institutional outputs, particularly for those outcomes that show relatively small variations among institutions.

TABLE 54
Career Choice and Final Field of Study:
Multiple Correlations of Residual Criterion Scores with College Characteristics
($N=246$ institutions)

RESIDUAL CRITERION SCORE[a]	STEPWISE MULTIPLE REGRESSIONS USING ALL 72 COLLEGE CHARACTERISTICS		
	Number of Variables Entering[b]	R	R^2
Career Choice:			
Biological scientist	7	.425	.181
Businessman	6	.468	.219
Clergyman	4	.361	.130
College professor	6	.530	.281
Engineer	9	.835	.697
Health professional	7	.427	.182
Lawyer	11	.682	.465
Performing artist	6	.391	.153
Physical scientist	9	.520	.270
Physician or dentist	6	.518	.268
Social scientist	8	.454	.206
Teacher	8	.604	.365
Scientist and Engineer (all[c] fields)			
Professional (all fields)	6	.497	.247
Final Major Field:			
Arts and humanities	10	.769	.591
Biological sciences	7	.470	.221
Business	6	.589	.347
Education	6	.543	.295
Engineering	8	.860	.740
Physical sciences	9	.561	.315
Social sciences	9	.659	.434

[a] Difference between the actual percentage at the institution and the expected percentage based on the student input characteristics (i.e., Actual percent minus Expected percent).
[b] College variables were entered into the multiple regression equation until no additional variable was capable of producing a reduction in the residual sum of squares exceeding $p = .05$.
[c] Not shown because of errors in the data.

The relation between the 21 mean residual criterion scores and the environmental characteristics of the 246 colleges were examined by means of stepwise multiple regression analyses. The dependent variable for these analyses was the residual criterion score; the independent variables were the 72 college characteristics used in Chapter 3. The results of these analyses are summarized in Table 54. The multiple correlation coefficients reveal that the success with which differential college effects can be accounted for by our 72 environmental measures varies considerably from one criterion to another. For example, while it was possible to account for a substantial amount (69.7 percent) of the deviation from expectation in the percentages of students who wanted to become engineers four years after entering college, relatively little of this deviation (13 percent) could be accounted for in the case of the career of clergyman. Since this pattern is very similar to the pattern of variances in residual scores (Table 53), it seems safe to conclude that the multiple

TABLE 55

Mean Residual Variance[a] Accounted For by Different Types of
Environmental Measures

($N = 246$ institutions)

CRITERION	PERCENTAGE OF RESIDUAL VARIANCE ACCOUNTED FOR BY:						
	8 EAT Measures	28 ICA Stimulus Factors[b]	12 ICA Image Factors[b]	All 36 ICA Factors	All 44[c] "Trait" Measures	21 "Type" Characteristics	All 72 College Variables
Final Major Field:							
Arts and humanities	51.0	40.9	38.4	46.2	54.9	32.1	59.1
Biological sciences	7.6	14.5	5.9	14.5	14.5	5.4	22.1
Business	23.9	22.1	18.2	23.5	33.5	16.7	34.7
Education	24.2	16.7	17.2	18.6	26.3	22.8	29.5
Engineering	48.0	21.8	15.4	22.3	54.0	69.7	74.0
Physical sciences	17.1	16.0	11.7	19.1	24.5	19.4	31.5
Social sciences	34.6	26.0	21.8	24.6	37.6	31.1	43.4
Career Choice:							
Scientist or Engineer (all fields)	35.7	17.7	15.0	20.8	35.9	—	—
Professional (all fields)	11.3	12.5	7.1	14.7	26.1	16.1	24.7
Biological scientist	5.7	9.1	4.3	9.1	9.1	8.7	18.1
Businessman	11.1	9.7	3.7	9.7	18.6	14.7	21.9
Clergyman	0.0	11.2	6.5	13.1	13.1	1.5	13.0
College professor	6.1	14.6	8.2	24.3	24.3	15.8	28.1
Engineer	49.2	18.2	13.5	26.9	52.7	65.6	69.7
Health professional	0.0	10.1	2.3	10.1	10.1	8.5	18.2
Lawyer	14.1	20.3	15.4	35.3	44.2	34.8	46.5
Performing artist	0.0	8.2	4.9	8.5	10.2	7.7	15.3
Physical scientist	8.5	9.2	0.0	9.2	13.9	16.6	27.0
Physician or dentist	16.0	19.5	14.2	22.8	24.0	10.9	26.8
Social scientist	2.3	12.9	5.6	12.9	12.9	10.9	20.6
Teacher	12.6	15.1	15.4	21.4	24.2	25.7	36.5

[a] $R^2 \times 100$ (as determined by separate stepwise multiple regression analyses, each of which was terminated at $p \geqq .05$).

[b] Four factors from the administrative environment were included among both the stimulus and the image factors. Also, an unlabeled factor (see Chapter 1, p. 11) was included in these analyses, bringing the total number of ICA factors to 36.

[c] Includes 8 EAT measures, 36 ICA factors, 21 type characteristics, five student input factors (Astin, 1965d), percentage of men in the student body, and per student expenditures for educational and general purposes.

R's shown in Table 54 are in part a function of the differential reliabilities of the residual outcome scores. That is, high correlations between environmental variables and differential college effects (i.e., residual scores) would not be found if the differential college effects had been measured unreliably. Note that the residual scores combine the errors in both actual and expected scores (see footnote 11).

The results of the separate environmental effects analyses using different subsets of college characteristics are shown in Tables 55 and 56. As was the case with the educational outcomes discussed in Chapter 3, the differential effects of colleges on the student's final major field and career plans are more dependent on the sophisticated trait measures than on the traditional administrative typologies. One notable exception to this generalization is the

TABLE 56
Career Choice and Final Major Field:
Amount of Mean Residual Variance Uniquely Attributable to
Different Types of Environmental Variables

| CRITERION | PERCENTAGES OF VARIANCE UNIQUELY ATTRIBUTABLE TO: | | | | | |
	"Trait" Variables *vs.*	"Type" Variables	EAT Measures *vs.*	ICA Factors	ICA Stimulus Factors *vs.*	ICA Image Factors
Final Major Field:						
Arts and humanities	27.0	4.2	8.7	3.9	7.8	5.3
Biological sciences	16.7	7.6	0.0	6.9	8.6	0.0
Business	18.0	1.2	10.0	9.6	5.3	1.4
Education	6.7	3.2	7.7	2.1	1.4	1.9
Engineering	4.3	20.0	31.7	6.0	6.9	0.5
Physical sciences	12.1	7.0	5.4	7.4	7.4	3.1
Social sciences	12.3	5.8	13.0	3.0	4.2	0.0
Career Choice:						
Scientist or Engineer (all fields)	—	—	15.1	0.2	5.8	3.1
Professional (all fields)	10.0	0.0	11.4	14.8	7.6	2.2
Biological scientist	9.4	9.0	0.0	3.4	4.8	0.0
Businessman	7.2	3.3	8.9	7.5	6.0	0.0
Clergyman	11.6	0.0	0.0	13.1	6.6	1.9
College professor	12.3	3.8	0.0	18.2	16.1	9.7
Engineer	4.1	17.0	25.8	3.5	13.1	8.7
Health professional	9.7	8.1	0.0	10.1	7.8	0.0
Lawyer	11.7	1.3	8.9	30.1	19.9	15.0
Performing artist	7.6	5.1	1.7	10.2	3.6	0.3
Physical scientist	10.4	13.1	4.7	5.4	9.2	0.0
Physician or Dentist	15.9	2.2	1.2	8.0	8.6	3.3
Social scientist	9.7	7.7	0.0	10.6	7.3	0.0
Teacher	10.8	12.3	2.8	11.6	6.0	6.3

choice of engineering—both as a major and as a career—which appears to be influenced much more by an institution's type characteristics than by its trait characteristics. The career choices of physical scientist and teacher also seem to be slightly more dependent on type characteristics.

Comparing ICA stimulus factors with ICA image factors, we arrive at results consistent with those in Chapter 3. A considerably higher proportion of the differential institutional effects on the student's career choice and major was uniquely attributable to the stimulus factors. Nevertheless, it is important to note that the image factors did account for substantial percentages of variance in certain outcome measures (e.g., lawyer).

The comparison of EAT measures with ICA factors (Table 56) yielded results antithetical to those discussed in Chapter 3. Whereas the ICA factors appeared to be much more important than the EAT measures in accounting for differential college effects on educational attainment and aspiration, the EAT measures had a greater influence on certain of the vocational outcomes —in particular, the student's final field of study. This finding makes good sense, since the six EAT personal orientations are assessed on the basis of the proportions of baccalaureate degrees awarded in different fields. Thus, it would seem that the student's final choice of an undergraduate field of study is affected more by the relative concentrations of his fellow students in various fields of study than by any other known characteristics of his institution.

The ICA factors accounted for a greater share of the differential college effects on the student's *career* choice (except in the case of engineer and businessman) than did the EAT measures. It is difficult to say why the EAT measures should not also be important determinants of the student's career choice. One possible explanation is that the larger effects of the EAT measures are to some extent artifacts of the curricular offerings of the institution and that these observed "effects" on the student's final choice of a major are not accompanied by comparable changes in his choice of a career.

Institutional Effects on Specific Careers

Table 57 summarizes the results of the analyses of college effects on career choice. For each of the 13 criteria of career choice, those college characteristics whose F-ratios in the final regression equation exceeded $p = .01$ are shown; they are listed in decreasing order with respect to their contribution to the reduction of the residual sum of squares in the regression equation. These F-ratios reflect the relative importance of each college characteristic in the final regression equation.

By far the largest F-ratio and largest zero-order correlation (last column of Table 57) were associated with the effects of technological institutions on the career of *engineer*. Apparently, students were much more likely to end up studying engineering (see also Table 58) and planning careers as engineers if they initially attended a technological institution. The considerable magnitude of this effect is underscored by the fact the seven institutions which had the highest mean residual scores for the career of engineer were all technological institutions. Their scores ranged from $+10.5$ percent to $+16$ percent; the score of the eighth-ranked institution ($+6.7$ percent) represents an abrupt drop. Since more than half of those students who initially chose engineering switched to some other career choice during the undergraduate years (see Table 43), and since relatively few students were recruited into engineering during this same period, it appears that this effect of the technological institution operates more as a greater holding power on students who initially choose engineering than as a program of recruitment of new students into the field. In other words, the dropout rate from engineering seems to be much lower in technological institutions than in other types of institutions. Inasmuch as the engineering student who attends a university or a liberal arts college has many alternative fields of study available to him, it could be argued that the technological institution's greater holding power (see Table 58) is an artifact of its more homogeneous curriculum, rather than a reflection of its genuine influence on the student's motivation and career plans. Even if this particular interpretation is valid, however, it should be pointed out that the curricular effect on major field has generalized to the student's choice of a career.

TABLE 57
Effects of Various College Characteristics on Career Choice

CRITERION: COLLEGE CHARACTERISTICS	SIGN	F-RATIO* IN FINAL REGRESSION EQUATION	r† WITH MEAN RESIDUAL SCORE
Biological Scientist:			
Organized dating (ICA)	−	15.6	−.18
Located in small town	+	13.9	.15
Competitiveness *vs.* Cooperativeness (ICA)	−	9.7	−.23
Women's college	+	9.4	n.s.
Rate of Cheating (ICA)	+	7.5	n.s.
Southeastern location	+	7.4	n.s.
Businessman:			
Organized Dating (ICA)	+	16.2	.27
Conventional orientation (EAT)	+	8.9	.30
Technical institution	−	7.1	−.26
Severity of Administration Policy against Drinking (ICA)	+	6.9	n.s.
Clergyman:			
Leisure Time (ICA)	−	12.6	−.18
Drinking *vs.* Religiousness (ICA)	−	9.3	−.23
Friendliness of Dorm Counselor or Housemother (ICA)	−	8.8	−.14
College Professor:			
Expenditure per student	+	25.2	.22
Liberal arts college	+	21.5	.27
Organized Dating (ICA)	−	19.1	−.19
Permissiveness (ICA)	+	10.6	.14
Familiarity with Instructor (ICA)	+	4.0	.28
Engineer:			
Technical institution	+	192.4	.78
Enterprising orientation (EAT)	−	21.1	−.37
Men's college	−	19.7	n.s.
Social orientation (EAT)	−	16.5	−.31
Organized Dating (ICA)	+	9.5	n.s.
Health professional:			
Predominantly Negro institution	−	12.5	−.21
Leisure Time (ICA)	−	10.1	−.20
Realistic orientation (EAT)	+	7.6	n.s.
Severity of Administrative Policy against Heterosexual Activity (ICA)	+	7.4	.15
Lawyer:			
Men's college	+	61.5	.41
Enterprising orientation (EAT)	+	31.7	.38
Liberal arts college	−	26.2	n.s.
Technical institution	−	17.5	−.21
Emphasis on Social Life (ICA)	+	14.7	.22
Academic Competitiveness (ICA)	+	14.0	.16
Severity of Administrative Policy against Drinking (ICA)	+	11.0	n.s.
Predominantly Negro institution	+	9.2	.14
Conventional orientation (EAT)	−	8.9	.15
Performing Artist:			
Private—nonsectarian institution	+	10.4	.24
Student Employment (ICA)	+	8.8	.16
Artistic orientation (EAT)	+	6.8	.13
Physical Scientist:			
Technical institution	+	32.9	.24

TABLE 57—Continued

Criterion: College Characteristics	Sign	F-ratio* in Final Regression Equation	r† with Mean Residual Score
Masculinity	−	28.1	−.23
Involvement in the Classroom (ICA)	−	16.1	n.s.
Informal Dating (ICA)	+	7.3	.16
Liberal arts college	+	7.2	n.s.
Permissiveness (ICA)	+	7.2	n.s.
Cohesiveness (ICA)	+	6.8	n.s.
Physician or Dentist:			
Technical institutions	−	22.2	−.26
Informal Dating (ICA)	−	17.6	n.s.
Severity of Administrative Policy against Aggression (ICA)	+	9.7	.31
Drinking vs. Religiousness (ICA)	−	9.3	−.37
Social Scientist:			
Predominantly Negro institution	+	11.4	.15
Informal Dating (ICA)	+	9.4	.15
Career Indecision (ICA)	+	8.7	.18
Emphasis on Social Life (ICA)	−	7.9	n.s.
Technical institution	−	7.1	n.s.
Private—nonsectarian institution	+	6.8	.20
Teacher:			
Catholic institution	+	28.5	.15
Teachers college	+	24.8	.36
Permissiveness (ICA)	−	20.8	−.29
Women's college	−	13.3	n.s.
Intellectualism	−	8.5	−.37
Artistic orientation (EAT)	+	7.5	n.s.
Severity of Administrative Policy against Heterosexual Activity (ICA)	−	7.3	n.s.
Professional (all categories):			
Men's college	+	43.0	.20
Technical institution	−	22.2	−.26
Drinking vs. Religiousness (ICA)	−	17.2	−.14
Snobbishness (ICA)	+	9.4	n.s.
Regularity of Sleeping Habits (ICA)	+	7.7	.14

* Based on the proportion of variance in the criterion which is independently attributable to the variable ($F_{01} = 6.7$).
† n.s. = zero-order correlation between the mean residual criterion score and the college characteristic was not significant ($p > .05$).

An alternative to this "environmental effects" interpretation is that we failed to measure and control adequately all the relevant student input variables. It is possible, for example, that there are motivational differences between engineering students who enter technological institutions and engineering students who enter universities or liberal arts colleges and that these differences are not reflected in their initial choices of careers and major fields or in their academic abilities, high school achievements, and family backgrounds. Although this possibility cannot be tested empirically without additional data, it seems unlikely that these very large effects on the choice of a career in engineering are attributable solely to subtle differences in uncontrolled input characteristics.

Several explanations are possible as to why attendance at a technological institution has a positive effect on the student's choosing a career as engineer. Two potentially important sources of influence in any college environment are the student peer group and the faculty. Thus, in most technological institutions, the engineering student who begins to question the appropriateness of his career plans is not likely to find that these doubts receive much encouragement from his fellow students or his professors, most of whom are themselves committed to the career. Holland (1966*b*) has described this phenomenon as follows: "The student at a technological institute finds himself in a consistent environment . . . [where] nearly everybody is striving for the same goals. To strive for other goals or to express doubts about the value of scientific and technological goals is to swim against the current of student and faculty opinion" (p. 68). The uncertain student may be further discouraged from leaving engineering because such a change would necessitate his transferring to another institution. Engineering students enrolled at universities and liberal arts colleges, on the other hand, are more likely to find interpersonal support for their doubts and to have available to them desirable alternative courses of study at the same institution.

Although other institutional characteristics had a comparatively small influence on the career choice of engineer, one of them—men's colleges—merits some discussion. Although men's colleges, as a group, had no detectable overall effect on choosing a career in engineering (i.e., the zero-order correlation shown in the last column of Table 57 was not significant), colleges of this type received a highly significant *negative* weight in the final regression equation. It would seem that men's colleges *other than technological institutions* have a negative influence on the student's interest in becoming an engineer. The reason that men's colleges as a group did not manifest this effect is that they included a few technological institutions. Once the pronounced positive effect of these institutions was taken into account, the smaller negative effect of the remaining men's colleges became apparent. This instance demonstrates the value of linear multiple regression analysis in detecting subtle environmental influences that are not revealed in simple correlations.

These results may have important implications for manpower specialists concerned with future supplies of trained engineers. If, for example, most technological institutions were eventually converted into multipurpose universities, the number of students who end up pursuing careers in engineering would probably decline substantially. Such an outcome cannot be regarded as inevitable, in view of the methodological limitations already noted. But the magnitude of the relationships shown in our data suggests that it ought to be regarded as a serious possibility.

Another sizable environmental effect was associated with the career choice of *lawyer*. Here it appeared that students were more likely to end up aspiring to careers as lawyers if they attended a men's college which had a relatively high Enterprising orientation.[12] The likelihood appeared to be still greater if the college they attended was not a liberal arts college. The zero-order correlation, which was not statistically significant, obscured this relationship. Because many men's colleges are also liberal arts colleges, the negative effect that other types of liberal arts colleges had on a student's aspiring to a career in law was not revealed until the contribution of men's colleges was taken into account. This illustration again demonstrates the usefulness of multiple regression analyses in uncovering multiple causal factors.

The environmental effects on career choices in the three categories of *scientist*—biological, physical, and social—did not fall into any consistent pattern. The most substantial effect involved the career of physical scientist: Technological institutions appeared to have a facilitative influence on that choice. The presence of a sizable negative weight for the variable of Masculinity (which is based primarily on the percentage of men in the student body) indicates that, of the nontechnological institutions, those with a relatively high percentage of women in the student body facilitated the development of interest in a career as a physical scientist. This finding, taken together with those discussed previously, indicates that the role that men's colleges (other than technological institutions) play in the distribution of manpower is to channel students from potential careers in engineering and physical science and into careers in law.

The patterns of environmental effects for the career choices of biological scientist and social scientist suggest additional hypotheses about the interaction between a student's career plans and his college environment. A college's being located in a small town, for example, seemed to facilitate the choice of a career as a biological scientist. This finding, which is consistent with Harmon's (1961) observations concerning the geographic distribution of doctorate recipients in the biological sciences, suggests that a rural atmosphere may be conducive to the development of interests in biological science.

Another suggestive finding is that predominantly Negro colleges tended to foster the development of interest in careers in the social sciences. Since Negro college students tend to be concentrated primarily in Negro institutions (Astin, Panos, and Creager, 1967b), the positive relationship between being Negro and choosing social science as a final major field (Table 50) may, in fact, represent primarily an environmental effect. In other words, since attending a Negro college (beyond the fact simply of being a Negro) apparently increased the likelihood that the student would want to become a social scientist, it seems reasonable to assume that the magnitude of the environmental effect has been underestimated through extensive confounding of environment and input and that the "race" of the college is at least as important as the race of the student. The most plausible interpretation here is that, given the current widespread concern over the status of the Negro in American society, the faculty and students of the predominantly Negro colleges are more likely than are the faculty and students of other colleges to encourage the development of interest in the scientific study of social problems.

One of the most intriguing patterns of environmental effects shown in

Table 57 is associated with the career of *college professor*. The student's interest in this career appeared to be enhanced if he attended a relatively affluent liberal arts college. Of special note is the environmental factor labeled Familiarity with the Instructor, which had the highest zero-order correlation ($r = .28$) with the residual career choice of college professor. (Although this variable entered the regression equation first, its contribution was subsequently diminished as the other variables entered.) This finding suggests that more students would pursue careers as college professors if personal contact between faculty and undergraduates were more frequent.

Just why expenditures per student should have had a positive effect on the career choice of college professor is not immediately obvious, although it may be relevant that the principal item in these "educational and general" expenditures is faculty salaries. Per-student expenditures for faculty salaries are dependent, in turn, both on the faculty-student ratio and on the average faculty salary. Perhaps a career as a college professor is more attractive to students exposed to professors who themselves are relatively well off.[13]

The student's interest in pursuing a career as a *teacher* seemed to be increased by his attending a Catholic college, a teachers college, or an institution with relatively strict administrative policies regarding student conduct. As Table 57 indicates, the career of teacher had its highest zero-order correlation—a negative one—with Intellectualism, which is a measure of the academic ability and the scientific interests of the entering freshmen class (see Astin, 1965d). It seems reasonable to surmise that the career choice of schoolteacher—which tends to attract the less able students even at the freshman level (Astin, 1965d)—is not encouraged at institutions that enroll students high in Intellectualism. The contribution of Intellectualism was diminished primarily by the addition to the equation of two dichotomous characteristics, teachers college and Catholic college (both negatively correlated with Intellectualism) and by the addition of Permissiveness (which is positively correlated with Intellectualism). In other words, the negative effect of Intellectualism is accounted for in part by the fact that Catholic colleges, teachers colleges, and colleges low in Permissiveness also tended to be low in Intellectualism.

The facilitative effect of the teachers college on the career choice of teacher paralleled the effect of the technological institution on the career choice of engineer. Once again we are confronted with at least two plausible interpretations. It is possible, of course, that these apparent "effects" are really manifestations of subtle motivational differences between students entering teachers colleges and students entering other types of institutions, differences not fully accounted for in our various input measures. On the other hand, they may be true environmental effects, an interpretation that is consistent with the fact that the environment of the teachers college is such as to provide little interpersonal support to the student who is contemplating a change from teaching to some other career choice. Furthermore, the education student attending a teachers college is more likely than is the education student attending a liberal arts college or university to have to change institutions if he changes his career plans.

Several other environmental effects shown in Table 57 merit brief mention. Choosing a career as a *clergyman*, for example, seemed to be facilitated if the student initially attended an institution that fell toward the religious end of the environmental factor labeled Drinking vs. Religiousness. The same factor also had a substantial effect on choosing a career as a *physician:* that is, the choice of such a career seems to be encouraged in the more religious environment. The career choice of physician also appeared to be encouraged in environments where the rate of informal dating was relatively low and the administrative policy against student aggression relatively severe. It may be of some interest to point out here that colleges controlled by the Seventh-Day Adventist Church showed pronounced facilitative effects on the choice of a career in medicine; the four Seventh-Day Adventist colleges in our sample were all among the highest-ranked 5 percent of the 246 institutions in their mean residual scores for this career.

Institutional Effects on Specific Fields of Study

The effects of the different college characteristics on the student's final major field of study are summarized in Table 58. For two of the seven major field criteria, the findings were consistent with those for the comparable careers: technological institutions had a positive effect on majoring in engineering, and teachers colleges had a positive effect on majoring in education. Although these environmental effects may be attributable to the limited curricula of these institutions (i.e., the student had few alternative choices), such an interpretation seems less tenable in light of the fact that comparable effects were found for career choice, which is not constrained by the curriculum. In short, the similarities in the results suggest that the effects of technological institutions and teachers colleges on majoring in engineering and education respectively were reflections of actual changes in the student's motivation, rather than artifacts of the curricula of these two types of institutions.

Several other findings concerning environmental effects on career choice were confirmed by the data on major fields. Majoring in one of the physical sciences, for example, is negatively associated with attending an institution with a relatively large percentage of men in the student body. (It will be recalled that the *career choice* of physical scientist was negatively affected by attending a college for men.) In addition, choosing a final major in some field of business, like choosing a career as a businessman, was positively affected by the Conventional orientation (an environmental measure based primarily on the concentration of students in such major fields as accounting and business administration). Somewhat surprisingly, men's colleges apparently had a negative impact on the choice of business as a field of study. This effect

TABLE 58
Effects of Various College Characteristics on Final Major Fields

Criterion: College Characteristic	Sign	F-ratio* in Final Regression Equation	r† with Mean Residual Score
Arts and Humanities:			
Enterprising orientation (EAT)	+	62.3	.58
Drinking *vs.* Religiousness (ICA)	+	28.9	.39
Leisure Time (ICA)	−	19.4	−.27
Academic Competitiveness (ICA)	+	11.4	.36
Artistic orientation (EAT)	+	11.0	.22
Musical and Artistic Activity (ICA)	+	8.6	.28
Biological sciences:			
Organized Dating (ICA)	−	17.8	−.27
Realistic orientation (EAT)	+	15.9	n.s.
Liberal arts college	+	14.3	.20
Friendliness of the Dorm Counselor (ICA)	−	8.8	−.15
Technical institution	−	8.0	−.13
Organization in the Classroom (ICA)	+	7.5	.18
Business:			
Conventional orientation (EAT)	+	41.2	.35
Organization in the Classroom (ICA)	−	9.0	n.s.
Men's college	−	8.5	−.31
Independence (ICA)	−	8.3	−.35
Education:			
Status	−	29.2	−.38
Women's college	−	11.6	−.21
Teachers college	+	4.3	.41
Engineering:			
Technical institution	+	418.3	.80
Men's college	−	33.1	n.s.
Selectivity	−	22.1	n.s.
Organized Dating (ICA)	+	15.2	n.s.
Realistic orientation (EAT)	+	12.2	.46
Located in small town	−	8.9	−.21
Informal Dating (ICA)	−	8.7	−.15
Physical sciences:			
Masculinity	−	43.1	−.30
Cohesiveness (ICA)	+	21.4	−.23
Scientific orientation (EAT)	+	11.1	n.s.
Northeastern location	−	7.0	−.16
Social sciences:			
Enterprising orientation (EAT)	+	75.3	.51
Scientific orientation (EAT)	+	13.6	.17
Social orientation (EAT)	+	12.0	−.20
Severity of Administrative Policy against Aggression (ICA)	−	10.7	−.38
Severity of Grading (ICA)	−	7.9	−.31

* Based on the proportion of variance in the criterion which is independently attributable to the variable ($F_{01} = 6.7$).
† n.s. = zero-order correlation between the mean residual criterion score and the college characteristic was not significant ($p > .05$).

was mediated in part by the tendency for the peer environments of men's colleges to rank high on the environmental factor of Independence ($r = -.35$). Apparently, majoring in business tends to be discouraged at institutions which have highly independent student bodies.

Two of the largest environmental effects shown in Table 58 involved the Enterprising orientation (see footnote 12). Students attending institutions with highly Enterprising environments appeared to be more likely than typical students to end up majoring either in arts and humanities ($r = .58$) or in one of the social sciences ($r = .51$). These findings give substantial support to the hypothesis that "the Enterprising Environment will foster . . . the development of verbal and persuasive skills" (Astin, 1963b, p. 220).

The "Progressive Conformity" Theory

In recent studies (Astin, 1965b; Holland, 1966b; Holland and Whitney, 1968), it has been proposed that during the undergraduate years, students tend to change their career preferences in the direction of the dominant career preferences of their peers. This theory holds that the peer group operates to create a greater degree of conformity among its members and, at the same time, to resist trends towards heterogeneity. These effects may be regarded as a simple learning phenomenon, in which the dominant forces in the college environment selectively reinforce behavior which conforms to to the "party line" (Astin, 1965b, p. 34). To state the assumption in more psychological terms, individual students are inclined to support or reward the behavior of fellow students if it conforms to or agrees with their own choices and prejudices and to discourage or censure "deviant" behavior. Consequently, the likelihood that a student's decision to pursue a particular career will be supported by his peers is a direct function of the proportion of those peers who have made similar decisions. Note that the process operates in two ways: it discourages those students who plan to pursue a relatively popular career from abandoning that choice, and it encourages those students who plan to pursue relatively unpopular careers to switch to the more popular ones.

Our findings with respect to the effects of technological institutions and teachers colleges support this theory. To test it systematically, we must make specific predictions about many different types of career choices, taking, as our basis, information about relative concentrations of students with these choices. The six personal orientations from the Environmental Assessment Technique (EAT), which reflect the relative distribution of baccalaureate recipients in six broad fields of study, provide an ideal basis for generating such a set of predictions. These six EAT measures—Realistic, Scientific, Social, Conventional, Enterprising, and Artistic—are derived from Holland's (1966a) theoretical classification of careers in terms of personality types. Since most careers can be classified as belonging to one of these six personal types, it is possible to develop specific predictions about the effects that each EAT measure will have on each career choice. The specific source of these predictions has been reported earlier (Astin, 1965d, Appendix C); here, the degree to which each career choice and major field of study resembles each of the six EAT personal orientations is expressed quantitatively as either 1.00 (maximum resemblance, a pure type), .75, .50, .25, or .00 (minimal resemblance). The sum of the weights assigned to any career or major field is always equal to 1.00. For example, since the career of physicist was assigned a weight of 1.00 for the Scientific orientation (maximum resemblance), its weights on each of the other five orientations were set at .00 (minimal resemblance). On the other hand, the career of engineer, which was judged to be of a more "mixed" type, was assigned a weight of .75 for the Realistic orientation, a weight of .25 for the Scientific orientation, and weights of .00 for the other four orientations. On this basis, we would predict that the career choice of engineer will be positively affected in colleges with high Realistic and high Scientific orientations and that the effect of the Realistic orientation will be greater than the effect of the Scientific orientation.

Using these weights (see Table 59) as a guide, we made predictions con-

TABLE 59
Weights Assigned to Each Criterion on Each EAT Personal Orientation[a]

CRITERION	EAT PERSONAL ORIENTATION:					
	Realistic	Scientific	Social	Conventional	Enterprising	Artistic
Career Choice:						
Biological scientist		1.00				
Businessman				.75	.25	
Clergyman			.75		.25	
College professor[b]		.75	.25			
Engineer	.75	.25				
Health professional		.25	.75			
Lawyer				.25	.75	
Performing artist					.25	.75
Physical scientist		1.00				
Physician or Dentist		.50	.50			
Social scientist		.25	.75			
Teacher			1.00			
Final Major Field:						
Arts and humanities					.50	.50
Biological sciences	.25	.75				
Business[c]				.75	.25	
Education			.75			.25
Engineering	.75	.25				
Physical sciences		1.00				
Social sciences[d]		.25	.50		.25	

[a] From Astin (1965d, Appendix C, Table C1).
[b] Changed from an initial weight of 1.00 for Social, on the basis of recent findings (Astin, 1964b).
[c] Combines accounting (1.00 and .00) and business administration (.50 and .50).
[d] Includes political science and economics, as well as sociology, psychology and anthropology.

cerning specific environmental effects on each career choice and final field of study. Specifically, we predicted that a given career or major would be positively affected by every EAT personal orientation for which it had been assigned a weight of more than zero. Further, we predicted that "mixed" types of careers and majors would be affected most by the personal orientation with the highest weight for the type. Our categories of choice being mutually exclusive, some careers and fields of study will almost certainly be negatively affected by certain personal orientations. Since negative weights had not been assigned to any of the careers or majors in the earlier study, however, no specific predictions about negative effects were made.

In addition to the predictions about each specific career choice and major field of study, comparable predictions were made about each of the six personal orientations from the EAT. Thus, we predicted that each orientation would show its largest effects on those careers or major fields which had the highest associated weights.

Table 60 shows the correlations between each of the mean residual career choices and major fields of study and each of the six personal orientations from the EAT. The last column indicates whether or not the data in each row confirmed our prediction based on the theory of progressive conformity. For example, in the case of the career choice of lawyer, the theory predicts that the highest positive correlation will involve the Enterprising orientation, since the career receives its highest weight (.75) on that orientation (see Table 59). More simply, we would expect that a college with a high proportion of potential lawyers (Enterprising types) in its student body is more likely to encourage the development of interest in a law career than is a college with relatively few potential lawyers. In this particular example, the prediction was clearly borne out (the correlation of .38 between the criterion of lawyer and the Enterprising orientation being the highest positive correlation in the row); confirmation of the prediction is indicated by a "yes" in the last column of the row.

Of the 19 specific predictions concerning the expected highest positive correlation for each specific career choice, 13 were confirmed.[14] In three of the six predictions which were not clearly confirmed, the predicted relationship was the second highest positive correlation: Specifically, the career of biological scientist had its second highest positive correlation with the Scientific orientation, the career of health professional (non-M.D.) had its second highest correlation with the Social orientation,[15] and the career of physical scientist had its second highest positive correlation with the Scientific orientation. The results clearly failed to confirm our predictions about the major of physical sciences and the career choice of social scientist, which correlated only .05 and .01, respectively, with the Scientific and Social orientations. For the major field of social sciences, the prediction not only was unsupported but was contradicted by the negative correlation of $-.20$ with the Social orientation. However, the secondary prediction that majoring in

TABLE 60
The Relation of Career Choice and Final Major Field to the Six Personal Orientations (EAT)
(N = 246 institutions)

CRITERION	Realistic	Scientific	EAT PERSONAL ORIENTATION: Social	Conventional	Enterprising	Artistic	Is Highest + Coefficient the Predicted One?
Career choice:							
Biological scientist	−.20	.07	.11	−.14	−.13	.03	No
Businessman	−.17	.11	−.03	.30	.22	.03	Yes
Clergyman	−.08	.06	.09	−.06	−.08	.08	Yes
College professor	−.03	.19	−.06	−.02	.07	.07	Yes
Engineer	.44	.20	−.31	−.26	−.37	−.23	Yes
Health professional	.01	−.06	.06	.07	−.02	−.05	No
Lawyer	−.23	.03	−.04	.15	.38	.04	Yes
Performing artist	−.06	−.07	−.01	−.01	.06	.13	Yes
Physical scientist	.12	.11	−.03	−.18	−.21	.03	No
Physician or dentist	−.14	−.11	.29	−.02	.01	.03	Yes
Social scientist	−.10	.09	.01	.00	.07	.13	No
Teacher	−.12	−.23	.36	−.09	−.16	.09	Yes
Is highest + coefficient the predicted one?	yes	no	yes	yes	yes	yes	
Final Major Field:							
Arts and humanities	−.36	.07	−.27	.21	.58	.22	Yes
Biological sciences	.07	.12	.01	−.01	−.04	−.13	Yes
Business	.06	−.29	.08	.35	−.01	−.10	Yes
Education	.18	−.15	.27	−.18	−.37	−.03	Yes
Engineering	.46	.13	−.24	−.29	−.42	−.24	Yes
Physical sciences	.01	.05	.20	−.26	−.34	.13	No
Social sciences	−.27	.17	−.20	.18	.51	.01	No
Is highest + coefficient the predicted one?	yes	no	yes	yes	yes	yes	

Note: $r_{.05} = .15$; $r_{.01} = .19$.

social science will be positively affected by both the Scientific and Enterprising orientations (several of the specific social science fields received weights on these orientations) was supported by the data.

The last row under the heading of "Career Choice" and of "Final Major Field" in Table 60 indicates whether or not each of the six predictions about the environmental orientations was substantiated. For example, it was predicted that the Realistic orientation would have its highest positive correlation with the career of engineer, since engineer received a higher weight on this orientation than did any other career. Similarly, it was predicted that the Realistic orientation would have its highest positive correlation with the major field of engineering. In the two examples given above, the predictions were confirmed, as is indicated by a "yes" in the appropriate rows under the column headed "Realistic."

The predicted effects on career choices and on final major fields of study were confirmed for five of the six personal orientations, the exception being the Scientific orientation. It was predicted that the Scientific orientation would show the largest positive effects on the career choices of biological scientist, physical scientist, and college professor, since these three careers were assigned higher weights (1.00) on this orientation than were any of the other nine careers. Although the correlations for all three were positive (r's = .07, .11, and .19, respectively), they were exceeded by the correlation for engineer ($r = .20$). Since this career choice received a partial weight (.25) for the Scientific orientation, these findings can be regarded as offering partial support for the theory. Similar partial support can be seen in the patterns of correlations with final major fields of study, where the small positive effect of the Scientific orientation ($r = .05$) on majoring in physical science (the only major with a weight of 1.00) was exceeded by its effects on four other fields, three of which (biological sciences, engineering, and social sciences) received positive weights for the Scientific orientation.

In brief, the data in Table 60 offers strong empirical support for the theory that, as he progresses through the undergraduate years, the student's career choice and field of study come to conform more and more to the dominant or modal choices of his peers. The theory appears to be generalizable to all six personal orientations and to a wide range of specific careers and fields of study, with the exception of those in the social sciences. In future research, the extent to which the theory of progressive conformity applies to aspects of the student's personal development other than his choices of a career and field of study should be examined thoroughly.

College Effects: The Institution as the Unit of Analysis

The effects of 58 of the environmental characteristics were examined under conditions in which differential student inputs were first controlled using the *institution* as the unit of analysis. In this analysis, mean scores for each institution on each student input characteristic (e.g., the percentage of entering students with average high school grades of "A") were computed.

We then conducted a series of 19 two-stage, stepwise regression analyses in which the mean actual scores on the 19 criteria of final major fields and careers served as the dependent variables. In the first stage of each analysis, mean scores on 88 student input variables were entered into the regression equation until no additional input variable was capable of producing a reduction in the residual sum of squares exceeding $p = .05$. In the second stage, the 58 environmental characteristics were permitted to enter the regression equation until the same criterion of $p = < .05$ was reached.

Table 61 shows the results of these additional analyses. The median multiple R based on student input variables was .88; adding the environmental variables raised the median coefficient to .90. These data show clearly that most student outputs for a given institution can be predicted with considerable accuracy from a knowledge of its student input charac-

TABLE 61

The Prediction of Career Choice and Final Major Field Using the Institution as the Unit of Analysis

($N = 246$ institutions)

CRITERION	STEPWISE CONTROL OF STUDENT INPUT VARIABLES			ADDITIONAL CONTRIBUTION OF ENVIRONMENTAL VARIABLES		
	Number Entering* Equation	R	R^2	Number Entering** Equation	R	Increase in R^2
Career Choice:						
Biological scientist	10	.488	.238	4	.535	.062
Businessman	11	.854	.730	2	.870	.027
Clergyman	7	.837	.700	3	.851	.024
College professor	16	.861	.742	10	.898	.063
Engineer	13	.972	.945	3	.979	.014
Health professional	14	.899	.809	0	.899	.000
Lawyer	11	.939	.883	3	.944	.009
Performing artist	9	.645	.416	2	.666	.028
Physical scientist	15	.873	.762	3	.882	.015
Physician or Dentist	10	.878	.771	1	.881	.004
Social scientist	13	.679	.461	5	.726	.066
Teacher	14	.955	.912	1	.956	.002
Scientist or Engineer (all fields)	17	.949	.901	5	.959	.019
Professional (all fields)	17	.904	.816	2	.908	.008
Major Field of Study:						
Arts and humanities	17	.914	.835	6	.935	.039
Biological sciences	14	.765	.585	17	.784	.029
Business	9	.882	.777	5	.901	.035
Education	13	.912	.831	3	.920	.016
Engineering	17	.977	.955	5	.986	.016
Physical sciences	15	.852	.726	3	.866	.025
Social sciences	11	.804	.647	4	.827	.038

* $p < .05$.   ** After control of student input variables.

teristics and that a knowledge of the institution's environmental characteristics increases the accuracy of these predictions only slightly. Although
the relative accuracy of prediction differed markedly for the 19 student output criteria, particularly career choices, these differences closely paralleled
the differences shown earlier in the analyses in which inputs were controlled
using the student as the unit of analysis (Tables 49 and 50) and in the subsequent analyses of environmental effects (Tables 57 and 58). The career
choices of engineer, lawyer, and teacher were predicted with the highest
degree of accuracy, whereas the choices of biological scientist, performing
artist, and social scientist were the most difficult to predict. Once again, it
appears that the reliability of the output measure (as reflected in the degree of
variation among institutions on that measure) is a major determinant of the
accuracy with which it can be predicted.

We will not discuss in detail here the findings obtained in this analysis of
specific environmental effects. (The interested reader should consult Appendix F.) It is relevant, however, to point out some of the similarities and
differences in the findings obtained through these two alternative methods
of analysis. A comparison between the specific effects obtained when the
student was used as the unit of analysis (see Tables 57 and 58) and those obtained when the institution was used as the unit of analysis reveals the following general trends:

1. Although many of the effects found in the two analyses were
identical, the magnitude was almost always larger in the analysis
where the *student* was used as the basic unit in controlling differential
inputs.

2. When the *institution* was used as the unit in controlling student
inputs, fewer significant environmental effects were found; a very few
new effects appeared but there were no reversals or otherwise contradictory effects.

3. The theory of progressive conformity was supported by both
types of analysis.

In short, when the unit of analysis is the institution rather than the student, considerably more variance in student outputs is accounted for by
student input characteristics. The implication here is that a substantial
amount of the differential effects of college environments can be attributed
to the peer culture (as represented by aggregated student characteristics).
Thus, when the college environment is viewed independent of the characteristics of its student body, its effects on the individual student's career and
study plans appear to be trivial.

SUMMARY

In this chapter, we have attempted to identify some of the personal and
environmental factors that influence the student's career choice and field of

study during the undergraduate years. On the basis of data furnished by students when they first entered college and again four years later, the following conclusions seem warranted:

1. About three-fourths of the students changed their long-term career plans after entering college. The percentage of those who changed, however, varied greatly from field to field, ranging from less than 50 percent in a few fields to more than 95 percent in others.

2. The patterns of change in career choice and in field of study during the undergraduate years were not random. In general, those students who changed their plans tended to switch to fields that were related to their initial choice. The "balance of trade" over time, however, was not equal for all careers, since the popularity of many of them changed dramatically during the four years following matriculation. The relative net percentage change for specific fields during the four-year interval varied from decreases of nearly 75 percent to increases of more than 400 percent.

3. By far the best predictors of the student's final major field and career choice were his initial choices as reported four years earlier at the time of matriculation. The characteristic having the next greatest predictive value over the four-year interval was the student's sex. The trend toward greater differentiation of sex roles during the undergraduate years was pronounced, with men gravitating toward the more "masculine" careers (i.e., those that were initially preferred more by men than by women) and women gravitating toward the more "feminine" careers. The same was true for major field.

4. Students who received part of their financial support through a loan from the college were somewhat less likely than students who did not receive such support to end up pursuing careers in engineering or majoring in some field of physical science. Students on scholarships, however, appeared to be more likely than nonscholarship students to end up pursuing careers in medicine. Students whose parents supplied the major portion of their college finances appeared to be more likely than other students to end up pursuing careers in medicine and the health professions and less likely to end up pursuing careers in business.

5. Although the 246 institutions varied widely with respect to the percentages of their students who aspired to particular types of careers four years after entering college, these institutional variations were diminished considerably when differential student inputs were taken into account. In several instances, however, differences in outputs that were not solely attributable to differential student inputs showed substantial relationships to the environmental characteristics of the institutions.

6. In general, the student's career choice tended to move into closer conformity with the more popular career choices among his fellow students. This effect was particularly evident in the case of the fields of engineering, teaching, law, and business.

The findings for each specific career choice and corresponding field of study are summarized below:

Biological Scientist. Like most science-related careers, that of biological scientist proved very unstable over the four years: only one student in every seven who initially named biological scientist as their choice also chose it four years after matriculation. The net loss of students, however, was relatively small: from .8 percent in 1961 to .6 percent of the total sample in 1965. The degree of net loss was held down in part because a disproportionate number of those defecting from the career choice of dentist switched to biological scientist. Choosing a career as a biological scientist appears to be discouraged at colleges where organized dating (that is, prearranged and rather formal—as opposed to spontaneous and informal—social activity) is relatively frequent among the students.

Physical Scientist. As with biological scientist, the career choice of physical scientist (chemist, physicist, mathematician, etc.) had a very low rate of stability during the four years, with approximately four students out of every five who initially chose such a career switching to some other choice during the four years following matriculation.

The net loss of potential physical scientists during the four years was somewhat greater than the net loss of potential biological scientists, with only about half as many students choosing such a career four years after matriculation.

Those students who, four years after matriculation, planned to become physical scientists tended to be more able academically and were more likely to be men than were those students who, at the time of college entrance, said they intended to become physical scientists. Technological institutions and institutions with a relatively high proportion of women in the student body appeared to foster the development of interest in becoming a physical scientist.

Engineer. Although the career of engineer registered a net loss (7.9 percent in 1961 and 4.7 percent in 1965) comparable to that found for the career of physical scientist, the choice of engineer was somewhat more stable: Fewer than two-thirds of the students initially choosing this career switched to some other career during the four-year interval. Thus, engineering was less successful than were the physical and biological sciences in recruiting students to replace those who defected during the undergraduate years. Technological institutions, in comparison with other types of institutions, had a pronounced positive influence on the student's interest in becoming an engineer. This environmental effect—larger than any other observed in our data—was of sufficient magnitude to be regarded as a major factor in determining the supply of trained engineers. Among the nontechnological institutions, men's colleges appeared to have a negative impact on the student's interest in becoming an engineer.

Social Scientist. Although career choices in the social sciences showed very low stability during the four years (approximately eight in every nine who initially chose such a career changed to some other), this career category actually registered a small net increase in total students during the four-year period because it recruited a relatively large number of students from other career fields. In fact, among the seven broad categories of *major fields*, the social sciences showed the largest net gain between 1961 and 1965 (from 6.2 percent to 13.5 percent of the total sample of undergraduates). Compared with those students who majored in social science at the entering freshmen level, those whose final major field was in social science included a high proportion of Negroes. Furthermore, attendance at a predominantly Negro institution appeared to enhance the student's interest in pursuing a career as a social scientist. The magnitude of this effect, however, was relatively small.

Physician. The career choice of physician showed an average rate of stability during the four years: Slightly less than 75 percent of the students who initially chose this career switched to some other choice. However, the total net loss of students planning to become physicians was higher than the net loss for almost any other career (from 5 percent of all students in 1961 to only 2.6 percent in 1965). Medicine, it would appear, fares badly in the competition for defectors from other fields.

Compared with those students who, as entering college freshmen, planned to become physicians, the group intending to become physicians four years later included a high percentage of men, a high percentage of academically able students, and a high percentage of the offspring of Jewish parents. The choice of a career in medicine was negatively influenced at technological institutions and at institutions where the rate of informal dating was relatively high. Institutions with a religious atmosphere and with relatively severe administrative policies against student aggression—Seventh-Day Adventist Colleges, in particular—appeared to encourage the development of interest in a medical career.

Health Professional (non-M.D.). As a group, these careers showed an average rate of stability during the undergraduate years (approximately two students in every three who initially chose such a career changed to some other). There were considerable differences, however, in the stability rates of the specific careers in this group. For example, whereas six out of every seven students who initially planned to become laboratory assistants or laboratory technicians changed to some other career choice during the four years, fewer than half of those initially intending to become nurses changed careers during the same period. In fact, the career choice of nurse showed a higher degree of stability (57 percent) than did any other single career choice. Because of their relatively poor success in recruiting defectors from other fields, careers in the health professions showed a total net loss of 27 percent (from 5.5 percent to 4 percent of the total sample) during the four years following matriculation. The group of students choosing these careers four years after matriculation included higher proportions both of women and of Negroes than did the group choosing these careers as entering freshmen. Predominantly Negro colleges, however, appeared to have a slight *negative* effect on the student's interest in pursuing a career in the health professions.

College Professor. Although the career of college professor showed only average stability during the undergraduate years (approximately 75 percent of those students initially choosing this career switched to some other career), it registered a very large net gain: more than 400 percent (from .6 percent to 3.3 percent of all students) during the four-year period. Of those students who changed their choice to college professor, a disproportionate number were recruited from among those who initially planned to be mathematicians or schoolteachers. Students who chose college professor as a career four years after matriculation were initially more highly motivated toward graduate training (i.e., they stated as freshmen that they planned to get advanced degrees) and more able academically than were students who initially chose this career. The chances that the student would end up pursuing a career as a college professor seemed to be increased if he attended a relatively wealthy liberal arts college or a college where there was a fairly high degree of familiarity between the students and the instructors.

Schoolteacher. The choice of a career as a schoolteacher showed a rate of stability second only to that for the choice of nurse, with fewer than half of those who initially intended to become teachers switching to some other career choice during the four years following matriculation. However, this career choice showed almost no net gain in total students during the four-year interval; apparently, it was not successful in competing with other fields to recruit changers. Compared with those students who initially planned to become teachers, those planning to become teachers four years after matriculation included a very high percentage of women and a fairly high percentage of students whose fathers were also schoolteachers. The student's interest in becoming a teacher appeared to be enhanced if he attended either a Catholic institution or a teachers college. Institutions with relatively permissive administrative policies appeared to discourage the pursuit of a career in teaching.

Businessman. The total number of students choosing careers in business increased relatively more during the undergraduate years (from 6.8 percent of the total sample in 1961 to 13 percent in 1965) than did the total choosing most of the other specific careers. Compared with students initially planning careers in business, those who planned such careers four years after entering college included a high percentage of men, a high percentage of students from well-to-do families, and a low percentage of academically able students. Aspiring to a career in business appeared to be encouraged in institutions where there was a relatively high frequency of organized dating and where there were relatively high proportions of other students pursuing careers in business.

Clergyman. The career choice of clergyman appeared to be relatively stable over the four years, with only a little more than half of those students who initially chose this career switching to some other choice. The total number of students intending to become clergymen also registered little net change (from .9 to .8 percent of the total sample), a finding which suggests that the number of defectors is balanced by the number of recruits during the undergraduate years.

Compared with those who initially wanted to become clergymen, those who named this choice four years after entering college included a high percentage of men and a high percentage of students whose fathers were also clergymen. Desire to pursue a career in the the clergy appeared to be enhanced by attendance at institutions where the frequency of religious activity was relatively high and where the amount of student drinking and of leisure time was relatively low. These environmental effects, however, were rather small in magnitude.

Lawyer. The career choice of lawyer was not only fairly stable during the undergraduate years (approximately 60 switched to some other career after entering college) but also showed a modest net gain in total students (from 3 percent of the sample in 1961 to 3.8 percent in 1965). Compared with the group of students initially intending to become lawyers, the group who chose careers as lawyers four years after matriculation included a very high percentage of men and fairly high percentages of academically able students, students of Jewish parentage, students from relatively affluent families, and students whose fathers were also lawyers. Pursuit of a career in law appeared to be substantially encouraged by attendance at a men's college or a college characterized by an Enterprising environment and discouraged by attendance at a liberal arts college or a technological institution.

Performing Artist. The percentage of students intending to become performing artists or writers showed no net change during the four years following matriculation. The student's interest in becoming a performing artist seemed to be increased slightly by attendance at a private nonsectarian institution. Choosing a final *major field* in the arts or humanities, however, is substantially enhanced at institutions with a strong Enterprising orientation and at institutions where there is a relatively high frequency of drinking (*vs.* religiousness) among the students. Noncoeducational institutions, in particular, seemed to increase the student's interest in majoring in one of the arts or humanities.

REFERENCES

1. It might be argued that the greater rate of change found in our study was attributable either to the open-ended method of reporting or to the larger number of categories used to classify career choices (40 as compared to Davis's nine categories). However, a comparison of identical career choices in the two studies does not support this contention. The career choice of lawyer, for example, showed a retention rate of 56.3 percent in Davis's study, as compared with only 39 percent in the present study. Other com-

parable careers showing the same trends were engineer (51.3 percent *vs.* 36.1 percent) and physician (43.5 percent vs. 28.5 percent).

2. Cross-tabulations of initial and final career choice and initial and final field of study, separately by sex, are given in Appendix H.

3. The statistical significance of each possible pattern of change was determined by 2×2 chi-square tests in which only changers were used: popular career versus all others, and specific career versus all others.

4. Holland uses the label "intellectual," although nearly every occupation in the class is concerned with science.

5. Note that the number of degrees of freedom for an analysis of mutually exclusive dichotomous categories is equal to the total number of categories minus 1.

6. The correlation matrices have been deposited with the National Auxiliary Publications Service. Order NAPS Document No. 00385, remitting $1.00 for microfiche or $3.00 for photocopies.

7. The results of the analyses for the combined scientist and professional criteria (#13 and 14 in Table 48) are not reported here because of certain errors in the scoring of the criteria that were not detected until after the analyses had been completed. However, these errors have been corrected in some of the analyses of environmental effects reported in the next two sections.

8. In general, the nature of regression analyses with dichotomous dependent variables is such that the more extreme the split (i.e., the more it deviates from .5), the less accurate the prediction. This generalization is especially true in the case where the variable is an artificial dichotomy (i.e., a dummy variable) that has been imposed on a continuously distributed variable.

9. As a result of these differential trends, the percentage of men among students in unclassifiable ("neutral") careers increased slightly (from 55.5 percent to 58.3 percent) during the four years.

10. Since these racial categories were mutually exclusive, no information was lost by omitting "other" from the regression analysis (i.e., the number of degrees of freedom is equal to the number of categories minus one).

11. The psychometric concepts of "reliability" and "error of measurement" are probably relevant here. If we assume that the absolute amount of error variance is approximately the same for each of the 21 actual and 21 expected scores (a reasonable assumption in view of the fact that the same subjects were used to compute the 42 scores at any given institution), then the reliability of any score (i.e., one minus the proportion of error variance) is a function of the total observed variance.

12. As was mentioned in Chapter 1, the Enterprising orientation is assessed primarily on the basis of the proportion of students majoring in business, political science, and history.

13. Although it is also possible that the amount of contact between faculty and students increases with the faculty-student ratio, the correlation between expenditures per student and familarity with the instructor ($r = .01$) was not statistically significant.

14. Only one of the weights was changed from the original table (Astin, 1965d, Appendix C): The career of college professor was changed from the Social to the Scientific orientation, following some recent evidence (Astin, 1965d) that college professors do not resemble Social types.

15. This highly heterogeneous category includes nurse (.75 Social and .25 Scientific), therapist (1.00 Social), social worker (1.00 Social), and laboratory technician (.50 Realistic and .50 Scientific).

5

Summary and Implications
of the Findings

WE UNDERTOOK THIS STUDY primarily to identify factors in the undergraduate college environment that affect the student's educational and career development. In particular, we were interested in those institutional characteristics that influence his persistence in college, educational achievement, plans for graduate and professional school, and choice of a major field and a career. The basic assumption was that better information bearing on these questions would be useful not only as a guide in educational planning and manpower development but also as a means of increasing our understanding of the interaction between the undergraduate and his college.

The general plan of this chapter is to review briefly the design and methodology of the study and then to present a comprehensive summary of the findings and their implications. In the earlier chapters, we presented detailed summaries of the major findings by type of *outcome* (e.g., educational achievement, career plans); here we shall summarize the findings by *institutional type or environmental characteristic*.[1]

DESIGN AND METHODOLOGY OF THE STUDY

The institutional population selected for our study included all accredited four-year colleges and universities in the United States as of the fall of 1961. From this population, we selected a sample of 246 institutions, stratified so as to maximize institutional diversity. Information was collected from each entering freshman at each institution at the time of his matriculation in the fall of 1961; changes in the student's educational and vocational plans were determined by means of a followup survey conducted four years later in the summer of 1965. Measures of certain environmental characteristics of the 246 institutions were available from an earlier study.

Our design for assessing environmental effects on the student's development required three conceptually distinct categories of information:

1. *Student input data* (the student's abilities, achievements, family background, and educational and career plans at the time he entered college)

2. *Student output data* (the student's educational status and aspirations and his career plans four years after entering college)

3. *College environmental data* (the administrative and environmental characteristics of the student's institution)

The student output (criterion) data included the following specific measures:

1–2. *Educational attainment* (completion of four years of undergraduate college within the four years following matriculation; attainment of the bachelor's degree)

3–5. *Educational aspirations* (highest degree sought four years after entering college)

6–8. *Educational achievement* (scores on the three Area Tests of Graduate Record Examinations administered during the senior year)

9–15. *Final undergraduate major field of study* (seven different broad fields)

16–29. *Final choice of a career* (14 categories)

The input information obtained when the students entered college in 1961 was concerned with initial career plans, probable major field of study, highest degree sought, academic and extracurricular achievements in high school, and socioeconomic background. For each student, a total of 89 input variables was used in the analyses.

Information about the college environment was obtained from published sources such as publications of the American Council on Education and the U.S. Office of Education and from ratings of the college environment provided by the students earlier in 1962. The 72 environmental measures included administrative "type" characteristics (type of curriculum, type of control, etc.) and measures of an institution's social and intellectual climate based on the frequency of occurrence of various observable "stimuli" and on the students' subjective impressions of their college environments.

Complete data (i.e., both input and output information) were obtained from approximately 36,000 students, or an average of about 140 students per institution. Separate multiple regression analyses were conducted, using the student output measures as dependent variables. Each analysis employed a stepwise regression solution in which student input variables were selectively entered into the regression equation. The principal purpose of these analyses was to equate statistically the students entering different institutions in terms of their input characteristics. The resulting "adjusted" output characteristics (i.e., controlled for differential input characteristics) were subsequently correlated with the characteristics of the institutions in order to identify environmental factors that affect the student's educational and vocational development. Several different methods of controlling differential input characteristics were attempted, with essentially the same results (see Appendix F).

THE CLASS OF 1965

In this section we shall summarize the status of the Class of 1965 as determined through our followup survey conducted four years after the students' matriculation; we shall discuss also some of the changes observed in the students' plans between 1961 and 1965.

Nearly two-thirds of the Class of 1965 completed four or more years of college during the first four years following matriculation. However, only about half obtained the baccalaureate degree during this four-year interval. Substantially more women than men had received the bachelor's degree, but the proportions of the two sexes who completed four years of undergraduate credit during this period were roughly equal. Of those students who dropped out of their first college, more than half enrolled at a second institution. Only a small minority of the dropouts reported that either academic or disciplinary problems were major reasons for leaving college, and fewer than one in four indicated that inadequate finances had led to their decision to drop out.

The results of the regression analyses for controlling the student input variables indicated that the student who was most likely to drop out of college was one who had relatively low grades in high school, who was not planning to take graduate or professional work at the time he entered college, and who came from a relatively low socioeconomic background. Students who were married when they started college or who got married after entering college were more likely to drop out than were the unmarried students.

In spite of the substantial proportion of students who dropped out of college during the four years following matriculation, the Class of 1965, considered as a group, raised the level of their educational aspirations during this period. The most substantial increase occurred in the percentage of students who planned to obtain either a master's or a doctoral degree. The percentage of students intending to pursue professional degrees declined slightly during the four years. Nearly three-fourths of the total group indicated that they planned to obtain a graduate degree at the time of the followup.

Students were less likely to drop out of college if they received a major portion of their college finances from parents or if they attended college on a scholarship.

Initial choices of major fields and of careers proved to be highly unstable during the four years following matriculation, though fields varied considerably in their holding power. Only one-fourth of the students reported the same career choice in 1965 as they had in 1961. In general, those students who changed their career plans during the undergraduate years tended to switch to fields related to their initial choices. The number of students choosing careers in science-related fields declined substantially, whereas the number intending to become college professors, housewives, businessmen, and lawyers increased substantially. Patterns of changes in the students' major fields of study showed a similar trend: The natural sciences and engineering sustained large net losses, and the social sciences, business, and arts and humanities had sizable net gains during the undergraduate years.

Almost without exception, the best predictors of the student's career choice four years after entering college and of his final field of study in college were his initial choices at the time of matriculation. The student's sex proved to be the next most effective predictor, with the men gravitating toward "masculine" careers and the women toward "feminine" careers.

Although the 246 institutions differed markedly in their output rates with respect to the various criteria (proportion of students dropping out, proportion pursuing a given career at graduation, etc.), these differences were diminished considerably when the differential input characteristics of the various student bodies were taken into account. In other words, a substantial portion of the observed differences among the 246 institutions, with respect to the educational and vocational development of their undergraduates, can be attributed to differences among the student bodies that existed at the time of matriculation. Nevertheless, a variety of differential environmental effects were found for most output criteria. In the sections that follow, we shall attempt to summarize these environmental effects separately for different types of institutions and for different environmental characteristics.

ENVIRONMENTAL EFFECTS BY TYPE OF INSTITUTION

Perhaps the most important finding about how the environment affects the student's educational and vocational plans is that the student's field of study and career choice come to conform more and more to the dominant or modal choice of his peers as he progresses through the undergraduate years (the "progressive conformity" theory). In other words, a student is more likely to maintain his initial choice of a given career or to shift from some other choice into that career if a relatively high percentage of his fellow students also choose the same career. This pattern of effects was particularly evident in the case of careers in engineering, teaching, law, and business.

To facilitate the summary of other patterns of environmental influences, we have classified the 246 institutions according to five administrative type characteristics: type of curriculum (universities, liberal arts colleges, teachers colleges, or technological institutions), type of control (public, private-nonsectarian, Roman Catholic, or Protestant), sex (coeducational, men's, or women's), race (predominantly Negro or non-Negro), and geographic region (Northeast, Southeast, Midwest, or West-and-Southwest).

Type of Curriculum

Universities. The major influence of the university is to increase the student's chances of dropping out of college and to lower his educational aspirations. Although the university has a negative effect on the student's interest in pursuing graduate training and in obtaining the Ph.D. degree, it has a slight positive effect on his interest in obtaining a professional degree. These patterns are consistent with the tendency for the university to stimulate the student's interest in a career in either business or law and to lessen his interest in pursuing a career either as a teacher at any level (elementary, secondary, or college) or as a natural scientist.

Why the university manifests this particular pattern of environmental effects is not immediately clear, though it seems likely that the pattern is attributable, at least in part, to the relative lack of student and faculty involvement in the class, the rather impersonal relationship between instructors and students, and the relative lack of concern for the individual student that occurs in most universities.

Liberal Arts Colleges. The pattern of effects observed for the liberal arts colleges is the converse of the pattern observed for the universities. The dropout rates in the liberal arts colleges, for example, are substantially lower than would be expected from the quality of their student inputs. In addition, liberal arts colleges increase the student's interest in attending graduate school and in obtaining a Ph.D. degree. They tend to channel students out of majors in business, education, and engineering and into majors in the arts and humanities and the social sciences. With respect to the student's final choice of a career, liberal arts colleges appear to lessen interest in becoming either a lawyer or an engineer and to increase interest in becoming a physical scientist, a social scientist, a physician, or a college professor.

Although there are many possible explanations for the sharp contrast between liberal arts colleges and universities, one interesting hypothesis is suggested by the fact that these two groups of institutions differ markedly with respect to two environmental factors, Familiarity With the Instructor and Concern for the Individual Student. Perhaps the university professor, who spends relatively little time with his students and much time in pursuing his own scholarly interests, provides a relatively poor role model in comparison with the college teacher, who often takes a more personal interest in his students.

Technological Institutions. The technological institution has a decidedly positive influence on the student's choice of a major field or career in engineering. This environmental effect, the most pronounced in our study, is of sufficient magnitude to be regarded as a major factor in determining the nation's supply of manpower in engineering.

One aspect of this effect is that it steers students out of potential careers in medicine, business, and law. There is also a slight tendency for the technological institutions to increase the student's interest in becoming a physical scientist. The technological institution has no particular influence on the student's persistence in college or on his interest in going on to graduate school.

Teachers Colleges. The pattern of environmental effects observed in the teachers colleges was in many ways analogous, though smaller in magnitude, to the pattern found in the technological institutions: that is, teachers colleges increase the student's interest in majoring in education and in pursuing a career as a teacher. The net effect of this tendency is to deflect students from majors in the arts and humanities and the social sciences and from potential careers in business or college teaching. Like the technological institutions, the teachers colleges show no particular pattern of effects either on the student's persistence in college or on his interest in pursuing graduate study.

The most likely explanation of the patterns observed in the teachers colleges and technological institutions is that students who might otherwise be inclined to change from engineering or teaching into some other field are less likely to do so at these institutions because the number of available alternative courses of study is much more limited than in most liberal arts colleges and universities. Furthermore, because of the highly homogeneous interests of both students and faculty in the technological and teachers colleges, the student who contemplates a change of career choice is not likely to find encouragement and support for such a change at these institutions. The implications for manpower policy and planning are clear: The trend toward converting teachers colleges and technological institutions into more generalized and heterogeneous kinds of institutions is likely to reduce the total number of students who pursue careers in teaching and engineering, and, to a lesser extent, in the physical sciences.

Type of Control

To compare the effects of type of institutional control, we divided the 246 colleges in our sample into four subgroups: public, private-nonsectarian, Roman Catholic, and Protestant. The most distinctive pattern of environmental effects was observed in the public institutions. Attending a public institution increases the student's chances of dropping out and decreases his interest in attending graduate school. The public institutions also tend to shift students out of the arts and humanities and the social sciences and into business and education.

Of the three types of private institutions, the Catholic and private-nonsectarian colleges are most likely to show the opposite pattern of environmental effects. The principal difference between these two groups is that at the Catholic institution, the student is more likely to persist in college, whereas at the private-nonsectarian institution, the student's interest in pursuing a career either as a college professor or as a performing artist is increased. Protestant institutions, which account for nearly half of the entire private group, have no distinctive pattern of environmental effects on the students—a somewhat surprising finding, in view of the many unique features of their educational environments (Astin, 1968a).

Sex

Both men and women are more likely to drop out of college if they attend a coeducational institution. This finding is consistent with an earlier study (Astin, 1964), which indicated that highly able women students were more likely to drop out of college if they attended an institution with a relatively large percentage of men in the student body. The largest single environmental effect observed among the noncoeducational institutions occurs in the men's colleges (technological institutions excepted) which tend to steer students out of potential careers in engineering and physical science and into careers in law. Women's colleges do not show many pronounced effects on the various student outcomes, except for a slight tendency to channel students out of education and teaching and into the natural sciences. Colleges for men and colleges for women both have a slight tendency to stimulate the student's interest in majoring in arts and humanities and in attending graduate school. Men's institutions, of course, have a pronounced positive effect on the student's interest in obtaining a professional degree.

Race

Although only seven of our 246 institutions were classified as "predominantly Negro" by the U.S. Office of Education in 1961, we considered it important to examine their possible differential effects because of the current widespread interest in these institutions on the part of foundations and governmental agencies. In general, the actual outputs for students attending these institutions were very close to the expected outputs, predicted on the basis of their input characteristics. There was a slight tendency for the predominantly Negro institutions to steer students away from potential careers in the health professions and teaching and into careers in law, biological sciences, and college teaching. Moreover, they increased slightly the student's interest in attending graduate school, although they had no particular effect on his chances of dropping out.

Geographic Region

In order to analyze how the college's location affects the various student outcomes, institutions were divided into four broad regions: Northeast ($N=67$), Southeast ($N=50$), Midwest ($N=95$), and West-and-Southwest ($N=34$). The largest differential effects of geographic region were on the student's educational attainment. Students attending institutions located in in the Northeast, compared with those attending institutions in other regions, are much more likely to complete their baccalaureate degrees and much less likely to drop out during the four years following matriculation. Northeastern institutions also appear to stimulate the student's interest in going to graduate school, in obtaining the Ph.D. degree, and in majoring in the arts and humanities and the social sciences. The only other distinctive pattern of geographical effects was observed at institutions located in the Southeast, which have a slight tendency to steer students away from the arts and humanities, social sciences, teaching, and health professions, and into the fields of physical science, biological science, and medicine. Southeastern institutions also reduce the student's interest in obtaining a Ph.D. degree and increase his interest in obtaining a professional degree.

Since the pattern of environmental effects associated with institutions located in the Northeast is similar to the pattern observed in the noncoeducational institutions, it seems likely that these regional differences are attributable, at least in part, to the relatively high concentration of men's and women's colleges in the Northeastern states and by the relative absence of such institutions in the other three regions.

EFFECTS OF SPECIFIC ENVIRONMENTAL CHARACTERISTICS

In this section, the results of the analyses of differential college effects are summarized separately for certain environmental characteristics of institutions. We have selected only those characteristics which showed consistent effects on the student's educational and career development. It should be recognized that some of the environmental effects observed in particular "types" of institutions may be wholly or in part a consequence of differences among the institutions in some of the characteristics described below.

Selectivity or "Quality." Institutions that are highly selective (i.e., that enroll exceptionally able student bodies) tend to have a positive effect on the student's persistence in college and also on his intention to go to graduate school and to obtain a Ph.D. degree. In addition, the highly selective institution tends to channel students away from majors in education, business, engineering, and physical sciences and away from careers in medicine and teaching; it attracts them into majors in the arts, humanities, and social sciences. A similar, but less pronounced, pattern of effects was observed with respect to a second measure of institutional quality: per student expenditures for educational and general purposes. It is possible that these trends reflect the strong humanistic bias that predominates at many selective institutions.

One of the most unexpected findings of the study is that the student's achievement (as measured by the three Area Tests of the Graduate Record Examination administered during his senior year in college) is neither improved nor impaired by the intellectual level of his classmates or by the level of academic competitiveness or the financial resources of his institution. Similarly, no evidence was obtained to support the common belief that the bright student benefits more than the less able student from exposure to these traditional features of "high-quality" institutions. In general, differences among students in their achievement at the senior level are much more closely linked to variations in ability that existed prior to the students' entrance to college than to *any* characteristic of the undergraduate institutions.

Institutional Size. The pattern of environmental effects associated with institutional size is similar in most respects to the pattern already described for universities. Students are more likely to drop out of college if they attend a relatively large institution. The larger institutions also tend to shift students away from majors and careers in the natural sciences and into careers in business. In general, however, these effects were smaller than those observed for the university, a finding which indicates that the university's effects cannot be accounted for solely by its size.

A variety of specific environmental effects involving a few of the 28 measures of the peer, classroom, administrative, and physical environments of our 246 institutions were also observed. The principal findings are as follows:

Organized Dating. College environments where there is a lot of pre-arranged dating among the students tend to shift students away from careers in biological sciences and college teaching and into careers in business and engineering. Moreover, they have a negative impact on the student's interest in obtaining the Ph.D. degree.

Independence. Colleges where the students manifest a good deal of independence (defined primarily in terms of verbal aggressiveness and proneness toward protests) tend to shift the students away from potential careers in teaching, business, and physical science and into the fields of arts and humanities. These relationships account in large part for the previously mentioned effects of the private institutions (which tend to have highly independent peer environments) and of the teachers colleges (which tend not to have independent peer environments).

Cohesiveness. The cohesiveness of the peer environment (measured primarily in terms of the number of fellow students whom the student regards as close friends) has a pronounced positive effect on persistence in college. By contrast, colleges with relatively incohesive environments have dropout rates that are much higher than was predicted from their student inputs. Attending a college with a cohesive environment also appears to increase the student's interest in pursuing a career as a physical scientist.

Informal Dating. The frequency of informal or casual dating among the students showed a distinctly different pattern of effects from that associated with prearranged or organized dating. In colleges where there is a high frequency of informal dating, the dropout rate is higher than expected, and students tend to shift away from majors and careers in the arts and humanities and engineering and to move toward careers in science and business. The effects of this variable account in part for the effects of the noncoeducational institutions noted earlier, since the students in most men's and women's colleges tend to have very few informal dates (Astin, 1968*a*).

Drinking versus Religiousness. College environments where there is considerable amount of religious activity and little drinking (the two patterns of behavior being polar) tend to shift students away from potential careers in the arts and social sciences and into potential careers in the clergy, medicine, and teaching. Colleges with relatively high rates of drinking and low rates of religious behavior manifest the opposite pattern.

Career Indecision. At colleges high on the factor of Career Indecision (which is defined primarily in terms of the proportion of students who change their majors and careers) student interest in pursuing careers in the non-M.D. health professions and in social sciences is facilitated, but so is dropping out of college.

Student Employment. Colleges in which a relatively large percentage of students work for pay have considerably higher dropout rates than were predicted from their student inputs. Although attrition was the only student outcome associated with this characteristic, the magnitude of the effect was substantial and could not be attributed to any other environmental characteristic.

Administrative Permissiveness. Colleges with relatively permissive or liberal attitudes toward student conduct tend to shift students away from potential careers in medicine and teaching and into careers as college professors, performing artists, and physical scientists. Permissiveness also appears to have a positive impact on the student's interest in obtaining a Ph.D.

IMPLICATIONS FOR POLICY

Readers interested in exploring the full implications of our findings for educational policy should refer to the detailed accounts of these findings in Chapters 2, 3, and 4. The major policy implications of the results can be summarized as follows:

1. In spite of current widespread criticism of higher education, most undergraduates at most institutions are reasonably well satisfied with their college. These findings suggest that any drastic alterations in the character of American higher educational institutions would not necessarily better satisfy the expressed needs of the large majority of undergraduate students.

2. The career fields of engineering and physical science decline markedly in popularity at virtually all colleges and universities during the undergraduate years and will almost certainly continue to do so—and at a faster rate—if existing technological institutions are transformed into complex universities, as some educators have suggested doing. The overall rate of undergraduate defection from these fields would probably be reduced if the technological institutions were to increase their enrollments and, at the same time, maintain their relatively homogeneous curricula.

3. The net loss of potential scientists and engineers during the undergraduate years is attributable chiefly to the failure of the major fields of the physical sciences and engineering to attract defectors from other fields. The comparative lack of curricular barriers (prerequisite courses, early specialization, etc.) in fields such as business and law appears to account, in part, for

their relative success in recruiting defectors. These facts suggest that if special accelerated curricula were established for students recruited into the natural sciences and engineering late in their undergraduate careers, the supply of scientists and engineers might be increased.

4. Since coeducational and women's colleges tend to have a positive effect on the student's interest in pursuing a career as a physical scientist, the strengthening and expansion of undergraduate science programs in such institutions may be one device for increasing the supply of physical scientists.

5. Participation in independent scientific research at the undergraduate level appears to increase the student's chances of authoring a scientific publication and also to stimulate his interest in becoming a college professor and in obtaining the Ph.D. degree. These findings suggest that the supply of productive physical scientists going into college teaching could be increased if more opportunities for participation in research were provided at the undergraduate level.

6. The widespread trend toward converting teachers colleges into liberal arts colleges or universities is likely to reduce the total proportion of undergraduates who end up choosing careers as elementary or secondary school teachers. These results imply that the existing shortage of qualified teachers is likely to worsen with time.

7. Although the major factors that influence the student's chances of dropping out of college are still only dimly understood, it seems clear that the number of dropouts could be substantially reduced if more college students were persuaded to defer their marriage plans until after they have completed their baccalaureate work. In addition to increasing the student's chances of dropping out, getting married while in college also appears to decrease interest in going to graduate school.

8. A given college's dropout rate appears to depend more on the characteristics of its entering students than on the effects of its particular environment. However, there is evidence that dropout rates in some institutions could be reduced if a greater degree of cohesiveness in the student body were achieved.

9. When student input is statistically controlled, the dropout rates of most public institutions are much higher than those of most private institutions. Thus, the growing concentration of students in public institutions may result in an increase in the proportion of dropouts among undergraduate students.

10. Some evidence suggests that awarding a scholarship to a student reduces his chances of dropping out. Neither working during the academic year nor borrowing money from the college appears to affect the student's chances of dropping out or his motivation to attend graduate school.

11. While there may be many economic and educational justifications for coeducation and for the merging of existing men's and women's colleges, it should be recognized that noncoeducational institutions possess many unique and potentially advantageous environmental features which may be

lost if they are converted into coeducational institutions (Astin, 1968a). Our findings suggest, for example, that merging a men's college with a women's women's college would lower the level of academic competitiveness and raise the dropout rates.

12. Contrary to popular belief, the student's scholastic achievement does not seem to be enhanced by his attending an institution with relatively high concentrations of able students and abundant financial resources. These findings suggest that it is important to reexamine some of our traditional notions about institutional quality or "excellence."

13. The student's later intellectual achievement, educational plans, and career choice depends much more on his characteristics and plans at the time of matriculation than on his choice of an undergraduate institution. The implication here is not that his choice of a college is an unimportant factor in his development, but rather that the college environment is of relatively little importance, in comparison to his initial input characteristics, in determining the outcomes considered in this study.

IMPLICATIONS FOR RESEARCH

The major implications of this study for future research in higher education can be summarized as follows:

1. The findings reported in Chapter 4 strongly support the hypothesis that college environments operate so as to produce a greater degree of homogeneity among the students with respect to field of study and career choice. Future research should be conducted to determine whether this "progressive conformity" effect holds true for other student characteristics, including values, beliefs, personal traits, and behavior patterns.

2. A related hypothesis that should be subjected to further empirical tests concerns the significance of environmental homogeneity. Briefly, our findings suggest that the potential of the college environment for effecting significant change in the student is a direct function of its degree of homogeneity (see also Astin, 1963b; Holland, 1962, 1966b).

3. Although dropping out of college was found to be related to several personal and environmental variables, our understanding of the principal causal factors is still very limited. Future studies of college dropouts should employ a wider range of qualitatively different input characteristics and environmental variables. In addition, there is some reason to believe that, for purposes of data analyses, dropouts should be classified on the basis of their principal reasons for dropping out and that separate analyses should be conducted for men and for women.

4. Several questions concerning the role of parental and family background characteristics in affecting the undergraduate's educational and vocational development merit further exploration. Do the religion and occupation of the parents operate as environmental influences during the college years? Are the effects of socioeconomic variables mediated through subtle

motivational differences which were not detected in our freshman input measures?

5. Since most of the environmental effects of our 246 institutions appeared to be mediated through the peer environment rather than the classroom, administrative, or physical environments, further study of the nature and influence of undergraduate peer groups is clearly indicated. At the same time, a greater effort should be devoted to the identification of other effective environmental variables which are more directly manipulatable and not so highly dependent on the characteristics of the entering students.

6. The principal method of analysis employed in this study, whereby input characteristics are first controlled using the student as the unit of analysis, appears to offer a promising approach to the difficult problem of assessing the impact of a college. Thus, a college's influence on a particular student outcome is defined in terms of a discrepancy between its actual outcome and its expected outcome as predicted from its student input. Expressing such discrepancies as percentages based on dichotomous outcomes (e.g., the percentage of students who drop out vs. those who do not) makes it possible to assess the effects of the college on the basis of the actual number of students who are affected (i.e., percentage of actual dropouts either above or below the expected percentage). Using several such discrepancy scores, one could "profile" any institution's pattern of environmental effects, showing the actual numbers (or percentages) of students affected. In a sense, this pattern would represent the "environment" of the college, at least insofar as the particular set of student outcomes is concerned.

7. The environmental "stimulus" factors derived from the Inventory of College Activities appear to account for a substantial proportion of the differential institutional effects on the student's educational attainment and achievement and career plans, although they were relatively ineffectual (in comparison with the Environmental Assessment Technique measures based on the curriculum) in accounting for differential institutional effects on the student's field of study. With the exception of the effects of the technological colleges, the college "trait" measures account for most of the differential effects of various administrative "types" of institutions. These findings suggest that additional research on institutional "traits" is indicated. In particular, it is important to determine how to modify some of the institutional traits that seem to have the greatest impact on the student. In this way, it will eventually be possible for educators to design new institutions or to change existing ones so as to achieve the greatest benefit for the student.

REFERENCE

1. Readers who are interested in summaries of all institutional characteristics which were found to affect particular types of outcomes (e.g., dropping out of college) should consult Chapters 3 and 4.

A

Information Form Filled Out by the Entering Freshmen

FRESHMAN INFORMATION FORM Fall 1961

201274

	7-12

Name: Last / First / Middle — Circle one: Male 1 / Fem. 2 — **13**

Home Address: Number and Street / City / Zone / State — **14**

Size of your high school graduating class (circle one):

Less than 50 (1)	50-99 (2)	100-199 (3)	200-299 (4)	300-399 (5)	400-499 (6)	500-599 (7)	600 + (8)

14

Your high school average (circle one):

D (1)	C (2)	C+ (3)	B- (4)	B (5)	B+ (6)	A- (7)	A (8)	A+ (9)

15

Probable major field in college: — **16-17**

Highest degree planned (circle one):

Less than BA or BS (1)	BA BS (2)	MA MS (3)	PhD EdD (4)	MD DDS (4)	LLB BD (4)	Other: _____ (5)

18

Probable future occupation: — **19-20**

Father's education (circle one):

Grammar school (1)	Some high school (2)	H.S. grad. (3)	Some college (4)	College degree (5)	Post-grad. degree (6)

21

Father's occupation: — **22-23**

Indicate whether you have achieved any of the following by underlining the appropriate words. On the line before any item you underline, indicate the number of times you have achieved it.

First, second, or third place in: ......school science contest; ......regional or state science contest; ......national science contest — **24**

......leads in high school or church sponsored plays; ......first, second, or third in regional or state speech or debate contest; ......first, second, or third in national speech or debate contest — **25**

......elected to one or more student offices; ......elected president of my class; ......received award or special recognition for leadership of any kind — **26**

......participated in *national* music contest; received a rating of "good" or "excellent" in: ......state music contest; ......national music contest — **27**

......won a prize or award in art competition (sculpture, ceramics, painting, etc.); exhibited or performed a work of art (painting, musical composition, sculpture) at: ......my school; ......place other than my school — **28**

......edited school paper or literary magazine; ......had poems, short stories, or articles published in public newspaper or magazine (not school paper) or in state or national high school anthology; ......won literary award or prize for creative writing — **29**

B

Followup Questionnaires (1965)

Dear Student:

You may remember that when you first entered college in 1961 you filled out a brief questionnaire in which you indicated your future educational and career plans. The results of the study based on this questionnaire have recently been published in a small book, Who Goes Where To College? (Science Research Associates of Chicago, 1965).

Now that nearly four years have elapsed since the original study, we would like once again to ask you about your current activities and plans and also to get your impressions of your undergraduate college. The purpose of this follow-up study, which is being supported jointly by the National Science Foundation, the U.S. Office of Education, and the National Institutes of Health, is to examine changes in career plans that occur after the student enters college, and to determine some of the factors that influence students to drop out of college, to take up graduate study, or to pursue a particular type of career.

We should greatly appreciate your completing this booklet and returning it to us in the enclosed envelope. All of the information is to be coded and used in group comparisons for research purposes only, so your responses will be kept entirely confidential.

Since we are following up only a limited sample of students, it is important to secure as complete a response as possible. We hope you will be able to participate.

Thank you for your consideration.

Sincerely yours,

Logan Wilson

Logan Wilson
President

Is your name and address correct?
Please add your zip code and make
any other changes:

Bureau of the Budget No. 99-6503
Expiration Date: June 15, 1966

153

Social Security Number: [ ][ ][ ] [ ][ ] [ ][ ][ ][ ]

If you should move from your current address and we should lose contact with you, is there some person we could contact who would be likely to know of your whereabouts?

Name _____

Street Address _____

City and State _____

HOW TO MARK THIS BOOKLET: This questionnaire will be read by an automatic scanning device. Certain marking requirements are essential to this process. Your careful observance of these few simple rules will be most appreciated.

Use black lead pencil only (#2½ or softer).

Make heavy black marks that fill the circle completely.

Erase cleanly any answer you wish to change.

Do not make any stray marks in this booklet.

EXAMPLE: Will marks made with ball pen, fountain pen or colored pencil be properly read?   Yes ○   No ●

1. Please mark one answer in each column:

	Highest Degree Now Held	Highest Degree Planned
None	○	○
Associate (or equivalent) (A.A., A.S., etc.)	○	○
Bachelor's Degree (A.B., B.A., B.S., etc.)	○	○
Master's Degree (M.A., M.S., etc.)	○	○
Ph.D. or Ed.D.	○	○
M.D., D.D.S., or D.V.M.	○	○
L L.B. or J.D.	○	○
B.D.	○	○
Other _____	○	○

2. When do you expect to obtain your highest degree? (Mark one)

I have already obtained it ○   1968 ○
This year (1965) ○   1969 ○
1966 ○   Later than 1969 ○
1967 ○   Not sure ○

3. What occupation do you plan to pursue as a career? _____

4. What is your current (or most recent) undergraduate major field of study? _____

5a. Answer if male: Have you ever served on full-time active duty in the armed services?   No ○   Yes ... Less than 1 year ○
2 years ○
3 years ○
4 or more ○

5b. Answer if female: In the long run which one of the following do you really prefer and which one do you realistically expect? (Mark one answer in each column)

	Really prefer	Realistically expect
Housewife only	○	○
Housewife with occasional employment	○	○
Housewife for a few years, employment later	○	○
Housewife with regular employment	○	○
Employment only	○	○

6. The following activities cut across a number of jobs. How much of your <u>long-run</u> <u>career</u> work do you expect to devote to each activity? (Mark one for each activity)

	A major amount	A moderate amount	Little or none
Teaching	O	O	O
Research and development	O	O	O
Administration or management	O	O	O
Service to patients or clients	O	O	O

7. After completing your studies, which of the following do you expect as your <u>first</u> employer? As your long-run future employer? (If you are still a student, answer in terms of your expectations after you complete your studies.) (Mark one in each column)

		First Employer	Long-run Career Employer
Government:	Federal	O	O
	State and local	O	O
Education:	Elementary & secondary	O	O
	Higher education	O	O
Other non-profit organizations:	Hospitals, clinics	O	O
	Social welfare	O	O
	Church	O	O
	Other non-profit organization	O	O
Business and services:	Self-employed, or family business	O	O
	Private company	O	O
	Professional partnership	O	O
	Research	O	O
Other (Mark and specify) _____		O	O

8. Please account for your activities since entering college in 1961 by marking all activities that apply in each column below. (Please mark at least one in each column)

	Academic Year 1961-62	Summer 1962	Academic Year 1962-63	Summer 1963	Academic Year 1963-64	Summer 1964	Academic Year 1964-65	Summer 1965	Academic Year 1965-66
Full time student:									
for the entire period	O	O	O	O	O	O	O	O	O
for part of the period	O	O	O	O	O	O	O	O	O
Part time student:									
for the entire period	O	O	O	O	O	O	O	O	O
for part of the period	O	O	O	O	O	O	O	O	O
Employed:									
in career-related job	O	O	O	O	O	O	O	O	O
in non-career-related job	O	O	O	O	O	O	O	O	O
Housewife:	O	O	O	O	O	O	O	O	O
<u>Other</u> (vacation, illness, etc.)	O	O	O	O	O	O	O	O	O

9. Where have you lived since entering college in 1961 (exclude vacations; if you lived several places during any year, indicate the place you lived the majority of the time.) (Mark one in each column)

Year –	1961-62	1962-63	1963-64	1964-65
With parents	O	O	O	O
Other private home, apartment or room	O	O	O	O
College dormitory	O	O	O	O
Fraternity or sorority house	O	O	O	O
Other student housing	O	O	O	O
Other (mark and specify) _____	O	O	O	O

10. In what college did you <u>first</u> enroll (Fall of 1961)?

    Name of college _____

    Located in _____
                            City   State

11. Since entering this college, have you changed institutions or dropped out of college for any period of time? (Exclude graduation and summer vacations) (Mark one):

    No ⬜ .... If <u>No</u>, skip to item 17 on the next page.
    Yes ⬜ .... If <u>Yes</u>, please answer the questions below:

12. Under what conditions did you leave your first institution? (Mark one)

    I was asked to leave because of unsatisfactory academic work
    (mark and skip to item 15) .... ⬜
    I was asked to leave for disciplinary reasons (mark and skip
    to item 15) .... ⬜
    I left college voluntarily .... ⬜

13. In deciding to leave your first college, indicate the importance for you of each of the following factors (mark one in each row):

	A <u>major</u> reason for my decision	A <u>minor</u> reason for my decision	Unrelated to my decision
I had changed my career plans	⬜	⬜	⬜
I was dissatisfied with the environment of the college	⬜	⬜	⬜
My scholarship was terminated	⬜	⬜	⬜
I wanted time to reconsider my interests and career goals	⬜	⬜	⬜
Marriage	⬜	⬜	⬜
Pregnancy	⬜	⬜	⬜
I was tired of being a student	⬜	⬜	⬜
I could not afford the cost of further education	⬜	⬜	⬜
My academic record was unsatisfactory	⬜	⬜	⬜
I was drafted	⬜	⬜	⬜

14. If you had had greater financial resources at your disposal, would you have left this college anyway? (Mark one)

    Yes .... ⬜   No .... ⬜   Not sure .... ⬜

15. Have you attended any other undergraduate institutions since 1961? (Mark one)

    No (mark and skip to item #17) .... ⬜
    Yes, one other institution .... ⬜
    Yes, two other institutions .... ⬜
    Yes, three or more other institutions .... ⬜

16. What is the name of your <u>current</u> (or most recently attended) undergraduate institution?

    Name _____

    Located in _____
                            City   State

YOUR UNDERGRADUATE INSTITUTION

17. Note: If you did not attend college during the past academic year (1964-65) skip to question 30 on page 8.

Which of the following experiences applies to you during the past year? (Mark either "yes" or "no" for each item.)

	Yes	No
Elected to a student office	O	O
Played on a varsity athletic team	O	O
Changed your long-term career plans	O	O
Flunked a course	O	O
Changed your major field	O	O
Fell in love	O	O
Got married	O	O
Had a lead in a college play	O	O
Wrote an article for the school paper or magazine	O	O

18. Of which of the following college organizations were you a member during the past year?

	Active Member	Inactive Member	Not a Member
National Social Fraternity or Sorority	O	O	O
Local Social Fraternity or Sorority	O	O	O
Intramural athletic team	O	O	O
College athletic team	O	O	O
Choir or glee club	O	O	O
Marching band	O	O	O
Honorary (subject matter) Fraternity	O	O	O

19. Below is a list of things that college students sometimes do. Indicate which of these things you did during the past year in college. (Exclude things which you did only while on vacation.) If you engaged in an activity regularly with a frequency appropriate for that activity, mark the circle under "frequently." If you engaged in an activity one or more times, but not frequently, mark the circle under "occasionally." Mark under "not at all" if you never performed the activity. (Mark one for each item)

Columns: Frequently / Occasionally / Not at all

	Freq	Occ	Not
Stayed up all night	O	O	O
Came late to class	O	O	O
Prayed (not including grace before meals)	O	O	O
Listened to New Orlean's (Dixieland) Jazz	O	O	O
Gambled with cards or dice	O	O	O
Lost privileges for infraction of college rules	O	O	O
Played a musical instrument	O	O	O
Took a nap or rest during the day			
Drove a car	O	O	O
Discussed sex with friends	O	O	O
Drank beer	O	O	O
Voted in a student election	O	O	O
Studied in the library	O	O	O
Attended a ballet performance	O	O	O
Overslept and missed a class or appointment	O	O	O
Had a blind date	O	O	O
Drank in a bar or club	O	O	O
Attended church	O	O	O
Participated in informal group singing	O	O	O
Cheated on examinations	O	O	O

	Freq	Occ	Not
Became intoxicated	O	O	O
Drank wine	O	O	O
Went to the movies	O	O	O
Discussed how to make money with other students	O	O	O
Listened to folk music	O	O	O
Attended a public recital or concert	O	O	O
Made wisecracks in class	O	O	O
Arranged a date for another student	O	O	O
Went to an overnight or week-end party	O	O	O
Took weight-reducing or dietary formula	O	O	O
Argued with other students	O	O	O
Been interviewed as a client in the college counseling center	O	O	O
Called a teacher by his first name	O	O	O
Checked out a book or journal from the college library	O	O	O
Tried on clothes in a store without buying anything	O	O	O
Asked questions in class	O	O	O

20. What was the frequency of your dates during the past year? Indicate the average number of dates of each type that you had per month. If less than one every two months, mark "none". (If married, indicate the number of times you and your spouse went out together to these events.)

	Average Number Per Month					
	None	1	2 to 3	4 to 5	6 to 9	10 or more
Casual coke, coffee or study dates	○	○	○	○	○	○
Informal dates to movies, student gatherings, etc.	○	○	○	○	○	○
Formal dates to dances and big parties	○	○	○	○	○	○

21. Description of One of Your Classes:
Name below the course you took this past year which was most closely related to your primary field of interest.

_____
Name of Course

_____
Department   Time at which class met

What was the academic rank of the teacher? (Mark one)

Instructor ○   Assistant professor ○   Associate professor ○

Full professor ○   Lecturer (or other) ○

22. Approximate number of students in class: (Mark one)

14 or less ○   25 – 29 ○   40 – 44 ○

15 – 19 ○   30 – 34 ○   45 – 49 ○

20 – 24 ○   35 – 39 ○   50 or more ○

23. Number of class sessions per week. (Mark one)

One ○   Two ○   Three ○   Four or more ○

24. Please mark "yes" for all the following statements which apply to this course. Mark "no" if the statement does not apply. (If the course had a lab portion, mark "yes" only for those items which apply to the lecture portion.)

	Yes No		Yes No
The class met only at a regularly scheduled time and place	○○	Students had assigned seating	○○
The instructor had a good sense of humor	○○	Attendance was usually taken every day	○○
The instructor was often sarcastic in class	○○	The instructor spoke in a monotone	○○
Students were permitted to smoke in class	○○	The instructor was often dull	○○
The class was taught by a graduate student	○○	The instructor knew me by name	○○
The lectures followed the text book closely	○○	The instructor was engaged in research of some kind	○○
The instructor was a woman	○○		
The instructor called students by their first name	○○	We sometimes had unannounced or "pop" quizzes	○○
The instructor encouraged a lot of class discussion	○○	The examinations were usually of the "objective" type (multiple choice, matching, etc.) rather than the "essay" type	○○
The instructor was exceptionally well-grounded in the course subject matter	○○		
The instructor outlined the day's lecture or discussion at the beginning of each class	○○	I almost never spoke in class unless I was called on	○○
		If he had wanted, a student could probably have passed this course mainly on "bluff"	○○
I sometimes argued openly with the instructor	○○		
I took notes regularly in class	○○	I sometimes argued openly with other students in the class	○○
I usually typed my written assignments	○○	I knew the instructor's first name	○○
I was in the instructor's office one or more times	○○	I knew which institution awarded the instructor his degree	○○
I was a guest in the instructor's home one or more times	○○	I usually did all of the assigned reading in this course	○○
The instructor was enthusiastic	○○		

25. Impressions of Your Undergraduate College: Answer each of the following as it applies to your
     college (the one attended during the past year)

	Yes	No
The students are under a great deal of pressure to get high grades	○	○
The student body is apathetic and has little "school spirit"	○	○
Most of the students are of a very high calibre academically	○	○
There is a keen competition among most of the students for high grades	○	○
Freshmen have to take orders from upperclassmen for a period of time	○	○
There isn't much to do except go to class and study	○	○
I felt "lost" when I first came to the campus	○	○
Being in this college builds poise and maturity	○	○
Athletics are overemphasized	○	○
The classes are usually run in a very informal manner	○	○
Most students are more like "numbers in a book"	○	○

26. How many students did you call
     by their first names or by nickname?
     (Estimate this as best you can)

	5 or less	6-10	11-20	21-50	51-100	101-200	More
	○	○	○	○	○	○	○

     How many of these students did you
     consider close friends?

	5 or less	6-10	11-20	21-50	51-100	101-200	More
	○	○	○	○	○	○	○

27. To what extent does each of the following describe the psychological climate or atmosphere at
     this college? (Mark one column for each)

	Very Descriptive	In-Between	Not at all Descriptive
Intellectual	○	○	○
Snobbish	○	○	○
Social	○	○	○
Victorian	○	○	○
Practical-minded	○	○	○
Warm	○	○	○
Realistic	○	○	○
Liberal	○	○	○

28. What is your over-all evaluation of this institution? (Mark one)

Very satisfied with my college	○
Satisfied with my college	○
On the fence	○
Dissatisfied with my college	○
Very dissatisfied with my college	○

9. All in all, in terms of your own needs and desires, how much of the following did you receive
    during the past year? (Mark the appropriate column after each item)

	Too much or Too many	Just about the right amount	Not enough
Freedom in course selection	○	○	○
Social life	○	○	○
Personal contacts with classmates	○	○	○
Work required of you in courses	○	○	○
Outlets for creative activities	○	○	○
Sleep	○	○	○
Exercise	○	○	○
Personal contacts with faculty	○	○	○
Personal contacts with family	○	○	○
Advice and guidance from faculty and staff	○	○	○

RECENT AND CURRENT ACTIVITIES

30. Since the Fall of 1961 how many <u>years</u> of undergraduate and graduate education have you completed? (Try to convert any part-time attendance into full-time equivalents):

Less than one term (quarter, semester, trimester) .... O
Less than one year .... O
One year (but less than two) .... O
Two years (but less than three) .... O
Three years (but less than four) .... O
Four years (or more) .... O

31. How have you financed your college and living expenses during your undergraduate years? (Mark
the appropriate percentage in each row below):

		None	1-20%	21-40%	41-60%	61-80%	81-100%
a.	Support from your parents	O	O	O	O	O	O
b.	Support from your spouse	O	O	O	O	O	O
c.	Scholarship or fellowship from:						
	your college	O	O	O	O	O	O
	state or local government	O	O	O	O	O	O
	Federal government	O	O	O	O	O	O
d.	Earnings from your own employment	O	O	O	O	O	O
e.	Loans:						
	from the Federal government	O	O	O	O	O	O
	from your state or local government	O	O	O	O	O	O
	from your college	O	O	O	O	O	O
	commercial	O	O	O	O	O	O
	other	O	O	O	O	O	O
f.	Other sources (savings, etc.)	O	O	O	O	O	O

32. How much money have you earned from <u>summer work</u> since entering college? (Mark one response
in each row)

	None	$1-99	$100-199	$200-299	$300-499	$500-599	$600-699	$700-999	$10 or m
Summer 1962	O	O	O	O	O	O	O	O	O
Summer 1963	O	O	O	O	O	O	O	O	O
Summer 1964	O	O	O	O	O	O	O	O	O
Summer 1965	O	O	O	O	O	O	O	O	O

33. Estimate your average undergraduate grade (or grade point average) so far: (Mark one)

	Over-all	In major subject
3.75 — 4.00 (A or A+)	O	O
3.25 — 3.74 (A- or B+)	O	O
2.75 — 3.24 (B)	O	O
2.25 — 2.74 (B- or C+)	O	O
1.75 — 2.24 (C)	O	O
1.25 — 1.74 (C- or D+)	O	O
Less than 1.25 (D or less)	O	O

34. Do you plan to enroll (or are you enrolled) in graduate or professional school?

Yes, immediately after completing college
  (mark and skip to #35 on the next page) .... O
Yes, but not immediately after college .... O
Not sure .... O
No (mark and skip to #45 on page 10) .... O

Which of the following factors <u>best</u> describes your reason for not enrolling in graduate or professional school right away? (Mark only one)

Lack of finances .... ○
Decided to work, because of attractive job offer .... ○
Marriage or family responsibilities .... ○
Lack of necessary undergraduate course requirements .... ○
Not accepted in graduate school .... ○
Faculty advised against it .... ○

35. When will you enroll in graduate or professional school? (Mark one)

I am already enrolled .... ○
This year (1965) .... ○
Next year (1966) .... ○
Not sure when (mark and skip to #45)on the next page .... ○

36. To begin with, will you attend (or are you attending) graduate or professional school on a (mark one):

   Full time basis? .... ○   Part time basis? .... ○   Not sure ...... ○

37. To how many graduate institutions did you apply for admission, and how many acceptances did you receive?

	None	One	Two	Three	Four	5 or more
Number of graduate institutions applied to	○	○	○	○	○	○
Number of acceptances	○	○	○	○	○	○

38. Where do you plan to attend (or are you attending) graduate or professional school?

Name of Institution _____

Located in _____   _____
                          City   State

39. In what department or school will (or did) you enroll? _____

                                        _____
                                        Graduate Field of Study

40. Is the above your (mark one):

   First choice institution? .... ○   Second choice institution? .... ○
            Less than second choice institution? .... ○

41. <u>For Medical Students Only:</u> Which of the following best describes the kind of practice you expect to have after you complete your training? (Mark one)

Individual practice .... ○
Group practice .... ○
Clinic or hospital practice, on salary .... ○
Salaried practice for an institution or industry .... ○
Other (mark and specify) _____ .... ○

How large a part do you think formal research will play in your practice? (Mark one)

A major part .... ○
Some part, but not a major part .... ○
No part at all .... ○

42. Have you applied for or received any financial assistance (fellowships, assistantships, etc.) for your graduate or professional education? (Mark one)

   Yes ...... ○   No (mark and skip to item #45 on the next page .... ○

43. Mark all that apply below:

Source of Stipend	Applied for (or was nominated)	Award not offered	Award offered & accepted	I refuse
I. Federal Government				
A. Atomic Energy Commission	O	O	O	O
B. Department of Defense	O	O	O	O
C. National Science Foundation	O	O	O	O
D. Veterans Administration	O	O	O	O
E. National Aeronautics and Space Administration	O	O	O	O
F. U. S. Office of Education:				
National Defense Education Act	O	O	O	O
Other Office of Education	O	O	O	O
G. U.S. Public Health Service	O	O	O	O
N.I.H. Fellowship Program	O	O	O	O
N.I.H. Training Grant and Traineeship Program	O	O	O	O
Other Public Health Service	O	O	O	O
H. Other Federal Government	O	O	O	O
II. Woodrow Wilson National Fellowship	O	O	O	O
III. Other private source	O	O	O	O
IV. Directly from the school that I am (or will be) attending	O	O	O	O
V. Other	O	O	O	O

44. Which of the following best describes the type of stipend that you now hold? (Mark one)
   Teaching Assistantship ... O
   Research Assistantship ... O
   Work free stipend (equal to or less than tuition) ... O
   Work free stipend (tuition plus cash grant) ... O
   No stipend awarded ... O

45. In an average day during the past year, how much time did you spend in each of the following activities?

	Average number of hours per day
	0 1 2 3 4 5 6 7 8 9 10(+
Studying for class assignments ("zero" if not enrolled during the past year)	O O O O O O O O O O O
Reading for pleasure	O O O O O O O O O O O
Sleeping	O O O O O O O O O O O
Attending movies or plays	O O O O O O O O O O O
Playing games (cards, chess, etc.)	O O O O O O O O O O O
Domestic duties (including child care)	O O O O O O O O O O O

46. Since entering college in 1961, which of the following applies to you? (Mark "yes" or "no" for each):

	Yes	No
Participated in the Undergraduate Research Participation (URP) program sponsored by the National Science Foundation	O	O

   If "yes", please indicate when you participated:

   from _____ to _____
   Month   Year   Month   Year

	Yes	No
Been placed on academic probation	O	O
Assisted on a professor's research project	O	O
Worked on an independent research project	O	O
Been elected to "Who's Who in American Colleges"	O	O
Been elected to Phi Beta Kappa (or comparable academic honorary society)	O	O
Graduated (or expect to graduate) with honors	O	O
Served as a laboratory assistant	O	O
Participated in departmental honors program	O	O
Participated in general honors program	O	O
Was author or co-author of an article in a scientific publication	O	O
Was author or co-author of an article in other scholarly or literary publication	O	O

Dear Student:

 A few weeks ago we sent you a research questionnaire as part of a follow-up study of students who entered college in 1961. If you have already completed and returned the form, please accept our thanks for your cooperation.

 If you have not yet had a chance to return the completed form, we hope that you will be able to do so as soon as possible. If you do not feel that you will have the time to complete the form, we would appreciate your completing the attached postcard and dropping it in the mail box. These few items of information are vital to the validity of our research effort.

 Your cooperation is greatly appreciated,

Sincerely yours,

Logan Wilson   PRESIDENT

FOLLOW-UP INFORMATION FORM B

SOCIAL SECURITY NUMBER: ☐☐☐ ☐☐ ☐☐☐☐

	Less than one term	Less than one year	One year	Two years	Three years	Four (or more) years
Years of undergraduate and graduate education completed since Fall, 1961 (Circle one):	1	2	3	4	5	6

Highest degree now held (Circle one):	None	AA AS	BA BS	MA MS	PhD EdD	MD DDS	LLB JD	BD	Other
	1	2	3	4	5	6	7	8	9
Highest degree planned (Circle one):	1	2	3	4	5	6	7	8	9

Current or most recent undergraduate major field: ___

	A	A- B+	B	B- C+	C	C- D+	D or less
Undergraduate grade point average (Circle one):	1	2	3	4	5	6	7
Grade point average in undergraduate major field (Circle one):	1	2	3	4	5	6	7

Planned career occupation: ___

Note: If your name and address is incorrect, please make any necessary changes in the return address portion of this postcard.

C

A Preliminary Evaluation of the Undergraduate Research Participation Program of the National Science Foundation

FOR THE PAST TEN YEARS, the National Science Foundation (NSF) has been conducting a program designed to provide promising undergraduate students majoring in science with increased opportunities for independent research and study. Since its initiation in 1959, this Undergraduate Research Participation (URP) program has involved more than 30,000 undergraduate students and has cost over 42 million dollars. According to a recent NSF brochure, the principal aim of the program is to provide the undergraduate student with "relatively individualized experiences in scientific investigation comparable in intensity and as nearly as possible, in level of sophistication, with those which form the heart of graduate study." Applications for project support under the URP program, which are reviewed by committees appointed by NSF, are usually prepared by the professor who would have the principal responsibility for supervising the research experience. Although the program is not restricted to upperclassmen, most of the students participate some time during their last two academic years or during the summer following their junior year.

The purpose of this appendix is to present some preliminary findings concerning two aspects of the URP program: (1) the characteristics of the undergraduate students who are selected to participate, and (2) the possible effects of the program on the student's career plans and professional development.

METHOD

Data bearing on the URP program were obtained from the followup questionnaire administered in 1965 (see Chapter 1, pp. 5–6). Each student was asked to indicate whether he had participated in the URP program as an undergraduate. The responses indicated that 860 students, representing approximately 2.8 percent of all the respondents, had taken part in the program, most of them during the summer following their junior year, with the late part of the third or the early part of the fourth undergraduate years being the next most frequent times. The proportion of men who participated (2.8 percent) was only slightly greater than the proportion of women (2.7 percent).

URP participants in the subsample of 3,821 subjects (see Chapter 1, p. 14) numbered 110, or approximately 2.9 percent of the total subsample. Our first step in analyzing the data was to determine what freshman input characteristics predicted participation in the URP program. This analysis had two purposes. First, a description of the participants is useful in assessing how successful the program is in reaching the more promising students. Second, before attempting to evaluate the program's effects on the student's subsequent aspirations and achievements (as revealed by the followup survey), one must make appropriate statistical adjustments to compensate for the biases that operate

NOTE: An expanded version of this appendix appears as an article in the *Journal of Educational Research*, 1969, 62, 219–21.

TABLE C1
The Prediction of Participation in the URP Program from
Freshman Input Data (1961)

$(N = 3,821$ students)

INPUT CHARACTERISTIC	ZERO-ORDER r^a WITH PARTICIPATION	STEPWISE REGRESSION ANALYSIS		
		Step	R	F-ratio Associated with Beta Weight at Final Step
Completed four years of college[b]	.079	1	.079	11.27***
Average grade in high school—A+	.104***	2	.129	22.62***
Probable major—physical science	.084***	3	.149	20.30***
Probable major—mathematics	.060***	4	.161	12.85***
Placed in a regional science contest	.078***	5	.171	12.58***
Career choice—physical or speech therapist	.057***	6	.179	11.45***
Father's occupation—business executive	.041**	7	.185	8.25**
Parents' religion—Jewish	.057***	8	.190	6.70**
Average grade in high school—B	−.055***	9	.195	7.36**
Plans to obtain Ph.D.	.075***	10	.198	4.84*
Probable major—biological science	.028	11	.200	4.16*
Career choice—physical scientist	.058***			
Average grade in high school—A	.050**			
Sex—male	.047**			
Career choice—physician	.045**			
Plans to obtain only B.A. degree	−.041*			
Career choice—college professor	.036*			
Father's education—college graduate	.036*			
Probable major—education	−.035*			
Placed in a high school science contest	.034*			
High school class size—500+	.034*			

[a] Since all variables were scored as dichotomies, coefficients are really *phi's*.
[b] This variable, though not an input characteristic, was forced into regression at the first step.
* $p < .05$.   ** $p < .01$.   *** $p < .001$.

in selecting participants. Unless such adjustments are made, any observed relationships between URP participation and the student's subsequent career development could be attributable to selection biases rather than to the influence of the program itself. Thus, if the program recruits the more highly able students, the subsequent performance of the participant will tend to be superior to the performance of the nonparticipant, even if the program itself has no impact on the student's development.

To determine which of 85 student input variables predict URP participation, a stepwise linear multiple regression analysis was used, in which independent variables were entered into the regression equation until no additional variable was capable of producing a reduction in the residual sum of squares which exceeded $p = .05$. Before the independent variables were permitted to enter, however, another dichotomous variable —whether the student had completed at least four academic years since 1961—was entered into the regression equation. Our purpose was to adjust for any bias caused by students' dropping out of college before they had an opportunity to participate in the URP program. Without such an adjustment, the input correlates of leaving college before the junior year (when students normally become eligible to participate) would tend to be correlated (negatively) with URP participation, even if such correlates were unrelated to the actual selection of participants among enrolled students.

Table C1 shows the results of the stepwise regression analyses. The input variables that had statistically significant zero-order correlations with the URP participation are listed in the first column, in the order in which they entered the regression equation (second column). The third column shows the size of the multiple correlation coefficient (R) at each step in the analysis. Although nineteen student input variables are correlated significantly with URP participation, only nine of them (and one additional input variable whose zero-order correlation was nonsignificant) entered the multiple regression equation. The last column in Table C1 shows the F-ratios that were associated with each regression weight at the *final* (eleventh) step in the analysis. These ratios reflect the unique contribution that each variable makes in predicting URP participation.

These data indicate that URP participants, as compared with nonparticipants who completed four years of college, had high grades in high school and were likely to be planning to major in the physical sciences, mathematics, or the biological sciences when they entered college. URP participants were also more likely than were nonparticipants to have placed (first, second, or third) in a regional or state science contest during high school and to plan to obtain the Ph.D. degree. They were also more apt to be of Jewish parentage and to have fathers who were business executives. A somewhat unusual finding is that the URP participants were more likely as entering freshmen to be planning careers as physical therapists or as speech therapists. Although the last 10 variables shown in the first column of Table C1 had significant zero-order correlations with URP participation, they did not enter the regression equation during the stepwise analysis. This finding indicates simply that their contribution to URP participation can be accounted for by the contribution of the 10 variables that did enter the equation. In this sense, they are redundant with the prior 10 variables.

Although a substantial number of student input variables entered into the multiple regression analysis, one additional check was made to determine the extent to which participants and nonparticipants were equated. This additional analysis involved the students' scores on the National Merit Scholarship Qualifying Test (NMSQT), a test of academic ability and achievement taken during the junior year in high school. Test scores were available on a subsample of 1,590 of the 3,821 students. The partial correlations between URP participation and each of the five NMSQT subtests, holding constant the variables shown in Table C1, are given in Table C2. One of the NMSQT subtests, mathematics, does have a highly significant partial correlation with URP participation, a finding which indicates that the stepwise analysis shown in Table C1 did not fully equate the participants with the nonparticipants in terms of their average academic ability. The partial correlation of .044 between URP participation and the Natural Science Reading subtest, although not statistically significant, also suggests that the groups were not equated.

In view of these findings, we decided to limit our examination of the effects of URP

TABLE C2
URP Participation as a Function of Academic Ability[a]
($N = 1,590$ students)

National Merit Scholarship Qualifying Test	Partial Correlation with URP Participation
Mathematics	.076*
Natural Science Reading	.044
Social Science Reading	.018
English	− .003
Word Usage	− .009

[a] In this analysis, the effects of the freshman input characteristics listed in Table 1 and the effects of completing four years of college were held constant.
* $p < .01$.

participation to the subsample of 1,590 students for whom NMSQT scores were available.

Student Outcome Variables

The information provided by the student in the 1965 followup questionnaire was used to construct several measures of outcomes that seemed apposite to the purposes of the URP program. Perhaps the most relevant outcome variable, in the light of both the program's immediate objectives and the participant's long-range career development, concerns scholarly achievement. In the followup questionnaire, the student was asked whether during the previous year he had been either the author or the co-author of an article in a scientific publication. He was also asked to indicate his current career choice, his plans about going or not going to graduate school, the highest degree he was seeking, and his final undergraduate major field of study.

The possible effects of the URP program were estimated in a four-step analysis, the results of which are shown in Table C3. The first column of coefficients shows the correlations between URP participation and seven different outcome criteria, holding constant the effects of the 1961 student input characteristics and completion of four years of college. The second column of coefficients shows the same partial correlations, but with the five subtests of the NMSQT also held constant. The last two columns of data show the results of the analysis under increasingly stringent conditions of control. Some additional word of explanation about these last two stages of the analysis may be in order before we proceed to a discussion of the substantive findings.

As we have already indicated, the principal methodological problem in attempting to assess the impact of the URP program is that participants may not be fully equated with nonparticipants on all relevant variables that bias their being selected for the program. After student input variables, including scores on the NMSQT, were controlled, the student's career choice at the time of graduation and his final major field as an undergraduate had highly significant partial correlations with URP participation. Although these findings could be taken as evidence that URP participation encourages the student to stay in the field of science and to pursue a career as a scientist, they could also be interpreted as an indication that we had not adequately equated the students on two important input variables *at the time of selection into the URP program*. Thus, although we had controlled for initial career choice and initial major field of study, it is possible that students who changed their major fields or career choices subsequent to entering college, but prior to their junior year, may, as a result of these changes, have altered their eligibility to participate in the program. In order to explore the possible effects of these two sources of potential bias, we performed the additional analyses shown in the third and fourth columns of Table C3, where the student's current (1965) career choice of physical scientist and final major field of study (physical science or arts and humanities) are also controlled.

The first column of coefficients in Table C3 suggests that participating in the URP program increased the student's chances of being the author or co-author of a published scientific article. It also appears that participation in the program increased his interest in becoming a college professor and in obtaining a Ph.D. degree. Participation in the program did not, however, seem to have a significant effect on his intentions of going to graduate school *per se* (i.e., pursuing a master's, doctorate, or professional degree). As we have already indicated, participation in the URP program was positively associated both with majoring in physical science and with planning a career as a physical scientist four years after entering college, and it was negatively associated with majoring in some field of the arts or humanities four years after entering college.

A comparison of the coefficients in the first two columns of Table C3 makes it clear that controlling for the differential academic abilities of participants and nonpartici-

TABLE C3

Partial Correlations between Participation in the URP Program and Various Outcomes (1965)

($N = 1,590$ students)

OUTCOME	(1) Freshmen Input Characteristics and Completion of Four Years of College[a]	CORRELATION WITH URP PARTICIPATION AFTER CONTROL OF:		
		(2) (1) and Academic Ability (NMSQT)	(3) (1), (2), and Career Choice of Physical Scientist (1965)	(4) (1), (2), (3), and Final Major Field
Was author or co-author of article in a scientific publication	.112***	.112****	.106***	.103***
Career choice—college professor	.112***	.114***	.086***	.092***
Plans to obtain Ph.D. degree	.081**	.080**	.057*	.058*
Plans to go to graduate school	.029	.030	.026	.029
Career choice—physical scientist	.154***	.151***	—	—
Final major field—arts and humanities	−.079**	−.072**	−.059*	—
Final major field—physical science	.097***	.089***	.019	—

[a] From Table C1.

* $p < .05$.   ** $p < .01$.   *** $p < .001$.

pants had little effect on the relationships between URP participation and the various outcome variables. The third column of coefficients indicates that controlling for the final career choice of physical scientist reduced the apparent effect of URP participation on final major field of study. This finding is perhaps predictable, since choice of a major field and choice of a career in any point in time are obviously interdependent. The final column of coefficients in Table C3 indicates that the additional control of final major field of study had little effect on the relationship between URP participation and the other outcome variables.

DISCUSSION

These findings lend support to the assumption that participating in a program of independent research and study at the undergraduate level facilitates the early development of scholarly productivity among potential scientists. In addition, such participation seems to increase the student's interest in becoming a college professor and in pursuing the Ph.D. degree. Perhaps these interests are stimulated because the student, in the process of taking an active part in his professor's research activity, comes to identify more and more with the role of professor. The evidence also suggests that participating in the URP program encourages the student to choose a career in physical science and to major in science rather than in the arts and humanities, but these outcome variables could very well be artifactually related to URP participation because of changes in the students' field of study that may have occurred prior to their being considered for the program.

The results of the regression analysis using student input variables indicate clearly that students who are selected as program participants are superior to students who are not selected, both in their past academic achievement and in their measured academic ability in mathematics.

Although these findings indicate that the URP program tends to have a generally favorable influence on the achievement and career plans of its participants, one should remember that the possibility remains that these apparent "effects" were mediated by other selection biases not considered in the analysis. Ideally, it would be desirable to replicate these findings by first identifying all those students eligible to participate in the URP program and then randomly selecting certain students from this group and rejecting others. Since randomized experimentation of this type is not administratively feasible, the second best methodological approach would be to identify all candidates eligible for the program *at the time of selection*. Those who are rejected or who decline would thus constitute a crude control group that could be compared with the URP participants by means of longitudinal studies. Such studies would be especially valuable if a broader range of student outcomes were considered and if the student's professional and scholarly development were followed over a longer period of time.

D

An Analysis of the Effectiveness of Different Followup Techniques

TO EXPLORE THE EFFECTIVENESS of different mail followup techniques and to determine the extent of response bias, a random sample of 665 subjects was drawn from a final pool of 23,673 hard-core nonrespondents (i.e., subjects who failed to complete either the long or the short form of the questionnaire mailed out in 1965). The 665 subjects were randomly assigned to one of twelve treatment cells defined by a $2 \times 2 \times 3$ design. The effects of the following variables were studied: type of cover letter (autotyped with a personalized greeting and signature versus mimeographed with an impersonal greeting and signature); type of outgoing postage ("live" stamp versus metered stamp); and class of outgoing mail (certified, special delivery, and first class). In addition, the cost per subject contacted[1] and the cost per respondent were computed for treatment cell. Cost per treatment was regarded as including charges for postage, materials, special handling (for example, autotyping and personalized signature), and clerical costs on the basis of man-hours estimated at the rate of $1.25 an hour. Finally, the bias operating on the items of information obtained from the subjects in each treatment cell was tested.

RESULTS

The design and some of the results of the study are shown in Table D1. In brief, the percentage of respondents by treatment varied from 18 percent to 79.4 percent and the cost per respondent varied from $1.60 to $3.38. The autotyped-live stamp-special delivery method (cell E) yielded the lowest cost per respondent ($1.60) and the highest percentage of returns (79.4 percent). The mineographed-metered stamp-first class method (cell L) yielded the lowest percentage of returns (18 percent); although the cost per subject *contacted* by this method was only $.70, the cost per *return* obtained was $3.16.

A multiple stepwise regression analysis was utilized to test first-order interaction effects. This analysis was accomplished by defining for each subject a "dummy" dependent variable (respondent or nonrespondent) scored "0" or "1," and a vector of "dummy" scores also scored "0" or "1" according to which treatment cell the subject had been assigned across the main effects and their first-order interactions. After the main effects were forced into the regression solution (multiple *phi* coefficients), no significant ($p = .05$) interactions were observed. The main effects significantly associated with obtaining a response and the order in which they entered into the stepwise solution were: certified mail, special delivery, live stamp, and autotyped cover letter. Thus, we can conclude that using first class mail, metered stamps, or mimeographed cover letters reduces the chances of obtaining a response.

A nonorthogonal multivariate analysis of variance was performed to test whether there was any bias among the items of information obtained from the respondents in

---

[1] A subject was assumed to have been contacted if the post office did not return the piece of mail as undeliverable. Although the number of undeliverable questionnaires varied slightly from cell to cell, differences were not significant.

TABLE D1

Design of the Study Showing Number of Students Contacted in Each Cell,
Percentage of Respondents, Cost per Contact, and Cost per Respondent

CLASS OF MAIL	AUTOTYPE (PERSONAL LETTER)		MIMEO (IMPERSONAL LETTER)	
	Live Stamp	Metered Stamp	Live Stamp	Metered Stamp
Cell: (Certified Mail)	A	B	C	D
# students contacted	45	47	44	52
Percentage respondents	66.7	55.3	59.1	50.0
Cost per contact	$1.90	$1.87	$1.60	$1.40
Cost per respondent	$2.80	$3.38	$2.70	$2.80
Cell: (Special Delivery)	E	F	G	H
# students contacted	44	49	43	41
Percentage respondents	79.4	42.9	51.2	45.1
Cost per contact	$1.28	$1.27	$1.00	$1.10
Cost per respondent	$1.60	$2.95	$1.97	$1.95
Cell: (First Class)	I	J	K	L
# students contacted	50	51	50	50
Percentage respondents	34.0	33.4	28.0	18.0
Cost per contact	$0.88	$0.90	$0.60	$0.70
Cost per respondent	$2.59	$2.63	$2.07	$3.16

the various treatment cells. (The variables included: years of college completed in the four-year interval 1961–1965, over-all undergraduate grade point average and grade point average in major field, level of terminal degree obtained, and level of educational aspiration. None of the tests of the main effects and their interaction terms was significant ($p = .05$) among the ten variables included in the analysis.[2] Thus, we can conclude that the *type* of respondent did not vary by treatment, although the cost per respondent and the percentage of respondents varied according to the mail procedures used.

DISCUSSION

The results of this analysis show that the probability of obtaining a response from a mail followup is a function of the methods used. Paradoxically, the cheapest method in terms of cost per respondent also tended to be the best in terms of rate of response. Conversely, the cheapest method in terms of cost per contact tended to be the most expensive in terms of cost per respondent and the least successful in terms of rate of response. However, this study cannot be separated from its context; the subjects were young adults—most of them college trained—selected from a group of hard-core nonrespondents. Also, the form that they finally completed and returned was a short checklist printed on the back of a postcard. While such contextual factors undoubtedly played a part in determining the response in this particular study, the magnitude of the differences suggests that the rate of response in other mail followup studies may be dramatically affected by the techniques used.

The data shown in Table D1 can serve as a rough guide in selecting a followup technique. For example, one can get some idea as to which of the several methods would yield optimal results given such constraints as amount of money available for followups and minimum response needed. If the purpose of a followup of nonrespondents is to in-

[2] Although no significant bias was found among the variables by treatment within the sample of respondents in this study, there was considerable bias in the mean scores on many items between the responses of the early respondents and the responses obtained from the hard-core nonrespondents.

crease the percentage of respondents, then one of the initially more costly methods should be used. On the other hand, if an investigator's main concern is to estimate the nature of the bias among respondents, a less expensive technique may serve as well. Of particular significance, of course, is the final cost per respondent. This study shows that what may appear initially to be the least expensive method, may in fact prove to be both the most expensive and the least satisfactory.

A major problem in interpreting and generalizing from the results of a mail survey is that of determining the degree of bias among respondents. Obviously, it is important to obtain an estimate of this bias and to attempt to correct for it among the returns. The results of this study suggest that an investigator would be well advised to choose one of the relatively less expensive mail techniques for the initial wave of questionnaires and then to select a technique that will assure a high rate of return among nonrespondents in the followup. Not only will this method increase the over-all rate of return, but also it will make possible a more stable estimate of the bias among early respondents.

E

Effects of Controlling Scores on the National Merit Scholarship Qualifying Test and Within-College Environmental Variables

SINCE SCORES ON THE NMSQT were available for only a biased sample representing less than half of the subjects, we performed a series of preliminary analyses to determine if the conclusions concerning environmental effects would be altered substantially if these additional input variables were controlled. These analyses involved the 1,590 students (from the original one-eighth sample of 3,821 subjects) for whom NMSQT scores were available. Each residual outcome variable was regressed on the scores for the five NMSQT subtests and on 12 within-college environmental variables. Correlations between residual outcome scores and college environmental variables prior to the control of these 17 variables were compared with the equivalent partial correlations after control of the 17 variables.

These two sets of correlations are shown in Table E1. The correlations of several of the residual outcome scores with environmental measures were unchanged by these additional controls. Only those outcomes whose correlations were changed are included in the table. The environmental variables shown are those which had correlations of at least .09 with the criteria prior to control of these 17 additional variables.

TABLE E1

Correlations between Selected College Characteristics and Residual Outcome Measures, before and after Control of Five NMSQT Scores and 12 Within-College Environmental Variables

($N = 1,590$ students)

Residual Outcome Measure	X College Characteristics	Correlation Before Control of 17 Variables	Correlation After Control of 17 Variables
Major in arts or humanities	x Enterprising orientation	.10	.08
	x Private-nonsectarian	.09	.06
	x Independence	.09	.07
	x Drinking vs. Religiousness	.09	.06
	x Musical and artistic activity	.09	.05
	x Severe policy against aggression	−.11	−.08
Major in education	x Women's college	−.09	−.09
	x Realistic orientation	.14	.12
	x Social orientation	−.12	−.11
	x Enterprising orientation	−.14	−.14
	x Artistic orientation	−.13	−.10
	x Liberal arts college	−.11	−.10
Major in engineering	x Technological institution	.20	.19
	x Competitiveness vs. Cooperativeness	.10	.07
	x Musical and artistic activity	−.12	−.10
	x Use of the library	−.10	−.09
	x Familiarity with the instructor	−.10	−.10
	x Flexibility of the curriculum	−.09	−.08
Major in physical science	x Per student expenditures	−.09	−.11
	x Liberal arts college	.09	.09
	x Use of automobiles	−.09	−.07
	x Severity of grading	−.11	−.09
	x Familiarity with the instructor	.10	.10
	x Concern for the individual student	.10	.09
	x Spread of the campus	−.09	−.10
	x Severe policy against aggression	−.10	−.08
Career choice of college professor	x University	−.09	−.11
Planning the Ph.D. degree	x Enterprising orientation	−.11	−.11
	x Percentage of men in student body	.09	.07
Planning a professional degree	x Men's college	.10	.08
	x Independence	.10	.07

F

A Comparison of Three Methods of Assessing Differential College Effects

Method A. Weights for predicting each outcome were determined by means of step-wise linear multiple regression analyses in which the *student* ($N = 3,821$) was used as the unit of analysis. These weights were then applied to the input data for all students ($N = 36,405$) to obtain an expected performance on each outcome measure. Residual scores were computed by subtracting expected scores from actual scores. Mean residual scores on each outcome were computed for the students at each institution ($N = 246$) and were used as the dependent variables in the analyses of differential environmental effects.

Method B. Mean scores were computed on each student input variable separately by institution. Stepwise regression analyses were then carried out; in these analyses, the effects of the mean scores were controlled first, after which the environmental variables were permitted to enter the analysis. Note that in this method, the student input was controlled using the institution (rather than the student, as in Method A) as the unit of analysis. In assessing the effects of college environmental variables, however, both methods use the institution as the unit of analysis.

Method C. Residual scores on each outcome served as the dependent variables. Stepwise regression analyses were carried out, using a subsample of 1,590 subjects from the sample of 3,821 in Method A. The students' scores on the five subtests of the National Merit Scholarship Qualifying Test and on the 12 within-college environmental variables were forced into regression first, after which the between-college environmental variables were permitted to enter the analysis.

The results obtained through each of these three methods are shown in Tables F2–F24. At the top of each, the dependent variable is indicated. The 71 environmental variables are listed (in abbreviated form) in three columns. The coefficients are the partial correlations between the dependent variable and the particular environmental variable after the student input variables have been controlled or, in the case of Method C, after the effects of the NMSQT and of the 12 within-college environmental variables on the residual dependent variable have been controlled. Only statistically significant ($p < .05$) coefficients are shown. If a college variable entered the stepwise regression analysis of environmental effects and had a significant ($p < .05$) weight in the final regression solution, it is marked with an asterisk (*). If an environmental variable had a nonsignificant partial correlation with the dependent variable following the control of input variables but ended up in the final regression solution with a significant weight, the sign (plus or minus) of the final regression coefficient is shown in parentheses. Table F1 provides the key to the abbreviations and the order of the variables.

179

TABLE F1
Key to the 71 College Environmental Variables

FIRST COLUMN	SECOND COLUMN	THIRD COLUMN
Characteristics of Entering Class	*Administrative Type Characteristics (continued)*	*Environmental Factors from the Inventory of College Characteristics (continued)*
1. Intellectualism (INTELL)	24. Protestant (PROT)	
2. Estheticism (ESTHET)	25. Roman Catholic (CATH)	48. Regularity of Sleeping Habits (REGSLP)
3. Status (STATUS)	26. Private-Nonsectarian (PNS)	49. Use of the Library (USELIB)
4. Pragmatism (PRAGMA)	27. Predominantly Negro (NEGRO)	50. Conflict with Regulations (CONFLI)
5. Masculinity (MASCUL)	28. Located in Northeastern region (NORTHE)	51. Involvement in the Class (INVOLV)
6. Selectivity (SELECT)	29. Located in Southeastern region (STHEST)	52. Verbal Aggressiveness (VERBAG)
Personal (Curricular) Orientations from the Environmental Assessment Technique	30. Located in North Central region (NOCENT)	53. Extraversion of the Instructor (EXTRAV)
7. Realistic Orientation (EAT 1)	31. Located in West or Southwest region (WSW)	54. Severity of Grading (SEVGRD)
8. Scientific Orientation (EAT 2)	32. Located in town of 500,000 or more (500000)	55. Familiarity with the Instructor (FAMILR)
9. Social Orientation (EAT 3)	33. Located in town of 100,000–500,000 (100000)	56. Rate of Cheating in the Class (CHEATG)
10. Conventional Orientation (EAT 4)	34. Located in suburb of large city (SUBURB)	57. Organization in the Classroom (FORMAL[3])
11. Enterprising Orientation (EAT 5)	35. Located in rural area or small town (SMALLT)	58. Academic Competitiveness (ACADCO)
12. Artistic Orientation (EAT 6)	*Environmental Factors from the Inventory of College Characteristics*	59. Concern for the Individual Student (CONCRN)
Miscellaneous Characteristics	36. Competitiveness *vs.* Cooperativeness (COMPET)	60. School Spirit (SCHLSP)
13. Educational and General Expenditures per Student (BUDGET)	37. Organized dating (ARRDAT[1])	61. Permissiveness (LIBERL[4])
14. Percentage of Men in Student Body (PCTMAL)	38. Independence (INDEP)	62. Snobbishness (PRACTI[5])
15. Undergraduate Enrollment (SIZE)	39. Cohesiveness (COHES)	63. Emphasis on Athletics (EMPHAT)
Administrative Type Characteristics	40. Informal Dating (INFDAT)	64. Flexibility of the Curriculum (CURFLX)
16. Men's College (MEN)	41. Femininity (FEMIN)	65. Emphasis on Social Life (SOCACT)
17. Women's College (WOMEN)	42. Drinking *vs.* Religiousness (DRVREL)	66. Spread of the Campus (BIGNSS[6])
18. University (UNIV)	43. Musical and Artistic Activity (MUSART)	67. Friendliness of the Dorm Counselor or Housemother (FRIEND)
19. Liberal Arts College (LIBART)	44. Leisure Time (LEISUR)	68. Severity of Administrative Policy against Drinking (SEVDRK)
20. Teachers College (TCHCOL)	45. Student Employment (WORKST[2])	69. Severity of Administrative Policy against Heterosexual Activity (POLSEX)
21. Technological Institution (TECHNO)	46. Career Indecision (CAREER)	70. Severity of Administrative Policy against Aggression (POLAGG)
22. Private Control (PRIVAT)	47. Use of Automobiles (AUTO)	71. Severity of Administrative Policy Against Cheating (POLCHT)
23. Sectarian (SECTAR)		

---

[1] Originally called "Arranged Dating."
[2] Originally called "Work Status."
[3] Originally called "Formality in the Class."
[4] Originally called "Liberalness of Faculty."
[5] Originally called "Practicality" (scored inversely).
[6] Originally called "Bigness."

Completion of Four or More Years of College

COLLEGE VARIABLE NAME	METHOD A	B	C	COLLEGE VARIABLE NAME	METHOD A	B	C	COLLEGE VARIABLE NAME	METHOD A	B	C
INTELL				PROT				REGSLP	(+)*	.29*	.06*
ESTHET	.14			CATH	.26	.28*		USELIB		−.15*	
STATUS	.28			PNS				CONFLI	.20	.26	
PRAGMA	−.31			NEGRO		−.20	−.07*	INVOLV	.17		.05
MASCUL				NORTHE	.29			VERBAG	.32*		
SELECT	.26*			STHEST				EXTRAV			
EAT 1	−.39*	−.15*		NOCENT				SEVGRD	−.26		
EAT 2				WSW	−.27*			FAMILR	(−)*		
EAT 3				500000				CHEATG	−.36	−.15	−.05
EAT 4				100000				FORMAL	.16	.22	.05
EAT 5	.28*			SUBURB				ACADCO	.21		
EAT 6	.19			SMALLT				CONCRN	.38		
BUDGET				COMPET	−.21			SCHLSP		.15	
PCTMAL	−.14*		−.07	ARRDAT	.21			LIBERL			−.07
SIZE	.22			INDEP	.26	.19*		PRACTI		−.18	
MEN	.14	.14		COHES	.17*	.25*	.05	EMPHAT	−.14		
WOMEN	.29			INFDAT	−.21	−.29		CURFLX	−.22	−.22	
UNIV	−.29	−.19	−.06	DRVREL				SOCACT	−.13		
LIBART	.36*		.06	MUSART		−.19		BIGNSS	−.20		−.05
TCHCOL	−.15			FEMIN		−.21		FRIEND			
TECHNO				LEISUR				SEVDRK			.05
				WORKST	−.27*	−.17		POLSEX		.13	.05
PRIVAT	.38	.13	.07*	CAREER	*	−.14*		POLAGG	−.21		
SECTAR	.26	.14		AUTO	−.18			POLCHT	.33	.23*	

COLLEGE VARIABLE NAME	METHOD			COLLEGE VARIABLE NAME	METHOD			COLLEGE VARIABLE NAME	METHOD		
	A	B	C		A	B	C		A	B	C
INTELL				PROT				REGSLP	(+)*	.27*	
ESTHET				CATH	.18			USELIB		(-)*	
STATUS	.22			PNS			.05	CONFLI	.17	.16	.06
PRAGMA	-.26			NEGRO				INVOLV	.18	.22	
MASCUL				NORTHE	.34*			VERBAG	.33*		.08
SELECT	.20*	(+)*		STHEST				EXTRAV			
EAT 1	-.34*	-.14	-.05	NOCENT				SEVGRD	-.16		
EAT 2		(-)*		WSW	-.31*			FAMILR	.13		
EAT 3				500000				CHEATG	-.35	-.27	-.06
EAT 4			-.06	100000				FORMAL	.19*	.22*	.06*
EAT 5	.23			SUBURB				ACADCO	.20		
EAT 6				SMALLT				CONCRN	.38	.20*	.08
BUDGET			-.06	COMPET				SCHLSP			-.07
PCTMAL				ARRDAT	.19			LIBERL		-.24	-.06
SIZE	-.28	-.23	-.10	INDEP	.31	.17*	.09*	PRACTI			
MEN	.23	(-)*	.05	COHES	.25*	.30*	.08	EMPHAT			
WOMEN	.22	.19		INFDAT	-.30	-.21*		CURFLX	-.30	-.26	-.08
UNIV	-.32	-.28	-.09*	DRVREL		-.17		SOCACT	-.17	-.17	-.07
LIBART	.31	.21	.06*	MUSART				BIGNSS	-.20	(+)*	-.05
TCHCOL				FEMIN				FRIEND			
TECHNO		.20	.06	LEISUR	(+)*	(+)*		SEVDRK		.22	(+)*
				WORKST	-.35*	-.27*	-.06	POLSEX		.20	.06
PRIVAT	.41*	.28*	.11*	CAREER	-.21*	-.17	-.08	POLAGG	-.21		
SECTAR	.24	.17		AUTO	-.18		-.07	POLCHT	.39	.32*	.10*

TABLE F4

Plans to Pursue Graduate Training

COLLEGE VARIABLE NAME	METHOD A	B	C	COLLEGE VARIABLE NAME	METHOD A	B	C	COLLEGE VARIABLE NAME	METHOD A	B	C
INTELL	.23			PROT				REGSLP			
ESTHET	.15			CATH	.15		.08*	USELIB	.16	(+)*	
STATUS	.23			PNS	.26	.15		CONFLI			
PRAGMA	−.21			NEGRO	(+)*			INVOLV			
MASCUL				NORTHE	.39*			VERBAG	.34		
SELECT	.32*	(+)*		STHEST	−.23			EXTRAV			
EAT 1	−.27			NOCENT	(+)*			SEVGRD	−.32		
EAT 2				WSW	−.19			FAMILR			
EAT 3	(+)*			500000			.05	CHEATG	−.14		
EAT 4				100000				FORMAL			
EAT 5	.21*	.14		SUBURB				ACADCO	.26		.06
EAT 6				SMALLT				CONCRN	.33	.13	
BUDGET			−.06	COMPET				SCHLSP			
PCTMAL				ARRDAT				LIBERL		−.14	
SIZE				INDEP	.36	.20*		PRACTI	.21		
MEN	.16			COHES		.16		EMPHAT			−.06
WOMEN	.13			INFDAT	−.14			CURFLX	−.23*	−.13	
UNIV	−.24	−.20		DRVREL	.20			SOCACT			
LIBART	.22			MUSART	.19			BIGNSS			(+)*
TCHCOL	(+)*			FEMIN		−.13		FRIEND			
TECHNO				LEISUR	(+)*	(+)*		SEVDRK			
				WORKST	−.13			POLSEX			
PRIVAT	.37*	.20*	.08*	CAREER		−.13		POLAGG	−.25		
SECTAR				AUTO	.36*	−.14		POLCHT	.19		

TABLE F5

Plans to Obtain the Doctorate

COLLEGE VARIABLE NAME	METHOD A	B	C	COLLEGE VARIABLE NAME	METHOD A	B	C	COLLEGE VARIABLE NAME	METHOD A	B	C
INTELL	.26			PROT				REGSLP			.06
ESTHET	.13			CATH	.18	.13		USELIB	.13		
STATUS				PNS	.18			CONFLI			
PRAGMA	−.14			NEGRO				INVOLV			
MASCUL				NORTHE	.22*			VERBAG	.27	.15	
SELECT	.20			STHEST	−.19			EXTRAV			.05
EAT 1				NOCENT				SEVGRD	−.23	−.13	
EAT 2	.17			WSW				FAMILR	.18	.18	
EAT 3	−.14			500000				CHEATG			
EAT 4				100000				FORMAL			.06
EAT 5				SUBURB	.15			ACADCO	.18		
EAT 6				SMALLT	−.14			CONCRN	.31	.22	
BUDGET	(+)*	(+)*		COMPET			−.05	SCHLSP	−.18		
PCTMAL				ARRDAT	−.26*	−.22*		LIBERL	.23*		
SIZE	−.18	−.19	−.06	INDEP	.25	.16		PRACTI			−.06
MEN				COHES				EMPHAT			
WOMEN				INFDAT			−.06	CURFLX			
UNIV	−.29*	−.24*	−.10*	DRVREL	.21	(+)*		SOCACT	−.30	−.17	
LIBART	.22	.23	.06	MUSART				BIGNSS	−.14*		−.06
TCHCOL				FEMIN				FRIEND			
TECHNO	.16			LEISUR	−.16			SEVDRK	−.15		
				WORKST			.06	POLSEX	−.13		
PRIVAT	.31*	.24*		CAREER	.13*			POLAGG	−.27	−.20	
SECTAR		.14	.05	AUTO	−.21		−.06	POLCHT			

TABLE F6

Plans to Obtain a Professional Degree

COLLEGE VARIABLE NAME	METHOD A	B	C	COLLEGE VARIABLE NAME	METHOD A	B	C	COLLEGE VARIABLE NAME	METHOD A	B	C
INTELL				PROT				REGSLP			
ESTHET				CATH				USELIB			
STATUS	.31			PNS				CONFLI			
PRAGMA				NEGRO				INVOLV			
MASCUL	.18			NORTHE				VERBAG			
SELECT				STHEST	.14			EXTRAV			
EAT 1	−.25		−.07	NOCENT				SEVGRD			.07
EAT 2				WSW				FAMILR			
EAT 3				500000	(+)*			CHEATG	−.25*		
EAT 4	(−)*	(−)*	.05	100000				FORMAL			
EAT 5	.37*		.11	SUBURB				ACADCO	.19*		
EAT 6				SMALLT				CONCRN			
BUDGET				COMPET			.05	SCHLSP	.18	.15*	
PCTMAL			.07*	ARRDAT	.22			LIBERL			
SIZE				INDEP			.07	PRACTI	.27*		
MEN	.29*		.08	COHES			.06	EMPHAT			
WOMEN				INFDAT	−.25	−.14		CURFLX			
UNIV	(+)*			DRVREL	(−)*	−.13		SOCACT	.16*		
LIBART				MUSART				BIGNSS			
TCHCOL	(+)*			FEMIN				FRIEND			
TECHNO	−.29*	−.14	−.09*	LEISUR				SEVDRK			
				WORKST				POLSEX			
PRIVAT			.05*	CAREER	(−)*			POLAGG		.13	
SECTAR				AUTO				POLCHT	.24		

TABLE F7

Arts and Humanities (Major)

COLLEGE VARIABLE NAME	METHOD A	B	C	COLLEGE VARIABLE NAME	METHOD A	B	C	COLLEGE VARIABLE NAME	METHOD A	B	C
INTELL	.38			PROT				REGSLP	−.15*		
ESTHET	.21			CATH	.17			USELIB	.17		
STATUS	.61			PNS	.26		.06	CONFLI			
PRAGMA	−.22			NEGRO	−.18			INVOLV	−.18		
MASCUL	.23			NORTHE	.23			VERBAG	.33		
SELECT	.48			STHEST	−.13			EXTRAV			
EAT 1	−.36	−.23		NOCENT	−.13			SEVGRD	−.33		
EAT 2		−.13		WSW				FAMILR	.16		
EAT 3	−.27			500000				CHEATG	−.25		
EAT 4	.21			100000				FORMAL			
EAT 5	.58*	.27*	.08*	SUBURB				ACADCO	.36*		.05
EAT 6	.22*	.17*		SMALLT				CONCRN	.40		.05
BUDGET	.27			COMPET				SCHLSP		.14	
PCTMAL				ARRDAT	.23			LIBERL	.27		.06
SIZE				INDEP	.43			PRACTI	.36		
MEN	.27			COHES	−.26			EMPHAT	−.25		
WOMEN	.17			INFDAT	−.25*	−.15*		CURFLX			.05
UNIV				DRVREL	.39*		.06	SOCACT	−.13		
LIBART	.24	.13		MUSART	.28*	.17	.05	BIGNSS	−.14		
TCHCOL	−.32	−.15		FEMIN	(−)*	−.15*		FRIEND	.16		
TECHNO	−.17*	−.23*		LEISUR	−.27*	−.16*		SEVDRK	−.28		
				WORKST				POLSEX	−.26		
PRIVAT	.33		.05	CAREER	.21			POLAGG	−.42		−.08*
SECTAR				AUTO	−.18			POLCHT	.28		

TABLE F8

Biological Sciences (Major)

COLLEGE VARIABLE NAME	METHOD A	B	C	COLLEGE VARIABLE NAME	METHOD A	B	C	COLLEGE VARIABLE NAME	METHOD A	B	C
INTELL				PROT	.20	.16*		REGSLP			
ESTHET	−.19			CATH				USELIB			
STATUS				PNS	−.16			CONFLI			
PRAGMA				NEGRO				INVOLV			
MASCUL				NORTHE				VERBAG			
SELECT	−.19			STHEST				EXTRAV			
EAT 1	(+)*			NOCENT				SEVGRD			
EAT 2		.17*		WSW				FAMILR	.14		
EAT 3				500000	−.15			CHEATG	.15		
EAT 4				100000				FORMAL	.18*	.14*	
EAT 5				SUBURB				ACADCO			
EAT 6	−.13			SMALLT	.14			CONCRN			
BUDGET				COMPET		−.13		SCHLSP			
PCTMAL				ARRDAT	−.27*			LIBERL	−.18		
SIZE	−.17			INDEP	(+)*			PRACTI			
MEN				COHES	.16			EMPHAT	.20		
WOMEN				INFDAT				CURFLX			
UNIV	−.16			DRVREL	−.15	−.13		SOCACT			
LIBART	.20*	.17		MUSART				BIGNSS	−.14		
TCHCOL				FEMIN				FRIEND	−.15*		
TECHNO	−.13*			LEISUR			−.05*	SEVDRK	.18		
				WORKST				POLSEX			
PRIVAT				CAREER	−.15			POLAGG	.14		
SECTAR	.16			AUTO				POLCHT			

TABLE F9

Business (Major)

COLLEGE VARIABLE NAME	METHOD A	B	C	COLLEGE VARIABLE NAME	METHOD A	B	C	COLLEGE VARIABLE NAME	METHOD A	B	C
INTELL	−.29			PROT				REGSLP			
ESTHET				CATH				USELIB		−.13	
STATUS	−.13			PNS	−.20			CONFLI			
PRAGMA				NEGRO				INVOLV			
MASCUL				NORTHE	−.15			VERBAG	−.24	−.14	
SELECT	−.20			STHEST				EXTRAV			
EAT 1				NOCENT				SEVGRD	.15		
EAT 2	−.29*			WSW				FAMILR	−.31	−.20	
EAT 3				500000				CHEATG	.17	.17	
EAT 4	.35*	.21*		100000				FORMAL	(−)*		
EAT 5				SUBURB				ACADCO	−.23	(−)*	
EAT 6				SMALLT				CONCRN	−.38*	−.22	
BUDGET	−.17			COMPET				SCHLSP			
PCTMAL				ARRDAT				LIBERL		(−)*	
SIZE	.24	.20		INDEP	−.35*	−.19*		PRACTI			
MEN	−.31*	−.15		COHES		−.15		EMPHAT			
WOMEN				INFDAT	.28			CURFLX	.13		
UNIV	.25	.26*		DRVREL	−.16			SOCACT	.28	.16	
LIBART	−.13	−.18		MUSART	−.16			BIGNSS	.25		
TCHCOL				FEMIN	.20			FRIEND			
TECHNO				LEISUR	.20			SEVDRK	.13		
				WORKST				POLSEX	.13		
PRIVAT	−.17	−.16		CAREER	.14			POLAGG	.28	.19	
SECTAR				AUTO	.19			POLCHT	−.18		

188

TABLE F10

Education (Major)

COLLEGE VARIABLE NAME	METHOD A	B	C	COLLEGE VARIABLE NAME	METHOD A	B	C	COLLEGE VARIABLE NAME	METHOD A	B	C
INTELL	−.22			PROT				REGSLP			
ESTHET	−.16			CATH		−.18		USELIB			
STATUS	−.38*			PNS				CONFLI			
PRAGMA				NEGRO	.13			INVOLV		−.13	
MASCUL				NORTHE				VERBAG	−.25	−.19	−.05*
SELECT	−.32			STHEST				EXTRAV			(+)*
EAT 1	.18	.19		NOCENT				SEVGRD	.22		.06
EAT 2	−.15			WSW				FAMILR			
EAT 3	.27			500000				CHEATG	.20		.06
EAT 4	−.18			100000				FORMAL			
EAT 5	−.37	−.13		SUBURB				ACADCO	−.23		
EAT 6	(+)*			SMALLT				CONCRN	−.26	−.16	−.07
BUDGET	−.21			COMPET	.13		.06	SCHLSP			
PCTMAL			.07	ARRDAT	−.20			LIBERL			
SIZE		.20		INDEP	−.23			PRACTI	−.21		
MEN		−.16		COHES		−.16		EMPHAT	.22		
WOMEN	−.21*		−.09*	INFDAT		.18		CURFLX			(−)*
UNIV				DRVREL	−.17			SOCACT			
LIBART	−.26	−.16	−.07	MUSART	−.16			BIGNSS			
TCHCOL	.41*		.05	FEMIN				FRIEND			
TECHNO				LEISUR	.23*			SEVDRK			
				WORKST				POLSEX			(−)*
PRIVAT	−.34	−.17		CAREER				POLAGG	.31	(+)*	
SECTAR	−.19*	−.22*		AUTO	.16		.05	POLCHT	−.25		

189

TABLE F11

Engineering (Major)

COLLEGE VARIABLE NAME	METHOD A	B	C	COLLEGE VARIABLE NAME	METHOD A	B	C	COLLEGE VARIABLE NAME	METHOD A	B	C
INTELL	.19			PROT				REGSLP			
ESTHET	.19			CATH				USELIB	-.26		-.09
STATUS	-.29			PNS	.16			CONFLI			
PRAGMA	.32			NEGRO				INVOLV			
MASCUL				NORTHE				VERBAG			
SELECT	(-)*			STHEST	(-)*			EXTRAV			
EAT 1	.46*	(+)*	.12	NOCENT				SEVGRD	.13		.05
EAT 2	.13	(-)*		WSW				FAMILR	-.22		-.10*
EAT 3	-.24	(-)*	-.11	500000	.15		.05	CHEATG			
EAT 4	-.29		-.06	100000				FORMAL	-.20		
EAT 5	-.42		-.14	SUBURB	.17			ACADCO			
EAT 6	-.24		-.10	SMALLT	-.21*		-.06	CONCRN			
BUDGET				COMPET	.15		.07	SCHLSP	-.19		-.06
PCTMAL				ARRDAT	(+)*			LIBERL			
SIZE		-.15		INDEP				PRACTI			
MEN	(-)*			COHES	-.18		-.09*	EMPHAT			
WOMEN				INFDAT	-.15*		-.06	CURFLX	-.22		-.08
UNIV				DRVREL				SOCACT	-.16		-.05
LIBART	-.31		-.10	MUSART	-.21		-.10	BIGNSS	.16	(+)*	
TCHCOL				FEMIN				FRIEND			
TECHNO	.80*	.51*	.19*	LEISUR	-.15			SEVDRK			
				WORKST				POLSEX			
PRIVAT				CAREER	-.16	-.13		POLAGG			
SECTAR	-.17			AUTO				POLCHT			

Physical Sciences (Major)

COLLEGE VARIABLE NAME	METHOD A	B	C	COLLEGE VARIABLE NAME	METHOD A	B	C	COLLEGE VARIABLE NAME	METHOD A	B	C
INTELL	.17			PROT	(−)*			REGSLP			
ESTHET				CATH			(−)*	USELIB			
STATUS	−.25			PNS				CONFLI			
PRAGMA	−.14*			NEGRO				INVOLV	.22		.07
MASCUL	−.35			NORTHE	−.16*			VERBAG	−.14		
SELECT	−.22		−.09	STHEST	.13			EXTRAV			
EAT 1				NOCENT				SEVGRD			
EAT 2	(+)*	.18*		WSW				FAMILR			
EAT 3	.20		.07	500000	−.14			CHEATG			
EAT 4	−.26	−.13		100000				FORMAL			.05
EAT 5	−.34*	−.16*		SUBURB			−.06	ACADCO	−.13*		−.07
EAT 6	.13			SMALLT				CONCRN			
BUDGET	−.15		−.11*	COMPET	−.27			SCHLSP	(−)*		
PCTMAL	−.30*		−.05	ARRDAT				LIBERL	−.18		−.08
SIZE	−.24	−.18	−.06	INDEP	−.24		−.06	PRACTI	−.19		
MEN	−.20		−.05	COHES	.23*	.09*	.07	EMPHAT			
WOMEN	.18			INFDAT	.14			CURFLX			
UNIV	−.20	−.14	−.06	DRVREL	−.28		−.07	SOCACT			
LIBART				MUSART				BIGNSS			
TCHCOL	.15	.14	.07	FEMIN	.22			FRIEND			
TECHNO	(+)*			LEISUR				SEVDRK	.26		.06
				WORKST				POLSEX	.29		.09*
PRIVAT				CAREER	−.17		−.06	POLAGG			.05
SECTAR				AUTO				POLCHT			

TABLE F13

Social Sciences (Major)

COLLEGE VARIABLE NAME	METHOD			COLLEGE VARIABLE NAME	METHOD			COLLEGE VARIABLE NAME	METHOD		
	A	B	C		A	B	C		A	B	C
INTELL	.27			PROT				REGSLP	−.13		
ESTHET				CATH	.19*			USELIB			
STATUS	.47			PNS	.19			CONFLI			
PRAGMA	(+)*			NEGRO	−.22*			INVOLV	−.16		
MASCUL	.25			NORTHE	.21			VERBAG	.26	.15*	
SELECT	.36		.09*	STHEST	−.18			EXTRAV			
EAT 1	−.27	−.13		NOCENT				SEVGRD	−.31*	−.14	−.06
EAT 2	.17*	(+)*		WSW				FAMILR	.17		
EAT 3	−.20*	(+)*		500000				CHEATG	−.13		
EAT 4	.18			100000				FORMAL			
EAT 5	.51*	.20*		SUBURB				ACADCO	.21		
EAT 6				SMALLT				CONCRN	.36	.16	
BUDGET	.17			COMPET				SCHLSP			
PCTMAL				ARRDAT	.19			LIBERL			
SIZE				INDEP	.36	.17		PRACTI	.16		
MEN	.27	.15		COHES				EMPHAT	−.13		
WOMEN				INFDAT				CURFLX	(−)*		
UNIV				DRVREL	.26			SOCACT			
LIBART	.26	.13		MUSART	.19			BIGNSS	−.17	−.14	
TCHCOL	−.24			FEMIN				FRIEND			
TECHNO	−.18		(−)*	LEISUR	−.13			SEVDRK	−.14		
				WORKST				POLSEX	−.13		
PRIVAT	.32			CAREER	.18			POLAGG	−.38*	−.15	−.06
SECTAR				AUTO				POLCHT	.21		

TABLE F14
Biological Scientist (Career)

COLLEGE VARIABLE NAME	METHOD A	B	C	COLLEGE VARIABLE NAME	METHOD A	B	C	COLLEGE VARIABLE NAME	METHOD A	B	C
INTELL				PROT				REGSLP			
ESTHET				CATH				USELIB			
STATUS				PNS				CONFLI			
PRAGMA				NEGRO	.14			INVOLV	.15		
MASCUL	−.20			NORTHE				VERBAG			
SELECT				STHEST	(+)*			EXTRAV			
EAT 1				NOCENT				SEVGRD			−.07*
EAT 2				WSW				FAMILR			−.06
EAT 3			.05	500000				CHEATG	(+)*		
EAT 4	−.14			100000				FORMAL			
EAT 5	−.13			SUBURB				ACADCO			(−)*
EAT 6				SMALLT	.15*			CONCRN		(−)*	
BUDGET		(+)*		COMPET	−.23*	−.13	−.06	SCHLSP			
PCTMAL	−.18			ARRDAT	−.18*			LIBERL			
SIZE	−.20			INDEP				PRACTI			
MEN	−.13			COHES				EMPHAT			
WOMEN	(+)*			INFDAT				CURFLX			
UNIV	−.18			DRVREL	−.14			SOCACT	−.16	(−)*	
LIBART	.19	.13*	.06	MUSART				BIGNSS			
TCHCOL				FEMIN				FRIEND			
TECHNO				LEISUR				SEVDRK	(−)*		
				WORKST				POLSEX			
PRIVAT				CAREER				POLAGG			
SECTAR	.13			AUTO	−.14			POLCHT			

193

COLLEGE VARIABLE NAME	METHOD			COLLEGE VARIABLE NAME	METHOD			COLLEGE VARIABLE NAME	METHOD		
	A	B	C		A	B	C		A	B	C
INTELL				PROT				REGSLP			
ESTHET				CATH				USELIB			
STATUS	.17			PNS				CONFLI			
PRAGMA				NEGRO				INVOLV			
MASCUL				NORTHE				VERBAG			
SELECT				STHEST				EXTRAV			(−)*
EAT 1	−.17			NOCENT				SEVGRD			
EAT 2				WSW				FAMILR			
EAT 3				500000				CHEATG			
EAT 4	.30*	.27*		100000				FORMAL			
EAT 5	.22			SUBURB			.07*	ACADCO			
EAT 6				SMALLT				CONCRN		−.14	
BUDGET				COMPET				SCHLSP			
PCTMAL				ARRDAT	.27*	.18		LIBERL			
SIZE	.14	.14		INDEP				PRACTI			
MEN				COHES	(−)*			EMPHAT			
WOMEN				INFDAT				CURFLX			
UNIV	.19	.18		DRVREL				SOCACT	.19		
LIBART				MUSART				BIGNSS			
TCHCOL	−.23*	−.17		FEMIN	.13			FRIEND			
TECHNO	−.26*			LEISUR				SEVDRK	(+)*		
				WORKST				POLSEX			
PRIVAT				CAREER				POLAGG			
SECTAR				AUTO				POLCHT			

TABLE F16

Clergyman (Career)

COLLEGE VARIABLE NAME	METHOD A	B	C	COLLEGE VARIABLE NAME	METHOD A	B	C	COLLEGE VARIABLE NAME	METHOD A	B	C
INTELL				PROT				REGSLP	.17		
ESTHET				CATH				USELIB			
STATUS				PNS				CONFLI			
PRAGMA				NEGRO				INVOLV	.15		
MASCUL	−.15			NORTHE				VERBAG			
SELECT		.20		STHEST				EXTRAV			.13
EAT 1			−.05*	NOCENT				SEVGRD			
EAT 2		.15		WSW				FAMILR			
EAT 3				500000				CHEATG	−.14	−.14*	
EAT 4			.05	100000				FORMAL			
EAT 5				SUBURB				ACADCO			.15
EAT 6			(−)*	SMALLT				CONCRN			
BUDGET	−.14		(+)*	COMPET	−.18			SCHLSP	.16*		
PCTMAL	−.18			ARRDAT				LIBERL	−.19		
SIZE				INDEP	−.13			PRACTI			
MEN				COHES				EMPHAT			
WOMEN				INFDAT				CURFLX			
UNIV				DRVREL	−.23*			SOCACT			
LIBART				MUSART				BIGNSS			
TCHCOL				FEMIN				FRIEND	−.14*	(−)*	
TECHNO				LEISUR	−.18*	−.19*		SEVDRK	.22		
				WORKST				POLSEX	.14		
PRIVAT				CAREER				POLAGG			
SECTAR				AUTO	−.13	−.13		POLCHT		.14	

195

TABLE F17
College Professor (Career)

COLLEGE VARIABLE NAME	METHOD A	METHOD B	METHOD C	COLLEGE VARIABLE NAME	METHOD A	METHOD B	METHOD C	COLLEGE VARIABLE NAME	METHOD A	METHOD B	METHOD C
INTELL	.17			PROT	.15			REGSLP			
ESTHET				CATH				USELIB			
STATUS	.20			PNS				CONFLI	−.18		−.06
PRAGMA				NEGRO	.16	(−)*		INVOLV			
MASCUL				NORTHE	−.13			VERBAG			
SELECT	.15	(+)*		STHEST				EXTRAV			
EAT 1				NOCENT				SEVGRD	−.21		−.09*
EAT 2	.19	.20*		WSW				FAMILR	.28*		.10*
EAT 3				500000			−.06	CHEATG			
EAT 4				100000				FORMAL			
EAT 5				SUBURB				ACADCO	.20	.16	
EAT 6			.05	SMALLT				CONCRN	.25		.09
BUDGET	.22*	(+)*		COMPET	−.16		−.07	SCHLSP			
PCTMAL		(−)*		ARRDAT	−.19*	−.16		LIBERL	.14*	(+)*	
SIZE	−.13		−.06	INDEP	.17			PRACTI	.13		
MEN	(−)*			COHES				EMPHAT			
WOMEN		(−)*		INFDAT				CURFLX		−.22*	
UNIV	−.13		−.07	DRVREL	.21			SOCACT	−.22	−.21*	
LIBART	.27*	.13*	.09	MUSART		(−)*	.06	BIGNSS	−.15		−.10
TCHCOL	−.19			FEMIN				FRIEND			
TECHNO				LEISUR				SEVDRK			
				WORKST				POLSEX			
PRIVAT				CAREER				POLAGG	−.24		−.08
SECTAR				AUTO	−.13		−.07	POLCHT			

Engineer (Career)

COLLEGE VARIABLE NAME	A	B	C	COLLEGE VARIABLE NAME	A	B	C	COLLEGE VARIABLE NAME	A	B	C
INTELL	.27			PROT	−.14			REGSLP			
ESTHET	.24			CATH				USELIB	−.26		−.06
STATUS	−.23			PNS	.20			CONFLI			
PRAGMA	.29			NEGRO				INVOLV	−.15		
MASCUL				NORTHE				VERBAG	.14		
SELECT	.18			STHEST				EXTRAV			
EAT 1	.44	(+)*	.09	NOCENT				SEVGRD			
EAT 2	.20*		.05	WSW				FAMILR	−.17		
EAT 3	−.31*		−.10	500000	.15			CHEATG			
EAT 4	−.26		−.06	100000				FORMAL	−.15		
EAT 5	−.37*		−.11	SUBURB	.21			ACADCO			
EAT 6	−.23		−.07	SMALLT	−.18			CONCRN			
BUDGET				COMPET	.16			SCHLSP	−.21	−.16	−.05
PCTMAL				ARRDAT	(+)*			LIBERL			
SIZE	(−)*	−.15		INDEP				PRACTI			
MEN	(−)*			COHES	−.21		−.07*	EMPHAT			
WOMEN				INFDAT	−.17*			CURFLX	−.24	−.15	−.07
UNIV		−.15		DRVREL	.15	(+)*		SOCACT	−.16		−.05
LIBART	−.27			MUSART	−.18		−.06	BIGNSS	.13		
TCHCOL				FEMIN				FRIEND	(+)*		
TECHNO	.78*	.46*	.16*	LEISUR	−.16			SEVDRK	−.17		
				WORKST				POLSEX			
PRIVAT				CAREER	−.13	−.14	−.05	POLAGG			
SECTAR	−.18			AUTO				POLCHT			

TABLE F19

Health Professional (Non-M.D.) Career)

COLLEGE VARIABLE NAME	METHOD A	B	C	COLLEGE VARIABLE NAME	METHOD A	B	C	COLLEGE VARIABLE NAME	METHOD A	B	C
INTELL				PROT				REGSLP	.17		
ESTHET				CATH	.22*			USELIB			
STATUS				PNS				CONFLI			
PRAGMA				NEGRO	−.21*		−.06*	INVOLV			
MASCUL				NORTHE				VERBAG			
SELECT				STHEST	−.16			EXTRAV			
EAT 1	(+)*			NOCENT				SEVGRD			
EAT 2				WSW				FAMILR			
EAT 3	(+)*		(+)*	500000				CHEATG			
EAT 4				100000				FORMAL			
EAT 5				SUBURB			−.05	ACADCO			
EAT 6			−.07*	SMALLT				CONCRN			
BUDGET				COMPET				SCHLSP			
PCTMAL				ARRDAT				LIBERL			−.05
SIZE				INDEP			−.07	PRACTI			−.05
MEN				COHES				EMPHAT			
WOMEN	.14			INFDAT				CURFLX			
UNIV				DRVREL			−.06	SOCACT			
LIBART				MUSART				BIGNSS			
TCHCOL			(−)*	FEMIN				FRIEND			
TECHNO				LEISUR	−.20*			SEVDRK	.13		
				WORKST				POLSEX	.15*		.06*
PRIVAT				CAREER	.16*			POLAGG			
SECTAR			(−)*	AUTO				POLCHT			

Lawyer (Career)

COLLEGE VARIABLE NAME	A	B	C	COLLEGE VARIABLE NAME	A	B	C	COLLEGE VARIABLE NAME	A	B	C
INTELL		▓		PROT				REGSLP			
ESTHET	−.19	▓		CATH				USELIB	.15		.06*
STATUS	.28	▓		PNS		(+)*		CONFLI	.16		
PRAGMA		▓		NEGRO	.14*		.05	INVOLV	(+)*		
MASCUL	.31	▓		NORTHE		▓		VERBAG	.15		.05
SELECT				STHEST		▓		EXTRAV			
EAT 1	−.23			NOCENT		▓		SEVGRD			
EAT 2				WSW		▓		FAMILR			
EAT 3				500000		▓		CHEATG	−.15		
EAT 4	.15*			100000		▓		FORMAL			
EAT 5	.38*		.08	SUBURB	−.13*	▓		ACADCO	.16*		
EAT 6		.13*		SMALLT		▓		CONCRN			
BUDGET				COMPET	.19		.09*	SCHLSP	.20	.19*	.07*
PCTMAL	.25		.07	ARRDAT	.21			LIBERL			
SIZE				INDEP	.16		.07	PRACTI	.17		
MEN	.41*		.10	COHES	.13		.07*	EMPHAT	−.13		
WOMEN				INFDAT	−.24		−.07	CURFLX			
UNIV				DRVREL			.05	SOCACT	.22*		
LIBART	(−)*			MUSART				BIGNSS			
TCHCOL				FEMIN	−.16		−.06	FRIEND			
TECHNO	−.21*			LEISUR	.15			SEVDRK	(+)*		
				WORKST			.06	POLSEX			
PRIVAT		−.14		CAREER				POLAGG			(−)*
SECTAR		−.14		AUTO				POLCHT	.18		

TABLE F21

Performing Artist (Career)

COLLEGE VARIABLE NAME	A	B	C	COLLEGE VARIABLE NAME	A	B	C	COLLEGE VARIABLE NAME	A	B	C
INTELL	.15			PROT	−.15			REGSLP			
ESTHET	.17			CATH				USELIB	(−)*		
STATUS	.13			PNS	.24*			CONFLI			
PRAGMA				NEGRO				INVOLV			
MASCUL				NORTHE				VERBAG			
SELECT				STHEST				EXTRAV			
EAT 1				NOCENT				SEVGRD			
EAT 2				WSW				FAMILR			
EAT 3				500000				CHEATG			
EAT 4				100000				FORMAL			
EAT 5				SUBURB				ACADCO			
EAT 6	.13*			SMALLT				CONCRN			
BUDGET				COMPET				SCHLSP			
PCTMAL				ARRDAT				LIBERL	.22*		
SIZE				INDEP				PRACTI	.14		.05*
MEN				COHES	−.17			EMPHAT			
WOMEN				INFDAT	(−)*			CURFLX			
UNIV				DRVREL	.20			SOCACT			
LIBART				MUSART				BIGNSS			
TCHCOL				FEMIN				FRIEND			
TECHNO				LEISUR				SEVDRK	−.15		
				WORKST	.16*			POLSEX	−.15		
PRIVAT				CAREER				POLAGG	−.14		
SECTAR	−.18			AUTO				POLCHT			

TABLE F22

Physical Scientist (Career)

COLLEGE VARIABLE NAME	METHOD A	B	C	COLLEGE VARIABLE NAME	METHOD A	B	C	COLLEGE VARIABLE NAME	METHOD A	B	C
INTELL				PROT				REGSLP			
ESTHET	.20			CATH				USELIB			
STATUS				PNS				CONFLI	−.14		
PRAGMA				NEGRO			.08*	INVOLV	(−)*		.05
MASCUL	−.23*			NORTHE				VERBAG			
SELECT			−.06	STHEST				EXTRAV			
EAT 1				NOCENT				SEVGRD			
EAT 2		.14*		WSW				FAMILR			
EAT 3				500000				CHEATG			
EAT 4	−.18			100000				FORMAL	−.19		
EAT 5	−.21		−.06	SUBURB	.19*			ACADCO			
EAT 6				SMALLT				CONCRN			
BUDGET			−.05	COMPET	−.19			SCHLSP			
PCTMAL				ARRDAT				LIBERL	(+)*		
SIZE				INDEP				PRACTI			
MEN	−.14			COHES	(−)*	.15		EMPHAT			
WOMEN				INFDAT	.16*	.13*		CURFLX			
UNIV				DRVREL			−.05	SOCACT			.05
LIBART	(+)*			MUSART				BIGNSS			
TCHCOL				FEMIN				FRIEND			
TECHNO	.24*			LEISUR				SEVDRK			
				WORKST	−.15			POLSEX	(+)*	.17*	.06*
PRIVAT				CAREER			−.09*	POLAGG			.06
SECTAR				AUTO	−.13			POLCHT			

TABLE F23

Physician (Career)

COLLEGE VARIABLE NAME	METHOD A	B	C	COLLEGE VARIABLE NAME	METHOD A	B	C	COLLEGE VARIABLE NAME	METHOD A	B	C
INTELL	−.32			PROT	.23*			REGSLP	.22		
ESTHET	−.22			CATH				USELIB			
STATUS				PNS	−.21			CONFLI	.15		
PRAGMA				NEGRO				INVOLV	.22		
MASCUL				NORTHE				VERBAG	−.15		
SELECT	−.32			STHEST	.13			EXTRAV			
EAT 1	−.14			NOCENT				SEVGRD			
EAT 2				WSW				FAMILR			
EAT 3	.29			500000				CHEATG			
EAT 4				100000				FORMAL	.17		
EAT 5			.06*	SUBURB	−.16			ACADCO			
EAT 6				SMALLT				CONCRN			
BUDGET	−.18			COMPET				SCHLSP	(−)*		(−)*
PCTMAL				ARRDAT				LIBERL	−.30		
SIZE	−.16			INDEP	−.22			PRACTI			
MEN				COHES	.23			EMPHAT			
WOMEN				INFDAT	(−)*			CURFLX			
UNIV				DRVREL	−.37*			SOCACT			
LIBART	.16			MUSART				BIGNSS	−.14		
TCHCOL				FEMIN				FRIEND			
TECHNO	−.26*		−.06	LEISUR				SEVDRK	.34		
				WORKST				POLSEX	.19		
PRIVAT				CAREER				POLAGG	.31*	.13*	
SECTAR	.23			AUTO	.14			POLCHT			

202

TABLE F24

Social Scientist (Career)

COLLEGE VARIABLE NAME	METHOD A	B	C	COLLEGE VARIABLE NAME	METHOD A	B	C	COLLEGE VARIABLE NAME	METHOD A	B	C
INTELL	.17			PROT				REGSLP	−.15		
ESTHET	.17			CATH				USELIB	.16		
STATUS	.13			PNS	.20*	.16*		CONFLI			
PRAGMA	−.14			NEGRO	.15*		.07*	INVOLV			
MASCUL				NORTHE				VERBAG			
SELECT	.15			STHEST				EXTRAV			
EAT 1				NOCENT				SEVGRD	−.19		
EAT 2				WSW				FAMILR			
EAT 3				500000				CHEATG			
EAT 4				100000	.14			FORMAL			
EAT 5				SUBURB				ACADCO	.13		
EAT 6	.13			SMALLT				CONCRN	.18		
BUDGET				COMPET	−.13		−.05*	SCHLSP			
PCTMAL	−.14			ARRDAT		−.16*	−.07*	LIBERL	.18	.13	
SIZE				INDEP				PRACTI	.16		
MEN				COHES				EMPHAT			
WOMEN				INFDAT	.15*			CURFLX	(−)*	−.14*	
UNIV				DRVREL				SOCACT	(−)*		−.06
LIBART	.18			MUSART	.19			BIGNSS			
TCHCOL				FEMIN				FRIEND			
TECHNO	(−)*			LEISUR		(+)*		SEVDRK			
				WORKST				POLSEX			
PRIVAT	.15			CAREER	.18*			POLAGG	−.24*	−.15*	
SECTAR				AUTO	−.18			POLCHT			

203

TABLE F25

Teacher (Career)

COLLEGE VARIABLE NAME	METHOD A	B	C	COLLEGE VARIABLE NAME	METHOD A	B	C	COLLEGE VARIABLE NAME	METHOD A	B	C
INTELL	−.37			PROT				REGSLP	.27		
ESTHET	−.17			CATH	.15*			USELIB			
STATUS	−.28			PNS	−.26			CONFLI	.17		
PRAGMA	−.16			NEGRO	−.20	−.15*		INVOLV	.26		
MASCUL				NORTHE				VERBAG			
SELECT	−.23			STHEST	−.20*			EXTRAV			
EAT 1				NOCENT				SEVGRD			
EAT 2	−.23			WSW				FAMILR			
EAT 3	.36			500000				CHEATG			
EAT 4				100000				FORMAL	.21		
EAT 5	−.17			SUBURB				ACADCO	−.17		
EAT 6	(+)*			SMALLT	.17			CONCRN			
BUDGET	−.32			COMPET				SCHLSP			
PCTMAL				ARRDAT	−.22			LIBERL	−.29*	−.14	
SIZE				INDEP	−.18			PRACTI	−.29		
MEN				COHES	.19			EMPHAT	.19		
WOMEN	(−)*			INFDAT				CURFLX			
UNIV	−.19			DRVREL	−.26			SOCACT			
LIBART				MUSART				BIGNSS			
TCHCOL	.36*			FEMIN				FRIEND		.13	
TECHNO	−.15			LEISUR				SEVDRK	.24		
				WORKST				POLSEX	(−)*		
PRIVAT				CAREER				POLAGG	.20		
SECTAR	.14			AUTO				POLCHT	−.23		

204

G

Original Categories for Coding Open-Ended Responses to Questions about Major Field of Study and Future Career

TABLE G1
Major Field of Study

01	Accounting	28	Mathematics
02	Advertising	29	Military Science
03	Agriculture	30	Music
04	Animal Husbandry	31	Nursing
05	Anthropology[a]	32	Pharmacy
06	Architecture	33	Philosophy
07	Biochemistry[b]	34	Physical Education and Recreation
08	Biology (including Botany and Zoology)	35	Physics
09	Botany[b]	36	Political Science
10	Business Administration	37	Predentistry
11	Chemistry	38	Prelaw
12	Economics	39	Premedicine
13	Education	40	Preveterinary
14	Engineering	41	Psychology
15	English	42	Public Administration[d]
16	Fine Arts and Art	43	Religious Education and Bible
17	Forestry	44	Social Work
18	Geography[c]	45	Sociology
19	Geology	46	Speech and Dramatic Arts
20	Health Technology	47	Theology and Preministerial
21	History	48	Zoology
22	Home Economics	49	Natural Science, Other*
23	Industrial Arts and Trade	50	Social Science, Other**
24	International Relations	51	Humanities, Other***
25	Journalism and Writing	52	Mixed Majors and Others
26	Language (Modern Foreign Language)	53	"Undecided"
27	Library Science	54	No response

[a] Later combined with 50.
[b] Later combined with 49.
[c] Later combined with 52.
[d] Later combined with 10.
* Natural science, other:

Double Majors {
Biological sciences
Chemistry
Engineering
Mathematics
Physics
}

** Social Sciences, other:

Double Majors {
Anthropology
Economics
Political science
Psychology
Sociology
}

*** Humanities, other:

Double Majors {
English
History
Languages
Philosophy
}

TABLE G2
Probable Career

01	Accountant (CPA)	25	Housewife and occupation
02	Actor and entertainer (including theater)	26	Interior decorator (including designer)
03	Advertising man (including public relations man)	27	Interpreter (translator)
		28	Journalist (writing, newspaper work)
04	Anthropologist	29	Lab technician (medical, dental, X-ray, etc.)
05	Architect		
06	Artist	30	Lawyer (attorney)
07	Biological scientist (including research)	31	Mathematician (including research)
08	Businessman (unspecified)	32	Military service (no specific field)
09	Business executive (management, administration)	33	Missionary[c]
		34	Musician (including singer, performer, etc.)
10	Business salesman		
11	Chemist (including research)	35	Nurse
12	Clergyman (minister, priest)	36	Pharmacist
13	Clerical worker (secretary, stenographer, bookkeeper)	37	Physician
		38	Physicist (including research)
14	College professor or teacher	39	Pilot
15	College professor + scientist[a]	40	Psychologist
16	Dentist (including orthodontist)	41	Skilled tradesman
17	Dietitian; home economist	42	Social worker
18	Engineer	43	Sociologist
19	Engineer + business, sales, executive[b]	44	Speech therapist
20	Farmer	45	Teacher (including youth work, guidance counselor)
21	Foreign service worker (diplomat, politician)		
		46	Veterinarian
22	Geologist	47	Other (including double choices)
23	Government service worker	48	Undecided
24	Housewife	49	No response

[a] Later combined with 14.
[b] Later combined with 18.
[c] Later combined with 12.

H

Cross-Tabulation of Career Choice
and Major Field of Study (Weighted Data)
1961 *vs.* 1965

BECAUSE of its very large size, this table has been deposited at The National Auxiliary Publications Service of The American Society for Information Science. Order NAPS Document 00385 from ASIS National Auxiliary Publications Service, c/o CCM Information Sciences, Inc., 22 West 34th Street, New York, New York 10001; remitting $1.00 for microfiche or $3.00 for photocopies.

Bibliography

Astin, A. W. A re-examination of college productivity. *Journal of Educational Psychology*, 1961, *52*, 173–78.

———— An empirical characterization of higher educational institutions. *Journal of Educational Psychology*, 1962, *53*, 224–35. (a)

————Influences on the student's motivation to seek advanced training: another look. *Journal of Educational Psychology*, 1962, *53*, 303–9. (b)

———— Productivity of undergraduate institutions. *Science*, 1962, *136*, 129–35. (c)

———— Differential college effects on the motivation of talented students to obtain the Ph.D. degree. *Journal of Educational Psychology*, 1963, *54*, 63–71. (a)

———— Further validation of the Environmental Assessment Technique. *Journal of Educational Psychology*, 1963, *54*, 217–26. (b)

———— Undergraduate institutions and the production of scientists. *Science*, 1963, *141*, 334–38. (c)

———— Personal and environmental factors associated with college droupouts among high aptitude students. *Journal of Educational Psychology*, 1964, *55*, 219–27.

———— College preferences of very able students. *College and University*, 1965, *40*, 282–97. (a)

———— Effects of different college environments on the vocational choices of high aptitude students. *Journal of Counseling Psychology*, 1965, *12*, 28–34. (b)

———— Student achievement and the college environment. Evanston, Ill.: National Merit Scholarship Corporation, 1965. (mimeo). (c)

———— *Who goes where to college?* Chicago: Science Research Associates, 1965. (d)

———— *The college environment.* Washington: American Council on Education, 1968. (a)

———— Undergraduate achievement and institutional "excellence." *Science*, 1968, *161*, 661–68. (b)

———— & Holland, J. L. The Environmental Assessment Technique: A way to measure college environments. *Journal of Educational Psychology*, 1961, *52*, 308–16.

———— & ———— The distribution of "wealth" in higher education. *College and University*, 1962, *37*, 113–25.

————, Panos, R. J., & Creager, J. A. National norms for entering college freshmen, fall 1966. *ACE Research Reports*, 1967, *2*(1). (a)

————, ———— & ———— Supplementary national norms for freshmen entering college in 1966. *ACE Research Reports*, 1967, *2*(3). (b)

————, Richardson, G. T., & Salmon, Mary. A computer program for normalizing distributions of variables. *Educational and Psychological Measurement*, 1967, *27*, 153–57.

Astin, Helen S. Career development during the high school years. *Journal of Counseling Psychology*, 1967, *14*, 94–98. (a)

———— Patterns of career choices over time. *Personnel and Guidance Journal*, 1967, *45*, 541–46. (b)

Bayer, A. E. The college drop-out: factors affecting senior college completion. *Sociology of Education*, 1968, *41*, 305–16.

209

Bottenberg, R. A., and Ward, J. H., Jr. Applied multiple linear regression. *Technical Document Report* PRL-TDR-63-6, Texas: Lackland AFB, 1963.

Cartter, A. M. *American universities and colleges.* (9th ed.) Washington: American Council on Education, 1964.

———— *An assessment of quality in graduate education.* Washington: American Council on Education, 1966.

Centra, J. A., & Parry, Mary E. College achievement in social science, humanities, and natural science: an exploratory study. *ETS Research Bulletin* RB-67-23, 1967.

Creager, J. A., Astin, A. W., Boruch, R. F., & Bayer, A. E. National norms for entering college freshmen, fall 1968. *ACE Research Reports,* 1968, *3*(1).

Davis, J. A. *Great aspirations.* Chicago: Aldine Publishing Co., 1964.

———— *Undergraduate career decisions.* Chicago: Aldine Publishing Co., 1965.

———— The campus as a frog pond: an application of the theory of relative deprivation to career decisions of college men. *American Journal of Sociology,* 1966, *72,* 17–31.

Flanagan, J. C., & Cooley, W. W. *Project Talent one year follow-up studies.* Cooperative Research Project No. 2333. Pittsburgh: University of Pittsburgh, 1966.

Harmon, L. R. High school backgrounds of science doctorates. *Science,* 1961, *133,* 679–88.

Holland, J. L. A theory of vocational choice. *Journal of Counseling Psychology,* 1959, *6,* 35–45.

———— Some explorations of a theory of vocational choice: I. One- and two-year longitudinal studies. *Psychological Monographs,* 1962, *76,* 26 (Whole No. 545).

———— A psychological classification scheme for vocations and major fields. *Journal of Counselling Psychology,* 1966, *13,* 278–88. (a)

———— *The psychology of vocational choice.* Waltham, Mass.: Blaisdell Publishing Co., 1966. (b)

———— & Whitney, D. R. Changes in the vocational plans of college students: orderly or random? *ACT Research Report* No. 25, 1968.

Knapp, R. H., & Goodrich, H. B. *Origins of American scientists.* Chicago: University of Chicago Press, 1952.

———— & Greenbaum, J. J. *The younger American scholar: his collegiate origins.* Chicago: University of Chicago Press, 1953.

Michael, W. B., & Perry, N. C. The comparability of the simple discriminant function and multiple regression techniques. *Journal of Experimental Education,* 1956, *24,* 297–301.

Nichols, R. C. Effects of various college characteristics on student aptitude test scores. *Journal of Educational Psychology,* 1964, *55,* 45–54.

———— Personality change and the college. *American Educational Research Journal,* 1967, *4,* 173–90.

Pace, C. R. *College and university environmental scales.* Princeton, N. J.: Educational Testing Service, 1963.

———— & Stern, G. G. An approach to the measurement of psychological characteristics of college environments. *Journal of Educational Psychology,* 1958, *49,* 269–77.

Panos, R. J., & Astin, A. W. Attrition among college students. *American Educational Research Journal,* 1968, *5,* 57–72.

————, ———— & Craeger, J. A. National norms for entering college freshmen, Fall 1967. *ACE Research Reports,* 1967, *2*(7).

Plant, W. T. Changes in ethnocentrism during college. *Journal of Educational Psychology,* 1958, *49,* 112–65.

Roe, Anne. *The psychology of occupations.* New York: John Wiley and Sons, 1956.

Summerskill, J. Dropouts from college. In N. Sanford (ed.), *The American college.* New York: John Wiley and Sons, 1962. 627–57.

Thistlethwaite, D. L. College environments and the development of talent. *Science,* 1959, *130,* 71–76.

———— College press and changes in study plans of talented students. *Journal of Educational Psychology*, 1960, *51*, 222–34.

———— Effects of teacher and peer subcultures upon student aspirations. *Journal of Educational Psychology*, 1966, *57*, 35–47.

Wooster Conference Report. *Research and teaching in the liberal arts college.* Wooster, Ohio: College of Wooster, 1959.

AMERICAN COUNCIL ON EDUCATION

LOGAN WILSON, *President*

The American Council on Education, founded in 1918, is a *council* of educational organizations and institutions. Its purpose is to advance education and educational methods through comprehensive voluntary and cooperative action on the part of American educational associations, organizations, and institutions.